New Ears for New Music

Cover design:
H. J. Kropp, using a sketch by Krzysztof Penderecki
created for his opera
"Die schwarze Maske" / "The Black Mask" (1984/86).

Expanded version of:
Neue Ohren für Neue Musik.
Streifzüge durch die Musik des
20. und 21. Jahrhunderts.

By Constantin Floros.
© 2006 SCHOTT MUSIC, Mainz - Germany

Constantin Floros

# New Ears for New Music

Translated by Kenneth Chalmers

**Bibliographic Information published by the Deutsche Nationalbibliothek**
The Deutsche Nationalbibliothek lists this publication
in the Deutsche Nationalbibliografie; detailed bibliographic
data is available in the internet at http://dnb.d-nb.de.

Library of Congress Cataloging-in-Publication Data

Floros, Constantin.
  [Neue Ohren für Neue Musik. English]
  New ears for new music / Constantin Floros ; translated by Kenneth Chalmers.
    pages cm
  Translation of the author's Neue Ohren für Neue Musik.
  Includes bibliographical references and index.
  ISBN 978-3-631-63379-3
  1. Music--20th century--History and criticism. 2. Music--21st century--History and criticism. I. Chalmers, Kenneth, translator. II. Title.
  ML197.F6313 2013
  780.9'04--dc23
                                              2013015579

ISBN 978-3-631-63379-3 (Print)
E-ISBN 978-3-653-03230-7 (E-Book)
DOI 10.3726/978-3-653-03230-7

© Peter Lang GmbH
Internationaler Verlag der Wissenschaften
Frankfurt am Main 2013
All rights reserved.
Peter Lang Edition is an Imprint of Peter Lang GmbH.

Peter Lang – Frankfurt am Main · Bern · Bruxelles · New York ·
Oxford · Warszawa · Wien

All parts of this publication are protected by copyright.
Any utilisation outside the strict limits of the copyright law, without
the permission of the publisher, is forbidden and liable to prosecution.
This applies in particular to reproductions, translations, microfilming,
and storage and processing in electronic retrieval systems

www.peterlang.com

György Ligeti in Memoriam

# Table of Contents

Preface ..................................................................................................... 1

From Expressionism to Experiment –
Directions and Tendencies in New Music ........................................... 3

Arnold Schoenberg – Revolutionary, Humanist and Visionary ........ 11

"Music is not to be Decorative; it is to be True" –
Towards an Aesthetic of the Second Viennese School ...................... 17

The Problem of "German Music" ....................................................... 23

The Fate of Arnold Schoenberg and Alban Berg after 1933 ............. 29

Two Unknown Letters by Schoenberg and Berg ............................... 37

Beethoven and the Schoenberg School .............................................. 41

Principles of Vocal Composition ........................................................ 47

Schoenberg's *Gurrelieder* ................................................................. 51

The Melodramas of *Pierrot lunaire* ................................................. 59

"God's Eternity Opposes the Transience of Idols" –
On Schoenberg's *Moses and Aron* ................................................... 65

Nationalism and Folklorism ............................................................... 71

Nikos Skalkottas – A Schoenberg Pupil in Berlin ............................. 79

Beyond Schoenberg and Debussy –
Nikos Skalkottas's 32 Piano Pieces .................................................... 85

A Conversation with Luigi Nono ....................................................... 97

Olivier Messiaen's "Theological Music" ......................................... 101

Pierre Boulez's Masterpiece *Le Marteau sans maître* ................... 105

Fascinated by the Music of Ligeti ..................................................................109

Ligeti's *Hölderlin-Phantasien*. A Letter from the Composer ..........................113

Iridescent Sound ..................................................................................................117

"Folklore in Serious Music is a Lie" –
Ligeti's Relationship with Béla Bartók ..............................................................125

Multicultural Phenomena in the New Music .....................................................133

"A Music of the Whole Earth, All Countries and Races":
Karlheinz Stockhausen's Utopia of World Music .............................................137

The Philosophy of Time and Pluralistic Thought of
Bernd Alois Zimmermann ...................................................................................143

Alfred Schnittke and Polystylism .......................................................................147

And Always for a Better World –
Approaches to Hans Werner Henze .....................................................................153

So-called Postmodernism .....................................................................................161

"No Artist Works at a Distance from Humanity" –
In Praise of Wolfgang Rihm ................................................................................167

Afterword ..............................................................................................................171

Notes ......................................................................................................................173

Selective Bibliography ..........................................................................................205

List of Music Examples and Illustrations ..........................................................213

Plates ......................................................................................................................215

Index .......................................................................................................................229

# Preface

> "Why are we not allowed to write such beautiful music as Johann Sebastian Bach?"
> GYÖRGY LIGETI[1]

It is not just the literature and visual arts of a given era that are marked by a "Zeitgeist", but music is as well. Intellectual standpoints and social and political upheavals, and the reactions they provoke, are all reflected in the music of their time. The defining characteristic of 20th-century music was a dizzying multitude of different paths, with several occasionally contradictory currents often co-existing. And all these developments, even those that seem independent, have their roots in the spirit of the age.

The fact of dissonance as a marker of new music is intimately bound up with the human suffering that dates from the time of the First World War onwards, and the 20th century is rightly known as the bloodiest in the history of mankind. Such experiences found compelling artistic expression in Expressionist music.

Iwan Martynow put forward the theory that between the two world wars, music moved between two poles.[2] At one pole was despair, dread and hopelessness – the elements that permeate Alban Berg's inspired works. At the other was levity and lightness, superficiality and entertainment. Music was widely taken to be play, masquerade, a trick, irony or pastiche, "music about music". Much of what is termed Neo-Classicism or *Neue Sachlichkeit* (New Objectivity) belongs to this category.

The trauma inflicted by two world wars, the Holocaust, the bombing of Hiroshima and Nagasaki and repeated crimes against humanity left a mark on music as well. Since 1945 at least, politically engaged music has consequently been a more or less continuous strong current.

The 20th century was particularly characterised by huge technological advances, by the spirit of invention and the joy of discovery – all symptomatic of a drive to develop the world of sound in every way possible, that resulted in experimental, inventive and innovative music. There were, of course, "retrogressive" tendencies too, associated with religious and spiritual needs, and a human desire for emotion and beauty as well.

This book provides an overview of the trends and directions in new music, and presents various aspects of the most important composers. My concern was to shed light on the contemporary historical, intellectual, psychological and social background to this *ars nova* as well. The music of the 20th century will be interpreted from this perspective for the first time in its entirety.

Originally, at a time when I myself composed, my intense interest in new music was as an artist. In 1960 I decided in favour of scholarship and gave up

composing completely. Since that time, new music has been a constant field of research for me. Initially, I focused my efforts on research into the music of the Second Viennese School and the work and aesthetic of György Ligeti. Later I turned to other composers. At the end of 1992 Breitkopf & Härtel published my extensive book on Alban Berg, subtitled "Music as Autobiography", and at the beginning of 1996 my book on Ligeti was published by Lafite in Vienna. I was lucky enough to have extended conversations with Ligeti, Hans Werner Henze, Luigi Nono, Friedhelm Döhl and Peter Ruzicka, and also got to know Wolfgang Rihm, György Kurtág, Arvo Pärt, Alfred Schnittke, Krzysztof Meyer, Roman Berger, Peter Michael Hamel, Anatol Vieru, Stefan Niculescu, Klaus Stahmer, Wolfgang Andreas Schultz, Manfred Stahnke and Wolfgang von Schweinitz personally. I would like to convey my heartfelt thanks to all those who have contributed to the creation of this book in any way: Mrs Nuria Schoenberg-Nono, Dr Claudia Vincis (Archivio Luigi Nono Venice), Dr Eike Fess (Arnold Schoenberg Center Vienna), Universal Edition AG, Internationaler Verlag Schott in Mainz, Verlage Sikorski in Hamburg, and above all Dr Kenneth Chalmers, for his conscientious and subtle translation. Michael Bock (Hamburg) was responsible for the formatting of the volume, and Michael Rücker and Thomas Papsdorf of Peter Lang Verlag provided valuable advice on printing.
The original German version of the chapter "Towards an Aesthetic of the Second Viennese School" has been expanded for this English edition.

# From Expressionism to Experiment
## Directions and Tendencies in New Music

> "It is the interest in change that has accelerated change to its giddy pace"
> ERNST H. GOMBRICH[1]

Around 1320, the French composer and theoretician Philippe de Vitry wrote a treatise that would subsequently acquire wide renown, and which he entitled *Ars Nova*, with the intention of distinguishing the music of his time from that of the past, the so-called *ars antiqua*. Six centuries later, something similar happened in Germany. In 1919, the prestigious critic Paul Bekker talked about the "new music" that was superseding that of the late Romantics.[2] The salient features of this new music were the extension and dissolution of tonality, atonality, as it was known, twelve-note composition and the "emancipation of the dissonance". All were markers of a development that can mainly be traced through the works of the composers of the Second Viennese School. Arnold Schoenberg and his principal pupils, Anton von Webern and Alban Berg, represent the radical "modernists" of the first half of the twentieth century, the path that they took ultimately emerging from a conflict with the boldest achievements of "late-Romantic" music. In many of their late works, Wagner, Liszt, Bruckner and Mahler – to name only the leading composers – pushed music to the very brink of atonality, and in all four there are occasional, bold note-clusters and unresolved dissonances that anticipate Schoenberg's early Expressionist period.

The question of whether music develops in parallel with the other arts continues to be debated. Many music historians deny it categorically. The Romantics were of a different opinion. Robert Schumann, no less, claimed that, "the aesthetics of one art are the same as another; only the material is different".[3] No one today could deny that there are at least similarities of expression between the arts of a given period. If we can take it that the characteristics of literary Expressionism are a strong need for expression, compression of material, concentration on the essential, and rejection of decoration, then the same applies wholesale to the works that Schoenberg, Webern and Berg wrote in their atonal period. It is significant that all three had a preference for Expressionist poetry; Schoenberg wrote Expressionist dramas such as *Erwartung*, op.17 and *Die glückliche Hand*, op.18, and is said to have commented, "Music is not there to decorate, it should be true."[4] It is surely no coincidence that most of the works that date from his atonal period are either vocal pieces, or take their inspiration from a text. Of each published opus of Schoenberg's, up to op.22, it is interesting that only five are purely instrumental, while in Webern's output, vocal works far outstrip instrumental ones.

In his *Harmonielehre* of 1911, Schoenberg argued that art at its highest level should be exclusively concerned with reproducing "inner nature".[5] Wassily Kandinsky expressed similar thoughts in his near-contemporary groundbreaking book *Concerning the Spiritual in Art*, the manifesto of a new aesthetic that broke with the imitation of "external nature" and aspired to the "unnatural, abstract and to inner nature".[6] Kandinsky got to know Schoenberg and some of his works in 1911, and wrote enthusiastically about them: "Schoenberg's music takes us into a new realm, where the musical experiences are not acoustic ones, but purely spiritual. This is the beginning of the 'Music of the Future'".[7]

A statement made by Schoenberg in his *Harmonielehre* is highly characteristic of the Expressionist artist. It reads, "That which is new and unusual about a new harmony occurs to the true composer only because he must give expression to something that moves him, something new, something previously unheard-of. That can also be a new sound, but I believe it is far more than that: a new sound is a symbol, discovered involuntarily, a symbol proclaiming the new man who so asserts his individuality."[8] The literary scholar Walter H. Sokel rightly denoted the Expressionist artist as a "Poeta dolorosus",[9] and it has to be said that the musical idiom minted by Schoenberg and his pupils expressed anguish above all. Its sounds are mostly codes for fear, loneliness, despair and dread. Helene Berg once defined her husband as "a specialist in setting the gruesome to music"[10]. Indeed, no other composer could have set Georg Büchner's words "Der Mensch ist ein Abgrund, es schwindelt einem, wenn man hinunterschaut" (man is an abyss, you feel dizzy when you look down into it) in Act 3 Scene 1 of *Wozzeck*, or the eerie attic scene in the third act of *Lulu* so harrowingly. Adorno grasped an essential truth when he wrote, "The first atonal works are case studies in the sense of psychoanalytical dream case studies".[11] The emancipation of the dissonance does not seem to match *serenitas*, or exhilaration of any kind. In this light, Hans Werner Henze's comment that the Second Viennese School as well as the post-Expressionist school had "no vocabulary of mirth" seems justified.[12]

The development of each and every art is determined by diverging forces, and the dialectic of advance and retreat has a part to play. While many composers train their sights on the future, others take their bearings from the past. Wagner, who coined the phrase "music of the future", had set himself the goal of renewing the art of composition by every means possible, not least by "wedding" it to poetry. Brahms, on the other hand, was firmly convinced had music had already reached its highest point before him.

As an intellectual movement, so-called neo-classicism started in Paris, and quickly took hold in many areas of cultural life, literature, visual arts and music. The leading figures in the movement were Jean Cocteau, Guillaume Apollinaire and Erik Satie. As early as 1916, Cocteau had drafted his *Esthétique du minimum* and espoused economy of means. His call of "back to the classics" signified a plea for a return to "order" and "elegance", and at the same time for a distancing from emotionalism. He repeatedly invoked the work of Picasso, whom he felt to be a kindred spirit, and repeatedly sought to contact Stravinsky.[13] Apollinaire put forward something similar in 1918 in an essay entitled *L'Esprit nouveau et les poètes*. 1918 also saw the appearance, just as the First World War was ending, of Prokofiev's *Classical Symphony* and Stravinsky's *The Soldier's Tale*, and two years later Stravinsky wrote his *Pulcinella*, a suite on themes by Pergolesi (and others). In 1913, with his *Sacre du printemps*, Stravinsky had appeared to many to be a revolutionary and *enfant terrible*; with these two later works he completed his departure from the style of his Russian ballets, bound up as they were with Russian folklore and traditions.

Around the same time, in January 1920, Ferruccio Busoni wrote a letter to Paul Bekker that was later to become famous under the title of *Young Classicism*.[14] What he principally meant by this term was stripping out the sensual, choosing austerity over subjectivity, regaining serenity (*serenitas*) and above all "absolute music". He was articulating what many had in mind, and were calling for: the rejection of 19th-century art, freedom from the literary, and the expressive rejection of programme music – all of which he had already put forward in 1907, in his *Entwurf einer neuen Ästhetik der Tonkunst*.[15] It would be wrong, however, to think that Busoni's proposal found nothing but approval. Both Hindemith and Schoenberg, who had read the pamphlet closely and commented on it when it was republished in 1916, had many objections to it. Hindemith's comments on some of Busoni's ideas were not just sarcastic, but downright withering. On Busoni's definition of "absolute music" as something "sober, like orderly rows of instrumental desks, or a tonic-dominant relationship, or developments and codas", Hindemith observed, "This absolute music has long since ceased to exist. Those of its representatives who might still be alive are to be seen in the better class of natural history museum".[16] And Schoenberg could not resist commenting on Busoni's utter condemnation of programme music, "Music can mimic how a person is inside, and in this sense, programme music is possible".[17] It is odd that as intelligent a musician as Busoni could write the letter of January 1922 to Fritz Windisch, publisher of *Melos*, in which he attacked neo-classicism in the strongest terms.[18]

In 1939, Stravinsky was invited by Harvard University to give a series of lectures on musical poetics.[19] On a first reading of his ideas it is no small surprise to see how far they conform to the aesthetic Cocteau proposed.[20] Stravinsky espouses musical craftsmanship, order and construction. He criticises "modernism", and the idea of progress in the arts, and makes his own Verdi's admonition "Torniamo all'antico e sarà un progresso".[21] His ideals are "academicism" and the living tradition. His hatred of Wagner, of the idea of art as a religion and of the *Gesamtkunstwerk* is symptomatic. From this starting-point, it becomes easier to understand how he comes out in favour of the goal of art as "diversion".²² His whole mindset is diametrically opposed to that of Schoenberg. Stravinsky's call to order found an echo in many countries. A great many composers took it as an invitation to focus on construction and technical mastery. Stravinsky's sound-world, his personal style of extended tonality and above all his complex metrical and rhythmic schemes became internationally famous. And during his neo-classical period Stravinsky never tired of fighting passionately for music to be recognised as an independent art. He consequently moved an enormous distance away from the aesthetic precepts of his Russian period and the three great ballets (*The Firebird*, *Petrushka* and *The Rite of Spring*) that after their Paris premieres had established his fame in Europe. To a large extent, the astonishingly colourful nature of the music of these works derived from the exciting scenic and choreographic situations that they illustrated so wonderfully. This marked a genuine triumph of a specific kind of programme music.

Adorno's widely-read *Philosophie der neuen Musik* that appeared in 1949 contains an apologia for Schoenberg and twelve-note music, and a crushing criticism of Stravinsky that caused a furore. Schoenberg is identified with progress, Stravinsky, in contrast, with restoration. Based on his conviction that psychoanalysis should serve transcendental philosophy, Adorno draws on many psychiatric categories and accuses Stravinsky of infantilism, depersonalisation, schizophrenia (hebephrenia) and catatonia. Although much of this critique is compelling, Schoenberg himself felt the need to speak up for his rival Stravinsky. "By the way, it's disgusting," he wrote to Hans Stuckenschmidt on 5 December 1949, "the way he [Adorno] treats Stravinsky".²³ Several decades later, György Ligeti singled Stravinsky out as the most significant composer of the 20th century.²⁴ Adorno's criticism of Stravinsky is easier to understand in the light of his belief in humanity, which he found convincingly expressed in artistic terms in the music of the Second Viennese School composers, particularly in Berg's *Wozzeck*, while he ascribed "anti-expression" and "lack of feeling" to Stravinsky.²⁵

To a large extent, 20th-century music was marked by an attempt to explore every path in the world of sound, and to exploit areas of it that had not been dreamt of before. These common denominators cover a whole range of directions and trends, the most obvious being the idea of being able to renew music by using new materials and instruments, new tonal systems, with noise and other experiments. Let us look at the broad outlines.

Dating from round the beginning of the movement are the futurist manifestos of Filippo Tommaso Marinetti that appeared between 1909 and 1910.²⁶ They exalt the wonders of the technical world, machines and mechanical things, locomotives, the speed of trains and automobiles and above all the beauty of speed. Francesco Balilla Pratella, the first composer who thought up a *Musica futuristica per orchestra*, in 1912, declared in a preface, that Verdi's words

"Torniamo all'antico" were "abhorrent, stupid and cowardly". Luigi Russolo is certainly a significant figure: he turned to the acoustic world of noise and developed a system of classification for the futurist orchestra, dividing noises into six categories: crashes and thunder, whistles and hisses, murmurs and rustles, screeches and grating sounds, percussive sounds (booms), human and animal voices. To generate these noises, by 1916 he had constructed no fewer than 21 noise-makers, his so-called *intonarumori*.

There is no doubt that Russolo had an inventive mind: one of his constructions was an "rumorarmonio", a kind of harmonium with two bass pedals that was able to play not just whole tones and semitones, but micro-intervals as well. The musical impact of Futurism was admittedly limited, and lost any significance as the movement began to align itself with Mussolini's regime. Today we associate only two works with the term Futurism: Arthur Honegger's *Pacific 231* of 1924, and Max Brand's music-drama *Maschinist Hopkins* of 1929.

Russolo's futurist aesthetic was a crucial spur to the French musician and author Pierre Schaeffer, who created so-called *musique concrète*. From 1948 on, he began to experiment with noises in the RTF Studio in Paris, with the goal of making the world of acoustic processes serve an artistic purpose. His "Concerts de bruits" drew on every imaginable everyday noise, water sounds, scraps of speech, and the sounds of exotic instruments. His experiments attracted the attention of such renowned composers as Pierre Boulez, Jean Barraqué, Marcel Delannoy and Henri Dutilleux, and Olivier Messaien, no less, composed a piece of *musique concrète*, entitled *Timbres-Durées* in 1952.[27]

Busoni delighted in new, reforming ideas on music. As early as 1907 he declared a harmonic revolution, and wrote, "For some time the third-tone has been asking for admittance, and we are still ignoring its message".[28] He also made reference to the "dynamophon", the invention of a Dr Thaddeus Cahill in America. The enormous device that Cahill had constructed made it possible to divide the octave endlessly, and Busoni consequently thought it would be possible to design a sixth-tone system. It was also Busoni who prompted Alois Hába and Ivan Vishnegradsky to compose microtonal music. Hába wrote a great many works in semitone, quarter-tone, fifth-tone and sixth-tone systems,[29] and Vishnegradsky quite a few in quarter, third, fifth, sixth and twelfth-tone systems.[30] Harry Partch is a special case, having developed an extremely complex system of pure vibration. His principal successor is Manfred Stahnke, the most important representative of microtonality in Germany today. Very little can be said with any certainty about the aesthetic effect of microtonal music, since it can be only heard only extremely rarely.[31]

The composer Edgard Varèse must be counted among the most important experimental figures in music. He studied first in Paris with Charles-Marie Widor, Albert Roussel and Vincent d'Indy, then struck up a friendship with Busoni in Berlin, and in 1919 settled in the United States. Prompted by Busoni's observation, "Composition was born free, and to win freedom is its destiny,"[32] he spent his life striving to "free sound" using every means imaginable. He consequently explored the use of new instruments, tape and electronics. He was fascinated by Hermann von Helmholtz's experiments with sirens, which he used in some of his scores (*Amériques* of 1918-1921, and *Ionisation* of 1930-31). He represented the notion that music belonged to both art and science, and made Hoëné Wronski's definition of music as "the incarnation of the intelligence inherent in sound" his own.[33]

Three ideas above all have fascinated and inspired composers in the second half of the 20th century: firstly, the notion that one should ignore tradition completely and begin again from zero; secondly, the requirement to explore sounds and noises and the entire acoustical world in every direction in dedicated laboratories; and thirdly, the idea that composing should have a scientific basis. Interestingly, it was Cocteau who defined music as "science made flesh".[34]

In the 1950s, electronic music studios were set up under various names in several European cities, as well as in Tokyo and the United States. The first and most significant appeared as early as 1950, in the broadcasting centre of West German radio in Cologne, on the instigation of Herbert Eimert, who collaborated with the technician Fritz Enkel and the physicist Werner Meyer-Eppler. Electronic music was distinguished from traditional music in that it experimented with sine tones, which are devoid of all harmonics, with sound mixing, and what is known as white noise. The earliest electronic works were by Karel Goeyvaerts, Karlheinz Stockhausen, Giselher Klebe, Gottfried Michael Koenig and György Ligeti. The most widely-known piece was Stockhausen's *Gesang der Jünglinge* (1955-56), a work that includes speech sounds as well as sine tones and noise, and is intended for five groups of loudspeakers.

It is safe to say that electronic music opened up an almost limitless potential in terms of sonorities (new sounds and noises), and could prompt particular associations. Since the first experiments in this direction demonstrated quite chaotic relationships, Stockhausen was apparently the first to structure the rhythms of his electronic pieces serially.[35] There is clearly a connection between these experiments and the emergence of so-called serial music. Serialism takes up Schoenberg's method of composing with twelve different notes, but goes much further, organising *a priori* not just pitches, but every parameter of the composition according to a series – duration, intensity and even types of attack. This compositional principal was elevated to the status of avant-garde doctrine. Many young composers (Stockhausen and Boulez were joined by Luigi Nono, Bruno Maderna, Henri Pousseur and others) adopted it, and no less a figure than Ernst Křenek coined the witticism that serialism had conclusively freed composers from the tyranny of inspiration.[36] This dialectical reasoning is easier to understand if we take on board that what Křenek called "inspiration" was for him essentially fortuitous, and also that he himself discovered "chance" operations in what was known as "totally determined" music, since in his opinion consonances could not be regulated serially. These considerations led to the seemingly paradoxical conclusion that the gap between serialism and aleatoric composition (*alea* being Latin for "dice") is not so great as it appears at first sight,, since ultimately every freely-chosen row depends on chance and is therefore as random as chance. There is, however, an essential difference between the work of the serial composers and the operations of a dice thrower.

However promising a beginning it might have had as a compositional principle, serialism was not destined to have a long life. It was first rocked by the publication of an essay by Ligeti in 1958 that convincingly demonstrated that the apparent mathematical logic of this type of musical construction neither guaranteed musical coherence nor had an exact correlation in physical perception.[37] John Cage's aleatoric concepts contributed further to the essential general uncertainty: they countered the serialists' belief in completely determined elements, wherever possible, with chance and indetermination. Apart from that, Cage ensured a "non-intentional" art of chaos through his theories, influenced by East Asian Zen Buddhism.

The idea of the musical avant-garde is closely bound up with the term "progress" – a somewhat arresting, and dubious term, if taken to denote "artistic" progress. (In comparison, the question of historical, social, technological or ecological progress is easier to answer.) The serialists invoked the "tendency of the material" postulated by Adorno – a formulation that has become famous and which ultimately should have justified twelve-note technique. Interestingly, he did not define the term "material" merely in terms of music theory, but in psychological and sociological terms as "sedimented spirit, preformed socially by human consciousness". As an "objective" spirit, the musical material is subject to the same processes as society, of which it is, after all, the expression, and for Adorno these processes follow the law of progress. The material consequently "demands" that the composer discard everything outdated and threadbare in music and always use those means that match the most recent stage of musical technique – and of social development. Nevertheless, for Adorno, Schoenberg's twelve-note method represented the very latest stage of technique.[38]

It is true that as early as 1955, Boulez had spoken of serialism not just as fertile ground to be ploughed, but also raised the issue of its "limits".[39] Toward the end of the 1970s many commentators were stating that the voyage of discovery through the world of sound was at an end, that the material had been exhausted. The modernists seemed to have lost, and a wide-ranging discussion began on musical "post-modernism". Around the same time, in 1977, IRCAM, the Institut de recherche et de coordination acoustique/musique, was founded in Paris, an ambitious institution that, under the directorship of Boulez, was charged with marrying information technology and music.[40]

In 1978, Hans-Jürgen von Bose felt the need to take stock, as spokesperson for the younger generation of composers, and explicitly distanced himself from "assumed belief in progress".[41] He spoke passionately of the "yearning for a lost beauty and content" – a content that was to be formulated anew for everyone individually. This was an acknowledgement of expression and a commitment to the "post-modernism" that seems to be the dominant voice everywhere today. Its most prominent representatives are successful, possibly because they write music that is relatively simply – sometimes exceptionally simply – constructed, that takes up the familiar, fills the emotional deficit and satisfies spiritual needs as well. Interestingly, as early as December 1983 Messiaen took stock of this in the course of an interview, when he stated that "Serialism, abstraction, aleatoric music, they are all things of the past. The direction today is completely different," defining this with reference to emotion and sensibility.[42]

The musical avant-garde and the post-modernists have fundamentally different goals. In the final analysis, these come down to progress and regression, forward and backward movement, and refusal and readiness to compromise. The success of the post-modernists (which might be temporary) can be attributed not least to the fact that they meet the aesthetic and emotional needs of a broad audience far more than the former avant-garde.

Nevertheless, the impression should not be given that the erstwhile avant-garde has now completely disappeared from the scene. Brian Ferneyhough, who is active in Freiburg, and Helmut Lachenmann count among its most prominent representatives. Lachenmann has been, and continues to be, highly controversial. Famous as the representative of "musica negativa", he strives, on his own admission, to "treat familiar idioms with loving destructiveness" which he himself understands to be at the same time "creatively constructive". Music thus appears to him as both: "as a field of rubble and a new force field".[43] For Lachenmann, art is creative provocation, the mobilising of intellectual resistance to the culinary, to the temporary gratification of false yearnings.[44]

Ligeti once rightly remarked that many 20th-century composers owe their success to a few works that for some reason became popular. He pointed to Ravel's *Boléro* and Stravinsky's three great ballets, which continue to interest audiences. Yet with a certain puzzlement he asked the question, "But who today is interested in such a wonderful work as Stravinsky's *Symphony of wind instruments* of 1920?"[45]

# Arnold Schoenberg
## Revolutionary, Humanist and Visionary

> "For the great artist must somehow be punished in his lifetime for the honour he will enjoy later."
> ARNOLD SCHOENBERG[1]

On 13 September 1949 Schoenberg celebrated his 75th birthday in Los Angeles, surrounded by his family. Congratulations poured in from friends and pupils, and a few days later he wrote a thank-you letter entitled "To gain recognition only after one's death" which he sent in facsimile to everyone who had written to him. There are many documents that reveal something about great artists, but this letter is one of the most upsetting. It reads:[2]

"In these last few days I have met with much personal recognition, which has given me great pleasure because it testifies to the respect in which I am held by my friends and other well-disposed people.

On the other hand, however, I have for many years been resigned to the fact that I cannot count on living to see full and sympathetic understanding of my work, that is, of what I have to say in music. I do indeed know that more than a few of my friends have come to feel at home with my mode of expression and are familiar with my ideas. It is likely then to be such as they who will fulfil what I prophesied in an aphorism exactly thirty-seven years ago:

'The second half of this century will be spoilt by overestimation of whatever the first half's underestimation left unspoilt'.

I am somewhat embarrassed by all these hymns of praise. But I nevertheless also see something encouraging in them. For is it so much to be taken for granted if in the face of the whole world's resistance a man does not give up, but continues to write down what he produces?

I do not know what the great have thought about this. Mozart and Schubert were young enough not to have to come to close terms with this problem. But Beethoven, when Grillparzer called the Ninth a jumble, or Wagner when the Bayreuth scheme seemed about to fail, or Mahler, when everyone found him trivial – how could they go on writing?

I know only one answer: they had things to say that had to be said. Once, in the army, I was asked if I was really the composer A.S. 'Somebody had to be,' I said, 'and nobody else wanted to, so I took it on myself.'

Perhaps I too had to say things – unpopular things, it seems – that had to be said."

At the end of his life, Schoenberg was fully aware that his life's work had, on the whole, not been understood. At the same time, he was convinced that his work would gain recognition after his death – a conviction, incidentally, that Mahler also felt deeply. Early on – in an aphorism published in 1910 – Schoenberg had made the prediction, "The second half of this century will be spoilt by the overestimation of whatever the first half's underestimation left unspoilt".[3]

In common with many other creative artists of genius, Schoenberg was unswerving, unshakable, implacable and uncompromising in pursuing his artistic goals. At the opening of his unfinished oratorio *Die Jakobsleiter*, he puts the following words into the mouth of the Archangel Gabriel: "Whether right or left, forward or back, up hill or down dale, you must carry on, without asking what lies ahead or behind. It should be hidden: it was permitted, required, for you to fulfil the task".[4] These lines seem tailor-made for Schoenberg himself. To be true to oneself, true to one's own ideas, was a personal characteristic that he particularly valued. Schoenberg ended his belated obituary of his pupil Berg with the *aperçu*, "It is a mark of a great personality to make the belief in one's ideas into one's destiny".[5]

There is another quality in the letter quoted above, a profound humility, the unwavering conviction that the true artist is actually an instrument through which something important and possibly unpopular can be revealed.

Schoenberg was one of the greatest geniuses in the history of mankind, comparable to Leonardo da Vinci and Wagner: a composer, theoretician, poet, author, painter and inventor, producer and man of the theatre, constructor and philosopher. He united ingenuity with mysticism, calculation with emotion, and supreme rationality with the idiosyncratic and esoteric. His personality has yet to be fully studied in depth. It is reported that he could be cheerful. He was humorous and witty, and could be ironic, even sarcastic. He was argumentative and often involved in legal disputes, and occasionally aggressive. In both his published photos and self-portraits he is rarely if ever seen smiling. He generally appears to be serious, very focused and occasionally tense. Many pictures give the striking impression of a visionary – he has the severity of a prophet looking out beyond time and the transitory.

Of all 20th-century artists, he was one who was met with the most bitter hostility, and was attacked and defamed. No one experienced such malicious animosity as he did, no one had to endure such mortification. Typically, the war against him did not flare up just in the Nazi period, but several decades previously, and just as typically, it carried on with scarcely any less force after his death. Many people considered him a madman and a charlatan. The Viennese music-theory teacher Emil Petschnig went as far as to define him as a "psychopath".[6] His atonal and twelve-note works above all met with bitter opposition. Most of the criticism of the first performances of his compositions consists of gloating broadsides. It is understandable as a result that he had nothing good to say about criticism and critics. "At the risk of affording my enemies some pleasure," he once wrote, "I have to confess that every critical infamy, every rebuke and every attack rouses me to extreme anger. Even when I laugh. Then I'm laughing with rage. That is why I consider it insincere for me not to fight back vigorously when the opportunity arises."[7] Two of his paintings, incidentally, are pictures of critics, one of them a malicious caricature.[8] What is striking about it is not just the pointed, triangular head, goatee beard and outsize ears, but also the broad grinning mouth with its expression of malice. The feeling of being constantly persecuted and even the firm conviction that a great injustice was being done to him stayed with Schoenberg throughout his entire life. It is against this backdrop that sentences like the following from the *Modernen Psalmen* of 1950-51 become easier to understand: "This I shall never understand: that these criminals who prey on me and rob me are protected by good fortune and lead happy lives, while I have spent many years of my life in want and distress. Is that just? Why should I be just, when I experience only injustice? Lord God, I do not beseech you to improve my situation. But I will beseech you more ardently and fervently to chastise the criminals."[9]

Even after his death Schoenberg continued to be a target for pamphleteers, who took particular pleasure in pulling him to pieces.[10] They excelled in deliberate incomprehension and criticised everything, or almost everything about him: his personality, his theoretical writings on music, the texts of his poetry, his compositional methods and above all his music. In 1951 Pierre Boulez gave a landmark lecture at the Darmstadt summer courses for new music entitled *Schoenberg est mort*.[11] On closer inspection, it quickly becomes clear that the text is merely a pamphlet, but even then it cannot be forgiven on the grounds that Boulez and the avant-garde of his time wanted and had to break away from Schoenberg at all costs. Here Boulez spoke of the Schoenberg "case" and of his "failure", insisting that the integration of twelve-note technique with traditional forms that Schoenberg so keenly desired was invalid.

All through his life Arnold Schoenberg proclaimed that the greatest goal of artist was to strive for self-expression.[12] He was a firm opponent of the concept of art as pure craft, and opened his essay *Problems in teaching art* with a profession of faith: "I believe that art does not come from ability, but from necessity."[13] The ideal from which he took his bearings was not so much "external" as "inner" nature. Around 1910 he understood art and music to be the representation of this "inner nature". It was his proud desire to express his psychological life in art. In August 1930 he wrote to Alban Berg, "Everything I have written bears a certain intrinsic similarity with myself."[14] In 1928, when the anti-romantic mood was in vogue, he defined Expressionist art as "the art of the presentation of *inner* processes".[15]

These precepts hold true not just for his music, but for his paintings as well. In 1912 Kandinsky noted that "Schoenberg's paintings can be broken down into two types: on one hand there are people and landscapes painted directly from nature; on the other, intuitively perceived heads, that he calls 'visions'". "These two types," he continues, "are strongly differentiated. They come from within one and the same soul, that at one time is set vibrating by external nature, and at another by inner nature".[16]

It is significant that almost all Schoenberg's pictures are psychological studies, pictorial psychograms. Also in 1912, Karl Linke described them using the phrase "external pictorial representations of internal stories".[17] It is likely he was referring to the two complementary caricatures *The Vanquished* and *The Victor*.[18] If one bears the expression of someone crawling deep within himself, the other caricatures triumph, self-affirmation and vanity.

"The second half of this century will be spoilt by overestimation of whatever the first half's underestimation left unspoilt". Did Schoenberg's prognosis turn out to be correct? It did, but only in part. Schoenberg's overriding significance as one of the fathers, or rather, *the* father of new music, has been internationally recognised. The atonality that he vigorously advocated, and composition with twelve notes related only to each other experienced a belated triumph in the second half of the 20th century. It was not only Schoenberg's pupils, headed by Berg and Webern, who contributed to that, but countless other composers as well, who worked and experimented with twelve notes in unorthodox and individual ways.[19] Even Stravinsky, at one time Schoenberg's polar opposite, made twelve-note technique his own in his late works. And the "emancipation of the dissonance" that Schoenberg preached became the hallmark of 20th-century music.

It can nevertheless hardly be said that Schoenberg has been overestimated. His multifaceted output has yet to establish itself in its entirety. It is certainly true that the early works and many others from the atonal period are performed with increasing frequency, and they might almost be said to enjoy some popularity. Works that spring to mind are the *Gurre-Lieder*, the string sextet *Verklärte Nacht*, op.4, the symphonic poem *Pelleas und Melisande*, op.5, the first two string quartets, op.7 and op.10, the two chamber symphonies, op.9 and op.38, the *George-Lieder*, op.15, the *Five Orchestral Pieces*, op.16, the monodrama *Erwartung*, op.17, and *Pierrot lunaire*, op.21. Other works, however, have the reputation of being unwieldy and hard to grasp, like the Serenade, op.24 the Piano Suite, op.25, the Quintet, op.26, the third and fourth string quartets, op.30 and op.37, and the Orchestral variations, op.31, among others. Their enormous structural complexity is off-putting, as Alban Berg had already recognised in 1924. It is not so much so-called atonality that creates problems of understanding, as the different structure of Schoenberg's music, especially "the plenitude of artistic means applied here and everywhere in this harmonic style too, by the application of all the compositional possibilities provided by centuries of music, to put it briefly: by its immeasurable richness."[20] It generally seems to be the case that today Schoenberg's atonal works are better appreciated than the dodecaphonic ones. Wolfgang Rihm, for example, confessed in 1987 that the starting-point for his *Hamletmaschine* was Schoenberg's music theatre, that is, *Die glückliche Hand* and *Erwartung*. He finds that they are intrinsically "music theatre as psychological drama in sound, one that encroaches on thought and pushes it far beyond the conceivable."[21]

In this context there is one other aspect of real significance: the firm belief in the 1950s and '60s that the development of twelve-note composition that got under way with Schoenberg was irreversible. What is known as Stockhausen's and Boulez's serial music primarily derived directly from Webern. His "stylistic purity" and the unemotional tone of his musical language were admired by many, and some felt that they had even discovered attempts at serial thinking in a number of his compositions. The retreat of the avant-garde in music and the visual arts that began in the 1960s and was in full flight by the 1980s has been so extensive that the question has to be asked whether such a movement exists at all today.

Many musicologists and musicians have long considered it their duty to view Schoenberg's works purely or predominantly in terms of their structure. They analysed his compositions in minute detail and tried to tease out the rules of Schoenberg's tone-row technique – a legitimate and valuable process, no doubt. Yet Schoenberg's music is not just structural: it contains intensely meaningful emotional and spiritual depths, which should never be left out of the equation. In an important letter of July 1932 to Rudolf Kolisch, Schoenberg himself explicitly stated that he did not want to be labelled a draughtsman, and made the complaint that some of his followers, when they came to analyse his twelve-note music, were at pains to discover how it was "done", whereas he would always have helped to discover what it "is".[22]

Perhaps all this is easier to understand when we consider that at the beginning of his compositional career, Schoenberg, as a creative artist, had a distinct affinity with a literary kind of inspiration. A number of his completed works and many unfinished fragments clearly belong to the genre of expressive programme music. After the symphonic poem *Pelleas und Melisande* he scrupulously avoided giving a poetic or programmatic title to any work or even individual piece. Nevertheless, there is no doubt that a large part of his instrumental output is conceived as programme music – admittedly an individual type of programme music, with many autobiographical elements and based on a secret programme that, in many cases, Schoenberg referred to in conversation, but chose not to disclose officially. He was following the maxim that he wanted to keep his secrets to himself, guided by the conviction that the "aware" understand everything anyway.[23]

It is characteristic of Schoenberg that in later years he spoke of art and music as a message. Like Mahler, he proposed the notion that the artist of genius stands outside their time, and anticipates future developments.[24] An essay from 1946 puts it succinctly: "It is my personal opinion that music conveys a prophetic message that reveals a higher form of life on which humankind develops.

And it is precisely through this message that music has an effect on people of all races and cultures".[25] To my mind, there can be no doubt that several of his works spring from this very artistic concept. It holds true as much for *Moses und Aron* – a drama of ideas and a religious profession of faith – as for the *Ode to Napoleon*, op.41 and the distressing cantata *A Survivor from Warsaw*, op.46.

It must be stressed that Schoenberg was an independent thinker, and not just within the field of music. Both his theological and philosophical thinking warrant careful consideration.[26] Several works, as will be shown, need to be understood not least as the expression of his religious belief and view of the world. This is particularly true of the sacred opera *Moses und Aron*, which was originally conceived as an oratorio.

For Schoenberg, music's capacity to impart a message to the "new humanity" was bound up inextricably with its structure. The compression, concentration on the essential and rejection of decoration that characterise both his Expressionist and twelve-note works in equal measure were, as outlined above, for him necessary for music to express something authentic, for it to be "true" rather than "decorative". It will be shown below that with this aspiration, Schoenberg consciously placed himself within the tradition of "German" music, and also what influence the attempt to erase him, as a Jew, from the German musical tradition, had on the expressive content of his music.

It should also become clear what kind of importance tradition had for specific currents in new music. While for many of the composers involved tradition was something to surmount, or at best considered a collection of material to be exploited, the Second Viennese School saw itself as belonging to and continuing a line of development running from Bach by way of Beethoven and Mahler to Schoenberg's twelve-note music, and stretching on into the future.

# "Music is not to be Decorative; it is to be True"
## Towards an Aesthetic of the Second Viennese School

Beauty and truth – the two primary concepts of artistic theory – are essentially different from each other. While the beauty of a work of art is the main subject in aesthetics (a more recent discipline),[1] truth is one of the primary issues in the philosophy of art.

It is known that aesthetic problems are generally discussed in terms of controversy, and the relevant questions of the nature of music and its position in the system of fine arts are no exception. While Kant gave music the lowest place among the arts, because it "played merely with perceptions",[2] Schopenhauer declared it to be the highest of all the arts.[3] Eduard Hanslick, whose specific area of interest was music, defined it as "tonally moving form", while in contrast Siegmund von Hausegger termed it the art of expression. The Austrian composer Gottfried von Einem admitted that he wanted to rouse listeners to think and feel. He sought truth in beauty – a standpoint that Mahler and the composers of the Second Viennese School had taken up long before him.

In April 1896, in the course of a conversation with his confidante Natalie Bauer-Lechner, Mahler made a statement that warrants particular attention. That in his conception of the so-called "flower" movement of the Third Symphony he had achieved "the most precisely delineated expressive effects" he put down to the fact that he had "never written a single note that is not absolutely true".[4] It is a remark that immediately catches our attention: we wonder what the striking formulation "the truth of music" might mean. In the following passage, Mahler initially refers to tone-painting – flowers moving in the wind, the "innocent flower-like serenity" at the beginning of the piece, and then the change into the serious and oppressive: "A stormy wind blows across the meadow and shakes the leaves and blossoms, which groan and whimper on their stems, as if imploring release into a higher realm".[5]

There is no doubt that the truth in music that Mahler is referring to here is rooted in experience. In the summer of 1893 he said, again to Natalie Bauer-Lechner, on the subject of his first two symphonies, "My two symphonies contain the inner aspect of my whole life; I have written into them everything that I have experiences and endured – Truth and Poetry in music. To understand these works properly would be to see my life transparently revealed in them. Creativity and experience are so intimately linked for me that, if my existence were simply to run on as peacefully as a meadow brook, I don't think that I would ever again be able to write anything worthwhile."[6] A little later he explained to Bauer-Lechner, that a work of his had sprung "only from anguish and the hardest inner experience". A letter to the writer Oskar Bie written in April 1895 is hugely significant: "My music is lived, and how can those people relate to it who do not live and on whom no draught of our stormy times blows?."[7]

One particular passage in Theodor Adorno's *Philosophy of New Music*, the legendary book first published in Frankfurt in 1958, with its apologia for the Second Viennese School, has special relevance to this thorny question: "Schoenberg's attitude towards play is just as polemic as is his attitude towards illusion. He turns just as sharply against the New Objectivity music-makers and their collective retinue as he does against the decorative elements of Romanticism! He has formulated both attitudes in his theoretical writings: 'Music is not to be decorative; it is to be true': and 'Art does not arise out of ability but rather out of necessity'. With the negation of illusion and play music tends towards the direction of knowledge."[8]

Of the two quotations that Adorno gives here, I was for a long time unable to locate the first ("Music is not to be decorative; it is to be true") in Schoenberg's writings. The second ("Art does not arise out of ability but rather out of necessity") comes from Schoenberg's essay *Problems in Teaching Art*, published in 1911.[9] Here Schoenberg makes a fundamental distinction between the craftsman and the true artist, contrasting ability and necessity. The ability of the artist is, in his opinion, "different in essence from the ability of the craftsman". There it is a case of "an ability developed from an external compulsion, an ability to express oneself". While the true artist expresses himself, the writer, the craftsman expresses "someone else". And this strict differentiation also extends to the means applied. "The craftsman," says Schoenberg, "can make what the artist had to create. With his dexterity and adaptability he can apply, as an artistic method, something the creative spirit did unconsciously."

If we want to get a full grasp of all these strains of thought, we have to consider them in three ways. Firstly, at the time when he formulated these statements, Schoenberg had, since 1908, long moved definitively in the direction of atonality. Secondly, he was consequently tacitly turning away from the formal aesthetic of Hanslick, who, in an essay that had by then acquired some fame, *The Beautiful in Music*, had coined the phrase "art comes from ability; those who are not able have 'intentions'".[10] Thirdly, Schoenberg professed to an expressive aesthetic, not just here, but throughout his entire life's work. His Prague memorial address on Mahler consequently contains the words, "In truth, there is only one, great thing that the artist strives for: self-expression. (...) Mahler too sought only to express himself."[11] These convictions of Schoenberg's were confirmed by his pupil Anton Webern in 1912 when he wrote "The experiences of his heart became notes. Schoenberg's relationship with art is rooted exclusively in the necessity of expression. His emotion is that of scorching flames: it creates completely new standards of expression, thus it need entirely new means of expression. Content and form are inseparable."[12] Adorno's claims on Schoenberg's aesthetic are further confirmed in the way the composer inveighs against decoration, like his friend Adolf Loos, and postulates the artist's struggle toward veracity. In the *Problems of Teaching Art* he writes, "The belief in one saving technique must be suppressed; that in striving for veracity promoted."[13]

Veracity in music stands in contrast to the notion of art as play, and above all takes the artist's experience as a given. Many leading composers (Wagner, Mahler, Bartók, Webern and Berg, to mention only a few) were utterly convinced that experience was the indispensable prerequisite of creativity.[14] In a revealing comment from 1911, Schoenberg reproached Liszt for having borrowed his programmes from world literature whereas according to his aesthetic maxims he intended in his compositions to deal only with his own subjects, that is, his personal experience.[15] Comments in the later essay *Human Rights* are even more astonishing. Here Schoenberg writes, "Music speaks in its own language of purely musical matters – or, perhaps as most aestheticians believe, of matters of feeling and fantasy. One can pass over Richard Strauss' good joke: 'I can express in music the moving of a pencil from one place to another.' That is not the language in which a musician unconsciously gives himself away, as he does when he formulates ideas which might even frighten him if he did not know that no one can find out what he hides while he says it."[16] So for Schoenberg, music was a secret language. As he saw it, composers, through their music, disclose what moves them most intimately and profoundly, that otherwise they do not want to convey. It is therefore no surprise that a number of Schoenberg's works are unequivocally autobiographical.[17]

Webern too, at least for time, swore by experience as the key source of inspiration. On 12 July 1912 he asked Berg the significant question, "Tell me, how do you start to compose?" And he admitted, "This is how it is for me: an experience goes around within me for such a long time until it turns into music, with a specific connection to this experience. Often right down to details. And more often it becomes music".[18] In the same letter, he reveals to his friend that with the exception of the violin pieces and some of his most recent orchestral pieces, all of his compositions from the Passacaglia op.1 were related to the death of his mother, which occurred six years before, in 1906. He confirmed these statements a few days later (on 17 July 1912) in a further letter to Berg. Here he wrote, "I'd also like to say that my pain about my mother only continues to grow. Almost all my compositions have come about in memory of her."[19] And he continued, "It is always the same thing that I want to express. I bring it to her as an offering. A mother's love is the highest thing: the love of a mother."

Webern's Six Orchestral Pieces, op.6, of 1909, reflect the whole painful experience of his beloved mother's death. It is true that they do not bear any extra-musical titles, yet in a letter to Schoenberg, Webern described their content in the following words: "The first piece is intended to express my mood when I was still in Vienna and, knowing about the misfortune, still continued to hope that I would be able to see my mother alive." The second piece conveys the painful news of the death of his mother. The third tends toward synaesthesia, conveying "the impression of the scent of the heather" that he "placed on the bier." In the autograph the fourth bears the eloquent heading *marcia funebre* – a title that was left off the printed version of the score. The piece conveys Webern's impression as he "followed the coffin to the graveyard". Much later, in 1933, the composer designated the fifth and sixth pieces as "Epilogue: Remembrance and Resignation".[20] The fourth is undoubtedly the most affecting of the pieces. For long stretches we hear noisy sonorities from the percussion section: bass drum, side drum, timpani, cymbals, tam-tam and low bells. These are interspersed with lamenting individual and combined sounds in the middle, high and low register. A chorale-like melody on muted trumpets at bars 23-26 seems like a paraphrase of the opening lines of the *Dies irae* sequence.

As I have extensively detailed elsewhere, personal experience was an essential prerequisite for Berg's creative process as well. The biographical aspect was extremely important for him in composing, and all his mature instrumental works (from the String Quartet, op.3 on) are, despite their technical complexity the music of experiences. It is my opinion that Berg's entire output is nothing less than music as autobiography.[21]

The element of truth in art was a theme that Adorno was also much concerned with. It is telling that he headed his much-read *Philosophy of New Music* with the following words by Hegel: "For in human Art we are not merely dealing with playthings, however pleasant or useful they may be, but... with a revelation of truth".[22] In his unfinished *Aesthetic Theory* Adorno put forward the "enigmaticalness" of artworks as a condition for explaining their existence, and made these assertions: "That artworks say something and in the same breath conceal it expresses this enigmaticalness from the perspective of language".[23] "Artworks that unfold to contemplation and thought without any remainder are not artworks".[24] And further on, "The solution of the enigma amounts to giving the reason for its insolubility, which is the gaze artworks direct at the viewer".[25]

At this point, if not before, however, doubts begin to arise. It cannot be denied that many artworks seem enigmatic. In many other cases, on the other hand, the alleged enigmatic nature can be rebutted as soon as it becomes scientifically and credibly possible to determine the artist's intentions. The fact that today we are well aware what Beethoven's intentions were in composing many of his works (the "Eroica", "Pastoral" or Ninth Symphonies, for instance) does not mean that these are not artworks. Mahler gave his thoughts on this problem in an important letter to the Viennese critic Max Kalbeck when he wrote, "Beginning with Beethoven, there is no modern music that does not have its inner programme. But no music has worth if the listener first has to be informed what is experienced in it – or what he has to experience. So once again – let every programme perish! One simply has to bring one's ears and heart and – not least

– give oneself over fully to the rhapsodist. There is always a little mystery left – even for the creator!"[26]

It is a truism that over time artworks works can undergo various interpretations, if only because they are often complex and multi-layered. Even so, in my opinion, every interpretation should be always be measured against the author's intentions. Adorno nevertheless asserts quite irrefutably: "Yet the silent and determinate answer of artworks does not reveal itself to interpretation with a single stroke, as a new immediacy, but only by way of all mediations, those of the works' discipline as well as those of thought and philosophy".[27] .This formulation is followed by this debatable phrase: "The enigmaticalness outlives the interpretation that arrives at the answer". No less debatable is Adorno's notion that what is enigmatic about the artwork is nothing less than its "fracturedness". This formulation becomes easier to understand when we remember that Adorno, like Friedrich Schlegel before him, had a particular preference for the fragmentary. Nevertheless, one can rightly question whether works like Beethoven's Missa solemnis or the Ninth Symphony are fragmentary.

As mentioned above, it is a central plank of Adorno's aesthetic theory that the enigmaticalness of the artwork should be coherent with its "truth content". He makes the important observation that, "Ultimately, artworks are enigmatic in terms not of their composition but of their truth content."[28] An assertion such as the following is absolutely central to the writer's dialectic thinking, "The truth content of artworks is the objective solution of the enigma posed by each and every one. By demanding its solution, the enigma points to its truth content".[29] But what is one to understand by the term "truth content"? By way of answer, Adorno writes, "Philosophy and art converge in their truth content. The progressive self-unfolding truth of the artwork is none other than the truth of the philosophical content."[30] On this point, Adorno is manifestly in agreement with the notions of artistic theory of Beethoven, Hegel and Webern. Webern shared with Beethoven the opinion that music was above wisdom and philosophy. In long-unpublished letter to his teacher Schoenberg, dated 23 July 1912, he wrote, "What you have to say on philosophy and music is wonderful. Music is itself a philosophy, but one that does not come from the mind, but from an organ that reaches deeper than that of any other art, that reaches the deepest of all. I sense that so clearly when I hear music by Beethoven, Mahler and you".[31]

# The Problem of "German Music"

> "With German music I consider a number of precautions to be in order"
> FRIEDRICH NIETZSCHE[1]

Anyone attending a Berlin Philharmonic concert during the Third Reich could see, when they looked toward the stage, a vast swastika surmounted by a broad banner.[2] On the banner was a quotation from Wagner's *Die Meistersinger von Nürnberg* that read: "Honour your German masters". In the closing scene of *Die Meistersinger*, Hans Sachs does indeed call on Walther von Stolzing and the assembled people to honour the German masters. Wagner made no secret of his German nationalist sentiments and is well known as the most passionate 19th-century campaigner for "German art" and "German music" . In countless writings he tirelessly exalted the "German spirit" and "German character", invoking both Goethe and Schiller as well as Bach and Beethoven. The paired opposites "German" and "un-German" music not only denote specific artistic issues but have national, nationalist, chauvinist, ideological and political implications as well. To grasp some of these implications, it should be kept in mind that a characteristic feature of the 19th century was an overwhelming nationalism – an intellectual movement that seems quite alien and incomprehensible to us now. Since the time of the Franco-Prussian War of 1870 at the very latest, a latent rivalry existed between German and France. Those who took the side of German music were, at the same time, against the French and "foreign" ("welsch"). French *esprit* and Romance *grazie* were pitted against German "profundity".[3] Debussy, proud to call himself a "musicien français", had declared war on Germany music. Nietzsche had vainly warned, in *Beyond Good and Evil*, against the "pathological alienation that the nationalist idiocy has placed between the peoples of Europe", and decades were to pass before his dream of a united Europe, a Europe that "wishes to become one" began to take shape.[4]

In 1977 Hubert Kolland attempted to shine some light on the social aspects of the way conservative music journalism conceived of music history during the Weimar Republic.[5] To this end, he examined contributions to the prestigious journal *Zeitschrift für Musik*, which in 1923 acquired the subtitle "Campaigning journal on behalf of German music and nurturing of music", and found that the terms "German" and "un-German music" already formed a thread running through discussions in conservative music journalism under the Weimar Republic. Looking closely at the material Kolland assembled, it is immediately clear that the term "German" denotes not just the national, healthy and natural, but also a turning away from progress, that is, something conservative, regressive and reactionary. The terms "German music" and "national music" denote what was later to be deemed "rooted in the native soil" ("bodenständig"). The term "un-German", according to Kolland's work, can be applied to everything from Jewishness, progress, division of labour and specialisation, technique and its application to music by way of "foreign" and "international" elements, to democracy, socialism and communism. The terms "Bolshevism" and "Bolshevist music" that were to go on to be slogans of the Third Reich, actually first appear in 1919.

In terms of their ideological content, many of the definitions quoted can be traced back to Wagner and his era. The terms "German culture" and "cosmopolitan synagogue"[6] are a well-known pair of polar opposites in Wagner's utterances, and Wagner himself defined the character of the German in these words: "The German is conservative; his treasure is accumulated from that of all times; he saves the old, and knows how to use it. He places more importance on retaining than gaining; the new that has been gained is only of value to him if it serves to ornament the old. He craves nothing from outside, but wishes to be unhindered within. He does not conquer, but neither will he tolerate being attacked".[7]

There is an inherent paradox in this: after Liszt, Wagner is one of the most impassioned spokesmen for musical progress in the 19th century. He swore by the new, and constantly experimented with new technical resources, with the goal of broadening music's expressive range. The conservative writers on music in the Weimar Republic, in contrast, took up a position that was anti-progress. They openly rejected the new German progressive faction, criticized Liszt and Richard Strauss, and condemned the "German Musical Union" that Liszt had established on the grounds that it allegedly performed nothing but new music. They considered speculative and theoretical experiments in music to be destructive, judged atonality as contrary to nature, and as "fundamentally alien to and against the German soul", and they spoke of the "subversion" of German music.[8] It was only natural that the Jew Schoenberg, the boldest innovator in experimental music, should be the target of the fiercest attacks. Long before the advent of Fascism, Schoenberg was characterized in Vienna as a "fraud" and "fool".[9] In Leipzig in 1918 his First String Quartet was written off as "miserable caterwauling".[10] In the pages of the *Zeitschrift für Musik* he was quashed as the embodiment of "Bolshevism in music" (1919),[11] the representative of "Satanism"[12] as well as "criminal" (1923),[13] and as "vermin injurious to public safety" (1924).[14] He was seen as the personification of evil. Those who are struck by the extremely aggressive behaviour that Schoenberg at time displayed and attempt to diagnose psychopathic traits in him would do well to consider that no other composer has ever experienced such a level of violent and bitter animosity.[15]

Alban Berg, too, as Schoenberg's pupil and a representative of the infamous atonality was already the target of ferocious attacks in the 1920s. After the successful Berlin premiere of *Wozzeck* on 14 December 1925, some negative voices mingled with the predominantly positive response. Even at that date Berg was labelled the "troublemaker of German music" and described by Paul Zschorlich as a "musical fraud and a composer injurious to public health".[16] The rumour that Berg was Jewish seems to have started to make the rounds at this very time. After the Prague production of *Wozzeck* that prompted riots in November 1926, he was described by a Prague newspaper as "the Berlin Jew" and by a Berlin paper as "the Czech Jew".[17] Berg stated in a published interview that being reproached for being Jewish did not affect him; he did not in any way repudiate it. Within Schoenberg's circle, he and Webern were the non-Jews ("Judenreinen" in Nazi terminology). On his father's side his roots were in Bavaria, and on his mother's, Bohemia. At this date at the latest, Berg had recognised that opposition to his work could be ascribed not to artistic considerations, but chauvinistic and anti-Semitic ones.

There is an element of tragedy in the fact that the leading composers of the Viennese school, who were rejected for being the "troublemakers of German music" felt that it was precisely the culture of German music that they belonged to. They felt that they were German musicians (Schoenberg up until 1933), knew that their roots lay in the German musical tradition, acknowledged that they had learned principally from German composers, and repeatedly invoked them. Endless statements and writings by them contain solemn commitments to German music. The documentation below draws to a large extent on a review of the as yet unpublished correspondence between Schoenberg, Berg and Webern.[18]

A propensity for intolerance is inherent in mankind. During the First World War patriotism had gripped the peoples of all the nations involved in the conflict. Schoenberg, Berg and Webern, all of them Austrian, felt at home with German culture. Some of the statements that Webern made in his letters could have come straight from the pen of Wagner. On 11 August 1914 Webern wrote to his teacher Schoenberg, "I implore Heaven for the victory of our and the German armies. It is absolutely out of the question that the German Reich and ourselves with it should perish. An unshakeable belief has awakened in me in the German spirit, that created human culture almost single-handed."

Webern then wrote to Berg on 25 August 1914, "Yes, it is a terrible but a purifying time. In any event, the German spirit must prevail. Think of the clarity of Beethoven, Kant, Schoenberg and Mahler, and of the mistiness of the French and the Russians."

A combination of misunderstood patriotism and intolerance had led to a boycott of German music abroad and foreign music in Germany during the First World War. On 26 September 1914 Berg complained in a letter to Schoenberg that the conductor Oskar Nedbal had performed works by Debussy, Delius and Liadov in a concert by the Tonkünstlerorchester – "as there are no longer any native composers". Schoenberg replied in October, "It's absolutely disgusting that Nedbal is performing French, Russian and English music. I think one should protest. Do it!"[19].

Since his early days, Schoenberg seems to have been obsessed by the idea of German music and its superiority. Among his papers is a memo written in pencil on a sheet of yellowing paper that must date from the time of the First World War, which reads, "When I think of music, it is only ever German music, consciously or not, that comes to mind. Those who are against it will often have to suffer starvation before such insight becomes natural. But German music thrives on hunger; scrimped and saved for, its wordless power will build and fill the palaces of the spirit for eternity. And it will always reach for the skies, whereas worldly inferiority prides itself on variety shows".[20]

The deeper one delves into Schoenberg's statements and writings, the clearer it becomes that he was extremely exercised by the question of national hegemony in the arts. At the end of July 1921 he said to his assistant Josef Rufer, that "today he had invented something that would guarantee the primacy of German music for the next hundred years",[21] by which he meant the method of composition with twelve notes related only to each other. Schoenberg was aware of the significance of his discovery, and unshakeable in his belief that the future of music belonged to twelve-note composition, and often spoke to his pupils on the subject. That is clear not least from Berg's extended treatise *Why is Schoenberg's Music So Hard to Understand?* of 1924. This essay, written as a contribution to the Schoenberg-Festschrift, is far more than a homage to Schoenberg. It articulates the firm conviction that through the work that Schoenberg had given to the world up to his fiftieth birthday, "assured the supremacy of not only his personal art, but what is more, that of German music for the next fifty years."[22]

There is no doubt about it: Schoenberg and his pupils were, from time to time, inspired by a sense of mission. In February 1931, at the time when he was working on *Moses und Aron*, Schoenberg drafted the essay *National Music* in which he formulated his thoughts on the question of hegemony in the arts. The fundamental idea of the essay is that the arts are bound up with race and nationality. To illustrate these ideas, Schoenberg refers to Wagner, the cause of whose success he links to the rise of the German people. "Wagner's music", he writes, "was not only the best and most significant of its age – it not only surpassed Berlioz, Auber, Meyerbeer, Bizet, Rossini, Bellini and others – but it was also the music of 1870 Germany, who conquered the world of her friends and enemies through all her achievements, not without arousing their envy and resistance.[23] The essay, in which Schoenberg writes, among other things, that the campaign against German music during the First World War was principally a war against music, climaxes in a solemn commitment to German music: "remarkably, nobody has yet appreciated that my music, produced on German soil, without foreign influences, is a living example of an art able most effectively to oppose Latin and Slav hopes of hegemony, and derived through and through from the traditions of German music".[24]

According to Schoenberg, then, a crucial factor in the question of national music is the tradition in which a composer grows up, and in which he is rooted. In support of his argument, he claims to have learned exclusively from German and Austrian composers, naming as his teachers, first Bach and Mozart, then Beethoven, Brahms and Wagner, while acknowledging that he also learned much from Schubert, and from Mahler, Strauss and Reger. Having excluded no one, he is able to say that his originality stems from the fact that he immediately mimicked everything good that he saw, even when he did not first see it in others. The thought that the power of tradition builds a bridge between the past and the future, the old and the new is a central theme with Schoenberg. There is some justification in the description of Schoenberg as a "conservative revolutionary".[25] The essay *National Music* ends with the words, "I am convinced that eventually people will recognise how immediately this 'something new' is linked to the loftiest models that have been granted to us. I venture to credit myself with having written truly new music which, being based on tradition, is destined to become tradition."

When Schoenberg wrote this essay, cultural politics in Berlin, where he worked as director of a masterclass in composition at the Akademie der Künste, were coming dramatically to a head. National Socialist and anti-Semitic watchwords quickly gained currency. Schoenberg seems to have had some sense of foreboding. Webern consoled him on 15 July 1931 with the words, "[...] for, my dearest friend, we are indebted to you not just for German hegemony in music, but beyond that – if I may be allowed to generalise your ideas – for saving the highest good of all from the general chaos of this time".[26]

## The Fate of Arnold Schoenberg and Alban Berg after 1933

After the Nazis took power on 30 January 1933, Schoenberg and his pupils, who saw themselves as representatives of German music, gradually had to grasp that their work was not considered "German music". This nascent defamation of Berg and Schoenberg had a number of psychological ramifications. After Max von Schillings, President of the Berlin Academy of Arts had declared at an Academy meeting on 1 March 1933 that the Jewish influence had to be broken, Schoenberg decided to resign from his professorial post and leave Germany. One of the unexpected consequences of these traumatic experiences was Schoenberg's return to the Jewish faith, in Paris on 24 July 1933. In a highly revealing letter from Arachon to Webern he outlined his reasoning, writing that he had long since determined that he was a Jew and would work for the "national cause of Judaism".[1] He was planning an extensive tour of America, possibly of the world, with the goal of "soliciting assistance for the Jews in Germany". He considered his activities in service of the Jewish cause to be of greater importance that his art. And in the same letter he tells Webern that "although with difficulty and with much wavering" he had finally and definitively broken free from what held him to the West.

Deeply affected by this revelation, Webern sent Schoenberg's letter on to Berg, who read it with dismay. Berg immediately grasped the psychological situation, and was able to gauge the depth of the crisis that the prevailing situation had plunged Schoenberg into, and told Webern that he simply did not believe in his teacher's apparent "rejection of the West" and his "turn toward the Orient".[2] There was only one label for Schoenberg's musical creativity, and that was "German". "What I understand by German," he wrote to Webern, "I hardly need tell you; it is enough to mention the un-German name of Pfitzner, for example. But I could also cite lesser associates. It is a shame that we are not able to talk about this in depth." In the meantime, Berg had had his own encounters with National Socialist ideology and cultural policies. On 16 May 1933 he had heard Wilhelm Furtwängler give a talk in Vienna on Brahms that he found deeply upsetting. The following day he wrote to Webern, "It was a Nazi-tinged lecture on behalf of German music that – so he [Furtwängler] implied – was last represented by Brahms. Without naming names, he rejected everything written after Brahms, especially Mahler and the younger generation [Hindemith]. It was not even mentioned that the Schoenberg circle existed."[3]

For several years Berg served on the jury of the Allgemeiner Deutscher Musikverein, and in this capacity he championed avant-garde composers. In 1929 Hans Pfitzner mounted a press campaign to try to have Schoenberg's opera *Die glückliche Hand* removed from the programme of the Duisburg Tonkünstlerfest,[4] and Berg subsequently made a point of resigning from the music committee, although he then rejoined it in March 1931. On 9 May 1933, the chairman of the organisation Joseph Haas informed him that "in the light of the situation in music policy in Germany immediate changes to the committee personnel were unavoidable". He ordered him to give up his post, since he was viewed as an exponent of an artistic current "that is opposed in the strongest possible terms by the German national movement".[5] Berg tendered his resignation on 17 May, but did not neglect to point out that he had "not a single drop of Jewish blood" in him, and that he had never been politically active. This was an opportunity for him to make it clear that he considered the National Socialist concept that his music was not "German" to be fundamentally false and that it could be refuted. And he took his leave from Haas and the members of the music committee with the assertion that what had united him with the Allgemeiner Deutscher Musikverein "for all those years" had been their shared interest in music that "was German and therefore – like no other – universally valid".[6]

It is possible that at this date Berg had not yet fully grasped the seriousness of the situation. In any event, he noted with some satisfaction that Hindemith was toying with the idea of recruiting him for the Berliner Musikhochschule.[7] Certainly, the musical world soon began to become exercised over the question of whether Berg was "Aryan" or Jewish. Heinrich Strobel asked him outright whether he was "definitely of pure breed".[8] Berg seems to have reacted calmly to these rumours at first. But in December 1933 when he and Webern were described as Jewish composers in a broadcast by the Bayerischer Rundfunk, he felt compelled to issue a denial. In a courteously restrained letter to the broadcaster dated 20 December, he emphasized that both he and Webern were of "100%" Aryan and German descent.[9] Not only his grandparents, but also his great-great-grandparents were Aryan, and all his great-great-grandparents had been Catholic. He was indeed German, or, to be precise, "5/8 German and 3/8 Austro-German". He also pointed out that as a member of the Prussian Academy he could not have been either Jewish or of Jewish descent. To corroborate the correction, he enclosed a copy of his family tree.

Even as early as 1931 and 1932 Berg would not have been unaware that the increasing politicisation of the cultural sphere in Germany was bringing reservations about him and his work in its wake. Before a performance of *Wozzeck* in Brunswick on 9 January 1931 was allowed to go ahead, he had to verify his Aryan descent.[10] And Alfred Einstein's review of the performance of *Wozzeck* in Berlin under Erich Kleiber on 30 November 1932 hailed the conductor's enterprise with the comment that it took "double the courage" at a time when the term "cultural Bolshevism" was so readily used.[11] After the Nazis took power, *Wozzeck*, which had previously been so successful, disappeared from German stages. Up until then Berg's finances had been in a healthy state, thanks to the royalties from *Wozzeck*, but they rapidly began to go downhill. Nevertheless, Berg did not give up hope that his friend Kleiber would be able to go ahead with the premiere of *Lulu* in Berlin. Kleiber was supportive, but still had to submit the libretto first to Hermann Göring. When Berg realised that the decision was on a knife-edge, and that the outlook was not favourable, he sent two identical letters on 20 April 1934 to the General Intendant Heinz Tietjen and to Furtwängler with the intention of changing the Berlin authorities' minds.

The text of this hugely revealing letter contains a kind of apologia for Berg's creativity and above all another solemn (and one might be tempted to say desperate) affirmation of German music. He writes, "The complete exclusion of my works from German theatres and concert programmes is like a deep wound to me. All my life I have felt that I am a German composer, and I have never been considered anything else". He felt able to back up this self-evaluation on the grounds of music theory, music history and musicology, but limited himself to a few pointers. His musical training was not only informed by German classical and Romantic composers, but also (nearly thirty years before) by Bach and Brahms as well. His art was founded on the centuries-old German musical tradition and was fundamentally different from the art of "every other nation or race". The music that he writes could be not be called Roman or Slav or Oriental or in any other way exotic, in simple terms, un-German. And he finishes up with the comment that *Lulu* should be seen for what it is in age of the Third Reich, "a German opera".[12]

The letter did not achieve the desired effect. Furtwängler wrote back to Berg on 23 May 1934, saying, "You have no need prove yourself to me as a German composer. I know you, and have known your music for a long time, and would have no qualms about taking on *Lulu* if it weren't for the text, which seems to me quite impossible given the current public mood here in Germany [...] Incidentally it should not be a surprise to you that you are widely considered to be a Jewish composer. It is a result of your close relationship with Arnold Schoenberg, as simply his most prominent pupil."[13]

It is not difficult to understand that Berg was deeply wounded by the discrimination against his music. On 6 May 1934 he wrote to Webern, "This tacit suppression of our music from German programmes must either be reversed or it will have to be proved to me that our music is not German."[14] Several months later, on 27 February 1935, he complained in a letter to Hella Hertzka that despite fifty years of living and working in his native land, he was still considered not to be "native", and added that he had answered a survey in *Echo* on the theme of Bach and Handel, whose 250th anniversaries were then being marked, with the following words: "It is lucky that Handel and Bach were born in 1685 and not 200 years later! Because otherwise the 'native quality' of one of them would be equally thrown into doubt, and the music of the other would be considered cultural Bolshevism. I would be happy to elucidate, Alban Berg."[15]

Most of all, Berg was distressed by the fate of his teacher, who had been forced to leave his country and Europe by the political situation. Immediately after he heard that Schoenberg had left Germany and was living in Paris, he wrote to Webern: "That is truly dreadful. What a fate! Now, at the age of nearly sixty, cast out from the country where he could speak his mother tongue, without a home, without the certainty of knowing where and on what to live: in a hotel room [...]".[16] After Schoenberg emigrated to the United States, and after his painful experiences with the Berlin Opera, Berg decided to dedicate *Lulu* to his teacher to mark his approaching 60th birthday. The letter on 28 August 1934 in which he dedicated the opera to Schoenberg is yet another passionate affirmation of German music and a tacit protest against the injustice that had befallen Schoenberg. Berg writes, "Please accept it, not only as a product of years of work most devoutly consecrated to you, but also as an outward document: the whole world – the German world too – is to recognise in the dedication that this German opera – like all my works – is indigenous to the realm of that most German of music, which will bear your name for all eternity."[17]

If we look closely at the letters and essays that Schoenberg wrote in America after the outbreak of the Second World War, we repeatedly come across the idea of art being used to convey a message to humanity. For example, the essay *New Music, Outmoded Music, Style and Idea* that reached its final version in 1946 contains the concise formulation: "There is no great work of art which does not convey a new message to humanity; there is no great artist who fails in this respect."[18]

On 3 December 1944 Schoenberg wrote to the American composer Roger Sessions that that most important thing was that people should listen to his music "in the same way as every other kind of music".[19] His compositional method was of no concern to the listener – "but I would like my message to be understood and accepted". In 1943 he was invited to speak to address a conference of Californian school inspectors on the subject of the educational and cultural significance of music. On 19 September he wrote to the conference organiser, Miss Helen Hefferman, "However it has always been my belief that a composer speaking of his own problems, speaks at once of the problems of mankind. But he does it in a symbolical way, without having been able, up to now, to develop definite vocables [a defined vocabulary], expressing matters of philosophy, economy or problems of labour, society or morals."[20]

The close bond between the artist and humanity is an idea that engaged Schoenberg's intense interest as early as 1910. However, all the evidence suggests that he did not formulate the concept of art as message fully until his first years in America. There are many pointers to the fact that the political situation in Germany after the Nazi takeover, his emigration to the United States, return to the Jewish faith and finally the outbreak of the Second World War together affected him profoundly, and the result was a new spiritual attitude and a move toward deeply humanistic thinking. From this point on, Schoenberg saw art's mission as conveying a new message to humanity.

The *Kol nidre*, op.39, *Ode to Napoleon*, op.41, Piano Concerto, op.42 and the cantata *A Survivor from Warsaw*, op.46 are an eloquent testament to the fact that from at least 1938 Schoenberg understood his music as committed art, and put it to the service of religious, political and humanitarian ideas. He conceived the *Ode to Napoleon* – as he himself explained in a handwritten commentary – as a protest again war crimes, tyranny and Nazi ideology, whose psychological background he tried to shed a light on.[21] It showed – so he thought – individual lives measured against the totality of society or its representatives as worthless, and glorified sacrifice only with the goal of world domination. So Schoenberg considered it nothing less than a duty of the intelligentsia to take up a decisive position against tyranny, as Mozart had done in *Figaro*, Schiller in *Wilhelm Tell*, Goethe in *Egmont* and Beethoven in the "Eroica" symphony and *Wellingtons Sieg*. At the same time, he made no secret of the fact that he identified Napoleon with Hitler. There are many indications that he was profoundly shocked by the Japanese attack on the American naval base Pearl Harbor in December 1941, and was this the decisive spur for him to set Byron's ode to music.[22]

Among the most surprising aspects of this twelve-note work, written between March and June 1942,[23] are its tonal echoes, triadic structures and powerful close with an E flat major chord that Willi Reich early on interpreted as a possible allusion to Beethoven's "Eroica".[24] In an important letter to René Leibowitz of 4 July, Schoenberg detailed some of the features of the twelve-note works he had written in the United States, admitting to some relaxation of the "rigour" in his handling of the twelve notes, and wrote in particular about the Ode: "It is true that the Ode sounds like E flat at the end. I don't know why I did that. I may have made a mistake, but it doesn't feel that way to me at the moment."[25] Nevertheless, it is highly likely that Schoenberg deliberately used the many tonal echoes in the Ode, and the quite exceptional E flat major close to allude to Beethoven, the "Eroica" and the heroic key of E flat major. It also has to be taken into account that the underlying tone-row of the ode has an unusual structure. For the "first period", comprising the first six notes of the row, Schoenberg arranged three different versions, as can be seen in the tables below [see music example 1].[26] The first of these is made up of two triads (e″, c#″, g#′ and f″, c″, a′, at the beginning of the top system of the table).

The row is consequently laid out not just to make tonal structures and allusions possible, but actually to bring them immediately to mind.[27]

[Music example 1]
Table of rows in the *Ode to Napoleon*, op.41

Another striking feature is that the final section of the Ode, bars 247-267, marked *Maestoso*, which serves to glorify George Washington (Napoleon's fictional democratic adversary), is not simply suffused with tonal echoes, but actually reveals a latent tonal centre. There is a distinctive eight-note theme underlying the final section, that begins with the notes d, e flat, G, b flat (the second four-note motif is an inversion of the first) and recurs frequently.

[Music example 2]
Theme of the final section of the *Ode to Napoleon* (bars 247-250)

It is tempting to see a further allusion to the "Eroica" symphony's E flat major signals in the first four notes of this theme. A close look at the Ode's thematic and motivic development reveals that the d, e flat, G, b flat motif (created from the second version of the "first period" of the row) is the leitmotif of the whole work. It returns conspicuously at several key moments in the score: played first at bars 100-102 (*poco maestoso*), then transposed in bars 174-175, it reappears in bars 221-223 and, as mentioned above, comes to an apotheosis in the final *Maestoso* (bars 247-267).

In a letter of 15 January 1948 to Hans Heinz Stuckenschmidt, Schoenberg wrote, "Lord Byron, who had previously greatly admired Napoleon, was so disappointed by his simple resignation, that he showered the most scathing derision on him. And I don't think I've failed in that in my composition."[28] There can be no doubt that when Schoenberg made the decision to compose the Ode, he thought of Beethoven, who had an ambivalent attitude to the Emperor, and had originally dedicated the "Eroica" to him.[29]

# Two Unknown Letters by Schoenberg and Berg

Arnold Schoenberg, born into a Jewish family, converted to Lutheranism in 1898. From the summer of 1921 at the latest, after his disturbing experience at Mattsee (he was informed by postcard that as a Jew he was unwelcome at the holiday resort), he began to reflect deeply on his national identity and the "Jewish question". The fateful events of 1933 compelled him and his family (his wife Gertrud and baby daughter, the one-year-old Nuria) to flee Berlin in May and travel to Paris, where he ceremonially returned to the community of the Jewish faith. Ten days later he wrote the following hugely revealing letter to Anton von Webern from Arachon, a seaside resort on the Atlantic coast, not far from Bordeaux.

Schoenberg to Webern[1]

ARNOLD SCHOENBERG　　　　　　　　　　　　4 VIII 1933
VILLA STRESA
AVENUE RAPP
ARACHON

*My dearest friend, I have just received your letter of 1 August, and was pleased to read of your great, unwavering concern: I did not expect anything else from you and, as I'm sure you know, I fully reciprocate. This is something that needs to be said often, at this time. As I wrote to Rufer yesterday, it is fortunate that we few have to deal with it, that throughout the current uproar such friendships stand firm! A comfort in this terrible time. You are right that it is difficult to remain inactive at this time. Certainly the circumstances for action are different for me than they are for you. I have been prepared for what has happened now for "14 years". Over this long period of time I have been able to prepare myself for it, and, although with difficulty and much wavering, have finally and definitively broken free from what has bound me to the West. I have long been resolved that I am Jewish, and you will also have sometimes heard me speak about a piece about which I was not yet in a position to say anything more detailed, in which I have shown the way for action for the national cause of Judaism. A week ago I also returned to the community of the Jewish faith officially, although (as my* Moses und Aron *will demonstrate) it is not religion that separates me from it, but my view on how the church's position on the demands of modern way of life. My intention is to be active in championing such endeavours. For me that is more important than my art, and I am determined – if I am suited to this sort of activity – to do nothing else now than work for the national cause of Judaism. I have just now started, and have found agreement for my ideas almost everywhere in Paris. My next plan is to make a big tour of Ameri-*

ca, which might lead to a world tour, to solicit aid for the Jews in Germany. I have had pledges of significant support. It is progressing, if rather slowly. Because, as always seems to be the case with me, those who have been affected by what I have said, and have believed me, are not often able to pass their impression on to a third party and make that person believe; because it is not just question of the wording, but the tone as well, which is so hard to replicate, of what I have said. So the third party remains sceptical until they speak to me directly. I am going to have to address large gatherings (with a loudhailer) and on the radio. For these reasons I know don't know how long I'm going to be able to work here, and whether I will be able to complete Moses und Aron and rework Der biblische Weg.[2] I'm now anxious to get the Concerto for String Quartet ready for the Kolisch Quartet, because there is a distinct possibility that I can place it with an English publisher (for a tiny fee, it is true, but I'm pleased nevertheless because I absolutely have to earn money), and besides it is meant to be premiered in London in November.[3] Incidentally, I should be in Prague for the Zionist Conference on 20 August; perhaps I'll come by Vienna then. To be honest, however much I'd like to see you all and my children and grandchildren, I don't much feel like it. Görgi is still in Berlin, although I've provided him with the possibility of getting away.[4] But perhaps he'll go shortly. He still has some work, and has been living respectably, and it really is a disaster that it is right now, when he has made a life for himself, is when he won't be able to stay. – My wife is very well, but it's just that she has a lot of housework to do, since apart from my sister we still don't have anyone, and the child creates a lot of work and in the tiny house we live in there is still much to do. – Nuria is – for me at least – delightful. On 30 June she walked unaided for the first time, that was at 14 months, after she had been able to walk holding someone's hand for at least 6-8 weeks beforehand. She gives us enormous pleasure, and we get quite puffed up with pride when we're pushing the pram and hear people saying, "She's so lovely! She's so cute!" We were very sorry to hear that Mali is still suffering.[5] I wonder whether she should take a proper cure? If I were there, I'd spend so long persuading her that she would go along with me. She has to follow me! We'd like to send some pictures of Nuria, but at the moment we can't find any decent copies. Next time! Many heartfelt greetings to you and your family.
Yours,
Arnold Schoenberg

After Webern had read Schoenberg's letter, he sent it on to Berg, who in August 1933 was working on the second act of *Lulu* in his "Waldhaus" on the Wörthersee. Berg returned the letter with the following, equally revealing comments, that also make reference to the death of the architect Adolf Loos.

Berg to Webern

*"Waldhaus" in Auen am Wörthersee*                                 *26.8.33*

*Your report of Adolf Loos's death, although I had known about it for a day, affected me deeply.[6] It is a comforting thought to me that at least one of us saw him in the last few days, but also that he was in the care of Dr Schwarzmann. Otherwise, I consider this "end" (if the word were ever warranted) as a "release". He is being buried now: I would have liked to have been there, since it actually would be my duty. Schoenberg's letter is enclosed. It touched me deeply. Even if I were to consider his turning away from the West* humanly *possible (I really don't think so, or at least I consider his turning to the* Orient *impossible, since there, as much as here he would be driven to lofty solitude), there is still for me the unchanging fact of his musical creativity, and for that there is only one description:* German. *I surely don't need to tell you what I understand by German: I only have to mention the un-German name of Pfitzner, for example. But I could also point to lesser associates. It is a shame that were are not able to talk about this in depth. You are coming to Klagenfurt in the autumn (which is nearly on us), aren't you? I would so like to talk to you about the* practical *side of Schoenberg's plans, since I feel that they are unfortunately not possible either, however much I admire his* purpose *and endeavours, and however much I feel that his* tackling *this problem is shows the deepest insight. Thank you, too, for your* other *news, that, thank God, was cheering: your short stay in the Tyrol, the completion of your two songs on texts by Hildegard Jone,[7] your garden...*
*I'm still stuck in the second act: a difficult birth, but I now think, having substantially reworked it, that I'm on the right path. Farewell, my dear friend!*
*Yours,*
*Berg.*
*All my love from this house to yours, this garden to yours!*

# Beethoven and the Schoenberg School

> "Music is not merely another kind of amusement, but a musical poet's, a musical thinker's representation of musical ideas."
> ARNOLD SCHOENBERG[1]

There is no question that Arnold Schoenberg was a person of great self-assurance, someone who always jealously guarded his independence. It would never have entered his head to take a lead from another artist, follow him, or even identify with him. Any dispute he entered into with another artist was always creative, and when one thinks of his powerful, determined personality, as well as his maxim that the greatest thing an artist can aspire to is self-expression, this becomes easier to understand.

If one tried to formulate what Schoenberg's relationship to Beethoven was, the most appropriate term would be elective affinity. There were specific features of Beethoven's personality and art that spoke to Schoenberg, but at the same time there was no question of identification with the composer. Characteristically, when Charlotte Dieterle, the wife of an American film producer, approached Schoenberg in 1936 with a request to collaborate on a proposed film on Beethoven, Schoenberg politely declined. He gave as his reason that he would not be able to write a more or less objective "life-story" of Beethoven, or to adapt Beethoven's music to a text written by another hand, because he always created independently. It was Otto Klemperer that he consequently suggested as a potential collaborator, on the grounds that, as he wrote: "He knows and really understands Beethoven really quite wonderfully, has the ability to feel him as a hero, and has mettle and spirit enough not to hold any of that back. And even if he is a tyrant, then that would only benefit the whole project. For a slave cannot emulate a hero".[2] Alongside a reverence for Beethoven the man and artist in this letter to Mrs Dieterle, there is an unmistakable distancing from Beethoven the "hero".

In 1910 Schoenberg published a list of aphorisms in the journal *Die Reihe*. Here defined the essence of art: "Art is the cry for help of those who experience in themselves the fate of humanity. They do not resign themselves to it, but battle against it. They do not dully serve the engine of 'dark powers', but throw themselves into its running wheels to understand how it is made."[3]

There is an echo in these words of Beethoven's struggle against fate and his will to conquer it. It is symptomatic that while Beethoven was thinking of his own personal situation, Schoenberg projects his thoughts on fate on to humanity. The artist experiences the fate of humanity in himself, an idea that stayed with Schoenberg for his entire life.

One other point deserving of some attention is that Schoenberg had a firm belief in the moral mission of art, and held art and fundamental convictions to be reciprocal. His entire creative work utterly rejects art as entertainment, sound, polish, surface and virtuosity. Agreeing with the aesthetic assertions of Adolf Loos,[4] whose lecture *Ornament and Crime* caused such a sensation in his day, he raged against the notion of art as decoration and ornament: "I believe that art is born of 'I must', not of 'I can'", a declaration that appears at the beginning of his essay *Problems in Teaching Art*.[5] Here he finds a fundamental division between the ability of the artistic craftsman and the "expressive urge" of the artist, and declares that striving for "veracity" should be encouraged.

No discussion of Schoenberg's relationship with Beethoven should lose sight of the fact that he did not just live at a different time from the older composer, but above all in another world. This makes it all the more astounding that many of his tenets of artistic theory are in accordance with those of Beethoven, who was indeed inspired by ethical ideals, who ascribed the tremendous success of Rossini in Vienna to the "frivolous, sensuous" spirit of the age, and vigorously declared his belief in music's moral purpose. It is striking that almost all the great composers of more recent music history were moralists: Beethoven, Wagner, Mahler and Schoenberg. In this connection it is worth mentioning that Beethoven, Mahler and Schoenberg were the three composers Webern and Berg most revered, and felt most drawn to. Webern in particular had a close affinity with Beethoven's work and personality. Not only did he admire him as a spiritual and artistic model, but also saw him as an absolute ideal. So great was his enthusiasm for Beethoven that he even stated, "Beethoven's birthday ought to be celebrated as the greatest holiday by the whole of humanity!"[6]

Webern was keen to have the clichéd image of Beethoven revised. He cast aside the notion that he was some kind of "mad fool", and continually stressed that he should not be portrayed as a "wild man".[7] What particularly drew Webern to Beethoven was his humanity – significantly, of all Beethoven's symphonies it was the Ninth that he held in the highest esteem.[8] As we know from his pupil Frederick Deutsch Dorian,[9] Webern gave much thought to the interrelationships between music and humanity, and it was an artistic ethos deeply rooted in Beethoven's ideal of humanity that he found persuasive. Webern also shared with Beethoven the opinion that music was a kind of higher wisdom and philosophy. In a long unpublished letter to his teacher Schoenberg of 23 July 1912, Webern wrote, "Your words on philosophy and music are wonderful. Music is indeed itself a philosophy, but not one that comes from the mind, but from an organ that reaches deeper than that of any other art, that reaches the deepest of all. I sense that so clearly when I hear the music of Beethoven, Mahler and yourself."

The extreme, radical and modern stance adopted by Schoenberg, Berg and Webern dated back to before the First World War, but was fully established in the 1920s and 1930s. A study of their as yet unpublished correspondence shows that they found fault with the majority of other composers (Stravinsky, Milhaud, Les Six), and felt themselves equally superior and isolated. They certainly had no great success with audiences, but consoled themselves with the thought that the highly demanding music they cultivated was ahead of its time, and destined to be properly understood only by the next generation, or even the one after that. In that spirit, Berg pointed to the remarkable fact of Schoenberg dedicating his Wind Quintet, op.26 to an innocent child – his grandson "little Arnold".[10] Berg, who had a sense for detecting parallel situations, remembered that in 1847 – twenty years after Beethoven's death – disparaging comments on the Ninth Symphony (a work that he held in particularly high regard) could still appear in print.[11] This gave him a sense that genuinely demanding music always struggled to gain acceptance, and he resigned himself to the fact that there was consequently nothing else for it than to "fly from such a present into as distant a future as possible". Despite all that, the composers of the Second Viennese School stood firmly by their principles, and were not ready to make concessions of any kind. Their intransigence is another link to Beethoven, whose stubbornness and uncompromising stance in artistic matters have become legendary. Soma Morgenstern characterised his friend Berg in the following terms: "In life the kindest, most conciliatory man, in art what he loves is the combative, rigorous, uncompromising and unrelenting".[12]

The huge uproar that the twelve-note composers provoked in the 1920s, and continued to do so at the beginning of the 1930s, and the lack of understanding and resistance that they encountered, drove the composers of the Second Viennese School further toward setting down a justification of their artistic goals. One of their principal concerns was to show their developing artistic path and give a historic justification for twelve-note music. In 1931 Webern told Schoenberg of his plan to offer courses in new music in Mondsee. Schoenberg found the plan "excellent in principle" and gave Webern some advice. "I would just recommend to you," he wrote to him on 22 January 1931, "to arrange the analyses (through the choice of works) so that the evolution of twelve-note composition emerges. So, for example, the Flemish school and Bach for counterpoint, Mozart for phrase-formation, but also for motifs, Beethoven, but Bach possibly as well for development, Brahms and possibly Mahler for varied, multiple interlocking procedures."[13]

Four weeks later, on 24 February 1931, Schoenberg completed his article *National Music*. Here he laid out his thoughts on the role of nations in the development of music, made an emphatic declaration of belief in German music, and expressed the opinion that he stood at a turning-point in the history of music, indeed, had initiated it. He compared the change from Bach's contrapuntal art to the "art of development through motivic variation" with the situation of composition in his own time, evoked a "historic parallel" and thought that "at the climax of art based on harmonic relationships" something quite new, "composing with 'twelve notes related only to each other'" was beginning.[14] The principal idea argued in this highly important essay and in the lectures on the "Path to the New Music" that Webern managed to give in Vienna in 1933 is the conviction that twelve-note composition is the necessary consequence of the development of music, and accordingly that all the processes of composition technique that Schoenberg, Berg and he himself had developed had demonstrable parallels in music history.

Particular relevance has to be attached to Schoenberg's emphatic declaration of belief in German music. Central to the essay *National Music* are the statements that his music is "produced on German soil, without foreign influences", that it derived "through and through from the traditions of German music", and that he learned principally or exclusively from Austro-German composers. Here, his "teachers" he names as "primarily" Bach and Mozart, and "secondarily" Beethoven, Brahms and Wagner. In particular he learned from Beethoven

1   *The art of developing themes and movements.*
2   *The art of variation and of varying.*
3   *The multifariousness of the ways in which long movements can be built.*
4   *The art of being shamelessly long, or heartlessly brief, as the situation demands.*
5   *Rhythm: the displacement of figures on to other beats of the bar.*

These five points of Schoenberg's broad artistic credo sum up the Second Viennese School's relationship to Beethoven, and also hold true for Webern, who admired Beethoven's formal mastery. In his Vienna lectures Webern repeatedly returns to the model of Beethoven and his historic significance. The fundamental "forms" of classical music, its periods and eight-bar phrases had found, in his opinion, "their purest expression" in Beethoven. But the larger forms too – sonata form, scherzo, Adagio and rondo – had reached the end of their development in Beethoven.[15] Webern after all considered variation form – of particular importance for Beethoven – to be a precursor of twelve-note composition.[16] He elucidated by referring to the last movement of the Ninth Symphony. The theme is monodic; everything that follows is based on the idea of this as the "Urform". The most extravagant things can happen, but it remains the same!

Bach's counterpoint, Beethoven's thematic-motivic work, and Wagner's harmonic complexity were the elements that Schoenberg tried to familiarise his students with in his teaching. Analysis and orchestration of well-known masterpieces, many of them by Beethoven, were obligatory in his composition classes. Hanns Eisler left a record of his lessons with Schoenberg: "Schoenberg did not allow his pupils to compose in a *modern* style: counterpoint and composition exercises had to be done in the classical style. Bach, Beethoven, Mozart, Schubert and Brahms were the great models from whom one had to learn one's craft."[17] And in a letter to Schoenberg, Berg remembered the failure of one of his early attempts to orchestrate a Beethoven piano sonata.

In addition to analysis and orchestrating great masterpieces, the lessons covered composing based on particularly important models. In his first attempts at composition, the self-taught Schoenberg carefully followed models. He had obtained second-hand copies of many of Beethoven's symphonies and string quartets, and initially modelled his works on pieces by Mozart, Brahms, Beethoven and Dvořák. To a certain extent he kept up this habit for some time after he had long since found his own path as a composer. If he was faced by a specific compositional problem, he would often seek advice from well-known masterpieces.[18] Works by Beethoven seem to have been the model for many of Schoenberg's movements in sonata, variation or rondo form.

Schoenberg himself indicated that he used the first movement of the "Eroica" as a model in the planning of his First String Quartet, op.7. The sheer expansiveness and the latent four-movement form of the projected work (part 1: exposition and development of the contrasting themes; part 2: Scherzo and Trio; part 3: Adagio and part 4: Rondo) posed particular problems for him. To solve them, he looked at the "Eroica", which prompted many ideas: "[…] how to avoid monotony and emptiness, how to generate diversity from unity, how to create new forms from the basic material".[19] He ultimately claimed to have also learned a great deal from Beethoven's masterwork on how to build up and release harmonic contrasts. To be clear, however, it should be stressed that when Schoenberg spoke about compositional models, he did not mean mechanical copying, but appropriating elements of compositional technique.

Berg too sometimes called on Beethovenian models when he needed to test his theoretical compositional ideas against a concrete example. In this context the extensive sketches for the Chamber Concerto that he wrote between 1923 and 1925 are very revealing. As notes in the sketches document, what he was looking for in the conception of the *Rondo ritmico* was to satisfy the demand of both comprehensibility (through repetition) and diversity (through a range of ideas).[20] He noted down on one sheet the incipits of the rondos of two Beethoven piano sonatas: the *Pathétique* in C minor, op.13, and the G major, op.31, no.1. It is also interesting to note a reference to the finale of Schoenberg's First String Quartet, a movement that takes an original approach to rondo form.[21]

In the essay *National Music*, mentioned above, Schoenberg states that his originality comes from the fact that he immediately imitated everything he saw that was good. And he quickly adds, "even when I had not first seen it in someone else's work. And I may say: often enough I saw it first in myself".[22] The comment refers back to appropriation of compositional techniques that Schoenberg had studied in many other composers, without which his challenging music would not be what it is. It could be concluded that individual appropriations that seem to be characteristic of the method of twelve-note composition are also to be found, or anticipated, in traditional music. The real point, of course, is that twelve-note composition represents something new in terms of method and style, for which there are no historical parallels.

It should have become clear that for Schoenberg and his pupils the intellectual content and veracity of a work lay not just in the expression of inner feeling and in ideological messages, but also in a composer's earnest striving to create a structure completely lacking in decorative ornament, and a rigorous internal coherence whereby every note is accounted for.

The use of texts opened up a further dimension in both expression and the formal structure of a piece of music. Before we turn to the many ways in which Schoenberg brought speech and music together, it is worthwhile taking an overview of the problems of vocal composition in new music.

## Principles of Vocal Composition

In chemistry, the term amalgam is used to signify the solution of bronze with mercury in order to obtain gold and silver. Amalgam can also be used in discussion of problems of vocal composition, of setting of language to music. For when music and poetry are joined together the "end product" is always more than the sum of the constituent parts. Something qualitatively new – a synthesis would be another term – comes into being.

Since at least the 19th century, theoreticians and composers have examined in depth the significance, possibilities and requirements of the symbiosis of music and poetry, art song and music drama providing them with much of the material for their deliberations. Not surprisingly, contrary positions were regularly expressed. While some saw the quality of a poem as a criterion for its suitability for setting to music, others took the element of musicality into consideration.

The view that a poem is less suited to musical setting the more finished it is might seem curious to us nowadays but had its advocates nonetheless. Brahms himself felt that Goethe's poems could hardly be enhanced by music because of their finished quality. "They are all so perfect," he once stated, "you can't do anything to them with music."[1] This explains why Brahms set relatively few Goethe poems. Mahler too admitted that it always seemed to him barbaric when musicians "undertake to set beautiful, finished poetry to music". "It is," writes Ida Dehmel, recording Mahler's own words, "as if a master has carved a marble statue and some painter wants to colour it."[2] The German psychologist Albert Wellek took the same approach when he proposed that the less significant the words, the more room there is for the music to develop and acquire its own individuality.[3]

The history of song-writing certainly demonstrates that the view that the high quality of a poem has an adverse effect on its setting is quite mistaken, not least because the 19th century offers many examples of "beautiful", perfectly-formed poems in terms of their musicality, being set as songs. The vast number of settings of Goethe, Heine, Eichendorff and Mörike, to take only three poets, immediately springs to mind. There is also the fact of the countless parallel settings, where the same verses were set to music by various composers, to demonstrate how many interpretations and readings a poem can offer.

The questions that immediately arise, however, are: on what level does the amalgamation of poetry and music take place? What influence does the poem bring to bear on the form of the composition, and what new dimensions are developed through the amalgamation of the poetry and music? In this regard, I believe there are five main levels to be differentiated.

The first level is that of form. The architecture of a poem, its structure, and the number and nature of the lines together pre-programme the way the composition is constructed as well. The composer can retain the strophic shape of the poem, but he can also choose a through-composed procedure. In new music, other procedures were developed in the way the structure of a poem affects the form of the composition.

The second level might be termed that of the material, where the spoken, chanted or declaimed word is turned into sound. The intonation, rhythm and metre acquire musical form. Here, the poem's phonetic material, articulation, and musical qualities such as rhyme, assonance and alliteration all come into play.

A third level consists of the affective relationships between poetry and music. Since the 18th century music has been taken to be the language of emotion, sentiment, and the heart. But poetry too possesses highly affective qualities. Many rightly see Romantic poetry in particular as an expressive tool for the direct articulation of emotion. It is a widely-held opinion that the emotional content of a poem is deepened and intensified when it is set to music. From that perspective, it is certainly no coincidence that it was precisely in the 19th century that art song reached its undisputed peak.

The fourth level, that of semantics, has a particular relevance. It is in the nature of music not to be semantically precise, but vague. The spoken word, in contrast, is indeed semantically precise, and poetry too has an inherent "meaning". Poets may make extensive use of metaphor and words with multiple meaning, but the principle is generally followed that a poem has an essential "sense". Many composers now treat the text as a bearer of semantic content. In this way music acquires meaning; it achieves that "certainty of expression" that Wagner felt was not inherent.

The fifth level is that of representation: poetic texts and poems show an abundance of images and figures that composers regularly transform into musical images and figures – as 16th- and 17th-century madrigals readily demonstrate .

These points about the various levels of the amalgamation of poetry and music hold true for traditional music, up to the modern period. If we turn to the music of the 20th century we are confronted by an altered situation. One of the reasons is that modern verse differs profoundly from traditional poetry in many aspects. One of its most conspicuous hallmarks is the loss of musicality. Rhyme, assonance, strophic structure and metre are considered threadbare and antiquated, and consequently avoided. The division into verses is often achieved exclusively through typography. Many modern poems are not mean to be recited, but only read. Gottfried Benn expressed the opinion as early as 1951 that he did not think modern poetry "could be recited".[4] It needed to be printed on paper, read, seen in black and white, it came to life when its exterior structure was visible, and became more intimate when leant over in silence. It is my feeling that his loss of musicality is one of the reasons why many contemporary composers pass over contemporary verse and turn back to older poetry.[5] One characteristic at least of a tendency in modern poetry, moreover, is hermeticism as a means of expression, an inclination toward the illogical, dreamlike and absurd.[6] Hallucinatory content becomes more frequent in poetry, a cult is made of metaphor and oxymoron, of contradictory pairing of opposites, and the sense of a poem is often encoded in a symbolist manner – one element that frequently has implications for the musical setting.

The way that vocal composition developed after World War II led to discussion of "linguistic disintegration" in new music.[7] It is easier to understand that judgement when we think of what is known as "speech-composition" (*Sprachkomposition*), that is, the various attempts to treat language as music, to take it exclusively as phonetic material, destroy its syntactic structure and ignore its semantic dimension, either partially or completely.[8] The dialectics of the phonetic and semantic elements of a text seems to be a crucial point for avant-garde vocal composition, and much depends on whether a composer is intent on taking the "meaning" of the text seriously. Many composers have actually been proud to have "stripped out" the meaning from the texts they have used. Clearly there is a significant issue involved.

The notion of "speech composition" can in a way be seen as an offshoot of the tendency to turn speech into music – a tendency established with the Romantic poets at the latest, then with the French Symbolists, and which took a concrete form with the Dadaists. Various nuances in Mallarmé and Rimbaud suggest that the poem has more to do with the sound of the words and the magic of language than the "sense". The avant-garde composers of the 1950s and 1960s – Karlheinz Stockhausen, Dieter Schnebel, Mauricio Kagel and György Ligeti – adopted these ideas, took a lively interest in linguistics and studied phonology They were all drawn to the idea of using the sound of language as a tone colour, a tonal duration.

Many trends in "speech composition" however must be understood against the backdrop of the conviction that language had become so conventional that it was now ossified and exhausted, and no longer conveyed anything. The destruction of language was the logical consequence of a fundamental critique of language, and also of the acknowledgement of being literally speechless.

No less significant is the spell cast by the philosophy of the absurd (think of Albert Camus[9]) over modern art, modern theatre (Beckett, Ionesco), modern poetry and contemporary music. In a thoughtful article, the Austrian musicologist Harald Kaufmann described Ligeti's *Aventures* and *Nouvelles aventures* as examples of "absurd music", and tried to show how their absurdity was not to be taken as a flattening, but rather as different from and an expansion of the intellectually meaningful.[10]

Any examination of thoughts on the aesthetic and philosophical premises of "speech-composition" must ultimately touch on the spiritual works of Dieter Schnebel (*Glossolalie, Madrasha II*). Their central idea is the synthesis of languages, the realisation and at the same time the dissolution of a Babel-like confusion of languages, the search for a complete, universal, global language.[11] In 1976 Werner Klüppelholz detected the end of *Sprachkomposition* and drew the following conclusion: "The actual intention of this kind of musico-linguistic writing is to offer a critique of human communication. Its random violations of syntax and semantics destroy a language, the damage to which should thereby be brought to light; the artistic disassociation of language is a reflection of the alienation of its users from the overly familiar as from that for which it stands.[12]

Certainly, other perceptions can be mentioned. At Darmstadt in 1961, for instance, Nono opposed Stockhausen's interpretation of *Il canto sospeso*, in particular against the assumption that in this work he (Nono) had "quite deliberately removed the meaning from specific points in the text".[13] Nono was emphatic in stating that as he saw it, words created a "phonetic-semantic unity" and that the music of all his recent choral compositions was to be understood as "the composed expression of the word". This was a plea for the notion of music as message.

It seems to me that this notion has gained ground in recent decades. It is striking, in any case, that when it comes to texts, various composers often choose the form of music drama. York Höller carried out an interesting experiment in this regard in his work *Schwarze Halbinseln* for large orchestra, vocal and electronic sounds, of 1982. The work is based on the poem *Die Nacht* by the Expressionist poet Georg Heym. However, it is only at the end that a female speaker recites the poem. Before that point, it is the linguistic and rhythmic structures of the poem, its expressive gestures and poetic images that secretly, as it were, shape the music.[14]

In artistic questions there is, of course, no absolute truth. Art can be perceived as much as a game as a message.

For Schoenberg, language was a medium for articulating states of mind and for setting down his beliefs. In many ways, texts thus had an influence on the musical structure, in that Schoenberg was always concerned with helping to provide adequate expression of the content of a poem or a libretto by musical means. Alienation or destruction of the linguistic sense would never have entered his head. The examples of *Gurrelieder*, *Pierrot lunaire* and the opera *Moses und Aron* should make this clear.

## Schoenberg's *Gurrelieder*

Arnold Schoenberg's monumental *Gurrelieder*, composed at the dawn of the 20th century, occupies a prominent position in the history of new music. It is one of the composer's most substantial and significant works, and in many ways it stands as the magnum opus of his first creative period, defined by his use of extended tonality. Schoenberg himself attached particular importance to it for his compositional development. In a letter of 19 August 1912 to Emil Hertzka, director of Universal Edition, he referred to it as "the key to my entire development. It shows sides of me that I no longer show, or if I do, on another basis. It explains how everything later had to come, and that is hugely important for my work: that the man and his development can be traced from this point on".[1]

The premiere in Vienna on 23 February 1913 (given in the Großer Saal of the Musikverein under Franz Schreker) was an unexpected and overwhelming success. For once, the normally indifferent press joined in the general chorus of praise. Webern enthused over the "roaring, unprecedented" sound of the "magnificent work", and counted himself fortunate to have at last experienced the recognition bestowed on his revered teacher. To this day, *Gurrelieder* remains Schoenberg's most successful work.

There are a number of elements to take into account in any consideration of the reasons for this quite exceptional success. After Wagner, many composers understood music as a medium for conveying ideological concepts, and *Gurrelieder* is one of those works by Schoenberg that need to be considered against an ideological background. It would not be inaccurate to identify it as a kind of redemptive mystery. As well as its rich range poetic imagery, the beautiful cycle of poems *Gurresange* (Songs of Gurre) by Jens Peter Jacobsen (1847-1885) is shot through with philosophical notions. The cycle relates the love story of Waldemar and Tove, and draws its strength from the properly Romantic concept of the affinity between love and death. Tove becomes a sacrificial victim of the jealous Queen Helwig, Waldemar's wife. But Tove also invokes "powerful, beautifying death". The idea of mortality runs like a leitmotif throughout the cycle. The message of the poetry is indeed a belief in the eternal cycle of life, and at the same time in the notion that love is stronger than death. The piece closes with a vision of the "laughing" rising of the sun out of the ocean of night.

Schoenberg must have been deeply affected by the beauty and richness of ideas in the poetry, which also includes the legend of the "wild hunt". In any case, he set out to express its grandeur using quite exceptional means, and his great oratorio calls for colossal forces: as well as five soloists and a speaker, the score stipulates three four-part male choirs, an eight-part mixed chorus, and a mammoth orchestra of eight flutes, five oboes, seven clarinets, three bassoons, two contrabassoons, ten horns, seven trumpets, seven trombones, contrabass tuba, four harps, celesta, a vast array of percussion and more than eighty strings. At the Vienna premiere there was a chorus of 600, and 150 players. It bears comparison with Mahler's "Symphony of a Thousand", which had its premiere in Munich on 12 September 1910.

Expressive excess goes hand in hand with this inflated sound-world. Schoenberg picks up where Wagner left off, and carries on further in the same direction. To justify their resentment of the newcomer and question his achievement, Schoenberg's opponents had indeed talked of "an emulation of Wagner" at the premiere of *Gurrelieder*. It is true, however, that in this respect as well Schoenberg here touches on unchartered territory. The more one explores the score, the clearer it becomes that this massive work has a great deal to divulge in terms of gaining a deeper understanding of Schoenberg's compositional development. Although many sections are clearly conceived in tonal terms, in others the extension of tonality is pushed so far that the step into atonality – Schoenberg's daring and much-resented move of 1908 – seems quite inevitable. Having said that, in the third section melodrama there are several atonal moments.

In 1897 the Leipzig publisher Georg Heinrich Meyer issued a German edition of Jacobsen's poetry in a translation by the Viennese scholar Robert Franz Arnold (a pseudonym for Levisohn). Schoenberg divided the *Gurrelieder* into three parts and began to set it to music in March 1900, making rapid progress. In a short time he composed the first two sections and a large part of the third but due to financial problems he had to break off work on it in April 1900 and orchestrate operettas. In March 1901 he was able to take up the composition again: he completed the remainder, and in August began to orchestrate it. Other tasks meant that he continually had to interrupt work on the orchestration, but by 1903 he had completed that of the first two parts and the beginning of the third. He subsequently put the piece aside for several years. He was aware of the huge difficulties involved in mounting a performance of this colossal work, which seemed to him insurmountable. Having lost heart, and any interest in the *Gurrelieder*, he abandoned his plan to complete the piece, and felt that he had to leave this task to posterity. Then, on 14 January 1910, the unexpected happened: as part of a Schoenberg evening in the Ehrbar Saal in Vienna, as well as the George Lieder, op.15 and the Three Piano Pieces, op.11, there was a performance of the first part of the *Gurrelieder* in Schoenberg's own piano reduction. The concert brought the highly controversial composer a conspicuous success: the general public was made aware of the existence of the *Gurrelieder* and they demanded a performance of the complete work.

Schoenberg was urged to complete the orchestration. In July 1910 he resumed work on it and finished the piece in 1911 in Zehlendorf in Berlin. As an aid to understanding the mammoth work, Universal Edition, which had agreed to publish the *Gurrelieder*, decided to print a "listeners' guide", and entrusted this task to Alban Berg.[2] In a letter to him, Schoenberg attempted to explain how he envisaged the content of this "guide". Berg was to indicate the most important themes and also point to the "most significant" places where they return. "Certain characteristic moods" were also to be described, "in simple, unbombastic (i.e., somewhat detached) style". Schoenberg had in mind something aphoristic, casual and loose in form. Berg took his teacher's advice to heart and set to work. He produced an enormous manuscript whose length appalled both Hertzka and Schoenberg. Despite the considerable cutting that he had to undertake, Berg's "guide" amounted to no fewer than 100 printed pages.

Berg had many reservations about the usual pamphlet style of musical commentary, and considered it his lofty duty to talk about the various musical aspects "avoiding all poetry and psychology", and indeed "on one hand – as in the discussion of the prelude – to deal with the harmonic structure, on the other the construction of the motifs, themes, melodies and transitions; to cover the form and structure of larger stretches of music, contrapuntal combinations, choral movements, part-writing, and finally the nature of the orchestration".

Berg's guide is without doubt the most thorough, detailed compositional analysis of the *Gurrelieder* yet produced, but certainly its tendency to avoid all poetry and psychology works against it. Just like Jacobsen's poem, Schoenberg's music lives not least through poetry and psychology. This is easier to understand if we consider that Schoenberg based his composition on an array of characteristic leitmotifs that are announced, varied in diverse ways, developed and combined. They denote perceptions, emotions, passions, ideas, states of nature and situations. They form deep intellectual relationships and give a psychological exploration of events. At the centre of this sophisticated system of leitmotifs are a love and death theme, a kiss motif, a theme for the "Ride of the Death" and a burial chorale.

It is only after an in-depth analysis of the score that one begins to recognise the overwhelming importance of this system. Not only is the huge orchestral interlude in the first part dominated by Tove and Waldemar's leading leitmotifs, but the other two parts also make repeated, varied references to what has gone before. This is Schoenberg's way of investing his music with semantic and psychological elements.

The first part of *Gurrelieder* is made up of a prelude, nine songs for Waldemar and Tove, a long orchestral interlude, and the Song of the Wood Dove. Waldemar and Tove sing alternately of their moods, their yearnings and the fulfilment of their love. Each song has its own, distinctive characteristics, an indication that Schoenberg managed to find an ideal musical expression for the mood of each poem. They are so well matched that it feels as if music and text are completely one.

Waldemar's first song "Nun dämpft die Dämm'rung jeden Ton" (Now twilight muffles every sound) evokes nature and the human spirit, the mood of twilight merging into a mystical sinking into one's self. With this, Schoenberg leaves his roots in Wagner's sound-world far behind. Wagner's chromaticism and altered harmonies are indeed among the hallmarks of the composition, but the way in which Schoenberg creates a sequence of differently structured sonorities is completely new and unique to him. One aspect that stands out in the prelude that serves as a symphonic introduction to the first song is its rather Impressionistic ostinato technique, in which a motif or a chord progression on which the movement is based is repeated several times. The same holds true for the augmented sixths (E flat, G, B flat, C, for example) and the frequent use of whole-tone chords, both of which Debussy frequently has recourse to.

There is an Impressionistic tint to Tove's song "O, wenn des Mondes strahlen leise gleiten" (Oh, when the moonbeams glide softly) as well. The poem expresses a feeling of pathos: in the moonlight, all nature appears to Tove to look like "a reflection of divine dreams". A distinctive mixture of pedal points, pentatonic motifs and whole-tone phrases gives the outer sections of the song their individual character, and harp sounds, glissando effects and harmonics from the multiple divided strings are some of the key colouristic effects in the orchestration.

Like the first two songs, the subsequent ones are also arranged in pairs. Waldemar's song "Roß! Mein Roß! Was schleichst du so träg!" describes the King of the Dunes' ride to Gurre and his impatience to see Tove. Tove's "Sterne jubeln, das Meer, es leuchtet" depicts her impatience to hold Waldemar, the "princely hero" in her arms. Both songs – linked by a common motif – are euphoric in mood. If Waldemar's song is characterised by impetuousness, Tove's song has an exhilarated, almost dance-like character.

The subject of the following two songs is Waldemar's and Tove's blissful love. Waldemar, proud to have Tove at his side, proclaims that he is not ready to exchange his happiness "for the glory of the Kingdom of Heaven and its deafening music". Naturally, the poetry's religious metaphor determined the chorale-like setting. Tove's love song "Nun sag ich dir zum ersten Mal" provides a lyrical counterpart, and is undoubtedly the most popular song in the entire work. Alban Berg, who spoke about the "irritating popularity" of this song, thought that the reasons were to be found in the syncopations and diminished seventh chords. What is certain is that the setting's particular expressivity also derives from Schoenberg's marked preference for wide intervals.

The theme of death is worked into the next two songs, but what a difference between the way the two poems, and the two settings, for that matter, are shaped! Waldemar's song "Es ist Mitternachtszeit" explores the idea of contrast: the subject of the poem is the difference between past and present, and the idea of mortality. "Accursed creatures" rise from their graves at midnight, look longingly at life, and sigh, "our time is over".

Waldemar however thinks of his present: "My time is now!". Schoenberg's setting takes account of this contrast, and intensifies it by musical means. The strikingly pale, ghostly sounds in the outer parts of the song (here the death motif and the burial chorale are heard for the first time) make a sharp contrast to the exuberant middle section.

Unlike Waldemar, Tove is not alarmed by death. In her song "Du sendest mir einen Liebesblick" she articulates her belief in the cycle of life and the immortality of love, and ends with the invitation "So let us drain the golden goblets to him, powerful, beautifying death". The setting – initially characterised by sumptuous chromaticism – is a telling example of indeterminate tonality, and culminates in a kind of Liebestod – the ecstatic climax of the first section – which establishes the key of G major.

Subtly, Waldemar's song "Du wunderliche Tove" that rounds off the group of what are essentially love songs, returns to the peaceful mood of the opening, both in the poetry and the music. The first and ninth songs share not only the same key (E flat major) and metre (3/4), but are also related in terms of mood. In the subsequent orchestral interlude the most important of the previously-heard themes are treated to symphonic development. These are Tove's love theme, the kiss theme, Waldemar's melodic phrase on the words "Mein Haupt wiegt sich auf lebenden Wogen", a "very soft" phrase from his song "Du wunderliche Tove", and finally (1 bar before rehearsal number 92) the Liebestod theme, that here undergoes a kind of apotheosis in A major. Toward the end of the interlude (5 bars after 94), the contrabassoon and bassoon play an attack-like motif that will later depict the murderous assault on Tove four times. After that (1 bar after 95), her love theme is heard in a strikingly distorted form.

The subsequent Song of the Wood Dove – a mixture of elegy and ballad – relates the dramatic evens of Tove's death and burial, and the king's pain and despair. The quasi-Expressionistic music moves between lamenting (typically sighing), funereal, poignantly agitated, and funeral cortege-like moments. At the end, the Wood Dove reveals that it was "Helwig's falcon" that "cruelly tore apart Gurre's dove". At this point the ten horns play the attack motif twice, triple forte.

Compared with the other two parts of *Gurrelieder*, the second is remarkably short. The poem deals with Waldemar's conflict with God. The king accuses God of being cruel and tyrannical, and blames him for robbing him of his only happiness. The orchestral introduction that leads into Waldemar's song is linked thematically to the Song of the Wood Dove. Waldemar's song itself, divided into three strophes, alternates between biting dissonances and sequences of solemn, consonant sounds, when the words touch on the glory of God. What is particularly striking is the movement's motivic and thematic density, and the way it pushes extended tonality to its furthest limits. Berg thought that the key of this song could be read as moving between C minor and B flat minor.[3] The movement does indeed close in B flat minor, but the prelude opens with an F sharp minor triad and is characterised by wandering harmonies. It is true that tonal centres are regularly established, but because of the endless modulations, the listener almost feels the ground giving way under his feet.

One of the great qualities of Jacobsen's poem is its range. Aesthetically, it embraces not just the lyrical and dramatic, but also has eerie, ghostly and grotesque elements. The enormous variety in the poem inspired Schoenberg to compose music that is equally varied, and this makes *Gurrelieder* the great piece it is.

The third part of this large-scale cantata is clearly divided into three sections, "Die wilde Jagd" (The Wild Hunt), "Des Sommerwindes wilde Jagd" (The Summer Wind's Wild Hunt), and the concluding Hymn to the Sun. The first ("Die wilde Jagd") ties together the saga of the ghostly rising of the dead and the story of the dead King of Denmark, who yearns for Tove and continues to accuse God, even in death. Different aspects of this subject-matter are elaborately treated across a sequence of five songs and two choruses.

The three motifs of the prelude to the third part paint a terse, vivid picture of the ghostly landscape where the "action" is played out. Significantly, these are the death motif and burial chorale from the first part, and the motif of the accusation of God from the second. Waldemar's first song, "Erwacht, König Waldemars Mannen wert!", combines the three-note waking call itself with the "Rising of the Dead" motif, created by Schoenberg out of the riding motif in the first part. Both these motifs are developed in the subsequent orchestral interlude with the involvement of the xylophone (the musical symbol of the grotesque).

The peasant's song "Deckel des Sarges klappert und klappt" treats the subject of the "wild hunt" from the viewpoint of a naïve and superstitious man, horrified by the "night fiend", who thinks he is protected by making the sign of the cross, repeating Christ's name three times. Matching the reproach in the poem, Schoenberg contradicts the first strophe of the song with the previously stated ghost theme, while he uses the new motivic material of the second as a basis.

The first chorus of Waldemar's Vassals ("Gegrüßt, o König, an Gurre-Seestrand!") paints a lively, colourful picture of the nightly activities of the band of riders: "Thus we hunt, as legend has it, every night till Judgement Day". Schoenberg set the text for three four-part men's choruses, and in his intermittent canonic writing he exploits every last technique imaginable. As logic would dictate, the orchestral part is dominated by the motif of the "rising of the dead". To conjure up a particularly ghoulish effect, Schoenberg makes extensive use of percussion, and at this point the score actually asks for iron chains.

Waldemar's second song "Mit Toves Stimme fluster der Wald" strikes an ardent note. Tove is always present in Waldemar's heart, and the poem ends with the lines "My dead heart swells and expands / Tove, Tove, Waldemar yearns for you!". The fervour of Schoenberg's setting exceeds that of all the love songs in the first part. Tove, incidentally, is present in the orchestral part in the form of quotes from her love song.

There is a powerful contrast to Waldemar's songs in the black humour of the song of Klaus Narr (Klaus the Fool), "Ein seltsamer Vogel ist so'n Aal". The treatment here of the themes of the wild hunt and humanity's apocalyptic fears is ironic, and tips over into the grotesque. Klaus, the fool from Farum, pokes fun at a whole host of things, and is confident that at the Last Judgement he will be able to talk his way out of most of his sins. Schoenberg gave a Scherzo quality to both this song and the following interlude. The mood is conversational, the music light, agile and fresh.

Waldemar's third and last song, "Du strenger Richter droben" goes back to the theme of the conflict with God. Waldemar urges God in heaven to let him and Tove be united "when the dead are resurrected", and threatens to burst into the Kingdom of Heaven with his wild hunt. The orchestral part of the setting is heavy with pathos, and interprets the poetic imagery with appropriate musical symbols (the love motif, the theme of the rising of the dead, and Waldemar's accusation of God).

The second chorus of Waldemar's vassals "Der Hahn erhebt den Kopf zur Krah" is a counterpart to the first. While one illustrates the nightly rising of the dead, the other describes their return to their graves each morning, and expresses their longing for rest and peace. Matching the accusation in the text, the setting is muted and sombre in tone. The music favours lower registers and the dynamics are mainly pianissimo. Only when the text deals with "life", that "with power and gleam, with deeds and beating hearts" does the music change to forte. At the same time. the opening motif of the work (c''- e flat' - b flat - b flat) is inverted to b flat' - g'' - c''' - c'''.

The melodrama "The Summer Wind's Wild Hunt" occupies a special place in the work's overall dramaturgy, effecting a decisive change of direction. The shadowy images disappear, and sombre visions give way to something brighter. The summer wind speeds across the lake, the cornfields and trees, and contemplates mortality and renewal. This melodrama deserves particular attention for two reasons: on one hand because here for the first time Schoenberg tries out his subsequently famous technique of *Sprechgesang* – a technique that he would later develop in the drama *Die glückliche Hand*, op.18 (1908-1913) and in *Pierrot lunaire*, op.21 (1912); on the other because specific points (particularly the sections beginning 3 bars before figure 77 and 4 bars before figure 79) are astonishingly progressive in terms of compositional technique. There is no perceived tonal centre here: Schoenberg composed this music as early as 1910/1911 in his atonal idiom.

*Gurrelieder* ends on an affirmative note. Schoenberg set the Hymn to the Sun that closes this vast work for eight-part mixed chorus and large orchestra. The music is striking for being so different, for its brilliance and colour, its palette of shimmering sounds and the alternation between chordal and canonic sections. This ties up with the opening of the work, creating a correspondence between the beginning and the end. The four-note motif of the opening (c" - e flat' - b flat - b flat) is now played by the trumpets, in the distinctive inversion (g' - e" - a" - a"). If the piece opens with an image of sunset, it ends with a picture of the rising sun.

## The Melodramas of *Pierrot lunaire*

The 21 (three times seven) melodramas of *Pierrot lunaire*, composed at the prompting of the actress Albertine Zehme in 1912, are today counted among the legendary works of new music. Albert Giraud's poems, and even more so, Otto Erich Hartleben's German re-workings of them that Schoenberg set to music, are far better than their reputation would suggest. (Hanns Eisler, no less, placed them in the "province of the demonic".) They explore in a range of ways variations on the literary motifs of the moon and Pierrot, but also draw in the motif of those poets who bleed to death at their verses, and there is a frequent ambivalent hovering between irony and pain (Nos. 6 and 7). When Schoenberg composed the first melodrama, *Gebet an Pierrot* (No.9), on 12 March 1912, he wrote in his diary: "I think it turned out very well, which is very inspiring. And I can sense that I am absolutely going in the direction of a new kind of expression. Here the sounds become *an absolutely brutal immediate expression of physical and emotional excitement.* Almost as if everything were directly transferred"[1] (my italics). The reciting voice is accompanied by an ensemble of five instruments in varying combinations. Berg noted in his hand-written copy of the score that each piece had its "own tone colour".[2]

Of the total of 56 poems that make up Hartleben's *Pierrot*, Schoenberg carefully selected 21 and organised them into a three-part cycle. In a letter to Alexander von Zemlinsky of December 1916, he referred to his melodramas, and gave a kind of personal interpretation of the work when he wrote, "My dearest friend, heartfelt wishes for Christmas 1916. It is a commonplace to say we are all moonstruck clowns; that is what the poet means when he writes that we take the trouble to brush away imaginary moonbeams from our clothes and yet pray to crosses. Let us be happy that we have wounds: they provide something that helps us not to value material things too much. Contempt for our wounds breeds contempt for our enemies, it is the source of our capacity to sacrifice our lives for a moonbeam. Pathos comes easily to us when we think of the *Pierrot* poetry".[3]

The fame of the melodramas rests not least on the original *Sprechgesang* approach, which has the twin advantage of being closer to speech, and having a richer, more nuanced range of expression.[4] The technique really advanced, however, when Berg took it up in *Wozzeck* and developed it further. Berg's enthusiasm for his teacher's idea still reverberates in his essay *Die Stimme in der Oper* ("Voice in Opera") of 1929, where he extols Schoenberg's *Sprechgesang* as a boundless artistic asset, and "one of the best mediums for comprehension".[5]

Of the many discussions of Schoenberg's cycle of melodramas, the most insightful come from the pen of Pierre Boulez, who performed *Pierrot* together with his own *Le Marteau sans maître* in Basel in 1962.[6] In an introductory essay to this concert, Boulez stressed the "theatrical" character of Schoenberg's work, likening it to a kind of "black cabaret" and pointed to the tendency to frequent changes of expression, the way all three parts "skip from one type of expression to another", which is their particular attribute. He cited as typical examples the "huge change in mood" between the "dark night-vision" and "the naïve irony in the 'Prayer to Pierrot'", as well as the contrast "between the deliberately pumped up horror of the 'Red Mass' and the dry informality of the 'Gallows Song'".

Boulez, however, found fault with Schoenberg's treatment of the voice. He spoke of an "error" that Schoenberg had made with regard to the relationship between the speaking and singing voice. According to Boulez, Schoenberg had not taken into consideration that many people's singing voice has a wider range and higher placing than their speaking voice, which has an inherent range and tends to the lower register. As a result, *Pierrot* lies both too high and too low. But Boulez's objection does not stand up: Schoenberg's *Sprechgesang* is neither speech nor song, but a hybrid. Schoenberg writes in the preface to the score that "realistic, natural speech" is not in any intended, and that the performance "should never call singing to mind".

As indicated, Boulez sought to locate the emotional mood of *Pierrot* somewhere between "naïve irony" and "hysterical obsession". But it would be more accurate to say that irony and pathos, lyricism and drama are the twin poles of the work, and that there is a wealth of nuances and different facets to the psychological universe they encompass. If we analyse the music, examine the treatment of the *Sprechstimme* and take account of what Schoenberg wrote, then the extent to which this *Sprechgesang* can be modulated appears no less remarkable. It has a palette that ranges from unpitched whispering (No.3) to an impressively musically realised scream – not, however, indicated as such – in No.15, "Heimweh", bar 24. In between lie the expressive spheres of seriousness (No.14) and intimacy (No.6).

If we take proper notice of Schoenberg's parenthetical comments, it becomes clear that they refer partly to the affective aspect and partly to the manner of delivery (the intonation). Examples of the affective character are the markings *kläglich* (pathetic, No.9) *ärgerlich* (angrily, No.18) and *erregt* (excited, No.18). In contrast, indications such as *gezischt* (hissed, No.9), *trocken, beiseite* (drily, aside, No.16) and *komisch bedeutsam* (comically meaningful, No.18) relate to the style of delivery. There is clearly a line running from here to Ligeti's *Aventures* and *Nouvelles aventures*.

In the same year that *Pierrot lunaire* was written, Schoenberg published his essay *The Relationship to the Text*.[7] It contains a number of striking statements, including the following sentence: "For me, even more decisive than this experience was the fact that, inspired by the sound of the first words of the text, I had composed many of my songs straight through to the end without troubling myself in the slightest about the continuation of the poetic events, without even grasping them in the ecstasy of composing, and that only days later I thought of looking back to see just what was the real poetic content of my song." If Schoenberg says so, then we have to believe him. However, in the case of *Pierrot*, the compositional process did not in fact work like that. If we study the score closely, we can discern a remarkable correspondence between poetry and music. As I see it, in composing most of the melodramas Schoenberg started from the poetic images, and transformed poetic ideas into musical ones. Here are some examples:

Several of the melodramas in *Pierrot* are conceived as character pieces, and in a number of cases the choice of a specific character is based on the poetic content. Naturally, the fifth melodrama, "Valse de Chopin", which in expressive terms is "a melancholy, gloomy waltz" is given the character of a slow waltz. It seems equally logical that Schoenberg composed the 20th melodrama, "Heimfahrt" (Journey Home) as a barcarole in 6/8. Yet the first strophe of the poem reads

*Der Mondstrahl is das Ruder,*
*Seerose dient als Boot:*
*Drauf fährt Pierrot gen Süden*
*Mit gutem Reisewind.*

*[The moonbeam is the rudder,*
*water-lily serves as boat,*
*on which Pierrot goes southward,*
*the wind behind his sails.]*

There are more revealing instances, however: in composing the fourth melodrama, "Eine blasse Wäscherin" (A pallid washerwoman), Schoenberg evidently pursued the concept of pallor, which dictated the dynamics and tonal and timbral scheme. The instrumental accompaniment – played by flute, clarinet and violin – comes across like a silhouette. As Schoenberg indicates in the score, the three instruments "play at exactly the same volume, all without any expression," at *ppp* throughout.

Giraud's "Madonna" – the sixth melodrama of the cycle – conjures up the image of the *mater dolorosa*, the "mother of all sorrows", invoked by the poet. In conceiving this melodrama, Schoenberg seems to have had models of sacred music in mind.[8] The piece is for flute, bass clarinet and cello, and it opens with a slow, three-part expressive first section (bars 1-14) for the three players. With its sighing figures and walking-bass pizzicato quavers from the cello, this section refers back to the slow movement of an old *sonata da chiesa*. The second section (bars 15-24) is, in contrast, in typical Expressionist style, a powerful intensification in which the reciting voice making dramatic points.

The eighth melodrama, "Nacht" is one of the most rigorously worked out pieces: a passacaglia on a predominantly chromatic, twelve-note theme. Appropriately for the sombre colouring of the poem ("Heavy, gloomy giant black moths / massacred the sun's bright rays"), dark sounds, from bass clarinet and cello, dominate. The piano part also favours the lower register, and the dynamics rarely rise above *piano*. It is only in the middle of the piece (bars 14-16) that Schoenberg makes a dramatic point with a crescendo. The third stanza evokes an image of heavy, oppressive melancholy:

*Und vom Himmel erdenwärts*
*Senken sich mit schweren Schwingen*
*Unsichtbar die Ungetüme*
*Auf die Menschenherzen nieder…*

*[And from heaven earthward bound*
*downward sink with sombre pinions*
*unperceived, great hordes of monsters*
*on the hearts and souls of mankind…]*

The 14th melodrama "Die Kreuze" also displays typical Expressionistic traits. Giraud here transfers the religious image of the crucifixion on to the situation of poets bleeding to death from their poetry:

*Heilge Kreuze sind die Verse,*
*Dran die Dichter stumm verbluten,*
*Blindgeschlagen von der Geier*
*Flatterndem Gespensterschwarm!*

*[Holy crosses are the verses*
*where the poets bleed in silence,*
*blinded by the peck of vultures*
*flying round in ghostly rabble.]*

The first two stanzas of the poem give a luridly-coloured description of bleeding, while the third conjures up an image of death with the setting sun as the "red royal crown". The musical setting responds to this antithesis: Schoenberg has the reciting voice in the first section (bars 1-10) accompanied by a dense, solid piano part, mostly playing *fortissimo*. It is possible that the repeated indication *martellato* was prompted by the poetic image of striking (see music example 3, p.64). In the second section, from bar 10 onward, the flute, clarinet, violin and cello join the piano, playing pianissimo. Schoenberg uses word painting to convey the image of the sinking sun. At the close – on the final declamation of the line "Heilge Kreuze sind die Verse" – Schoenberg again makes a dramatic gesture.

Because of its use of counterpoint, the 18th melodrama, "Der Mondfleck" is the most famous piece in *Pierrot*. Almost more interesting in terms of our exploration, however, is the 17th, entitled "Parodie", which tells of a grey-haired duenna, passionately in love with Pierrot, waiting for him in an arbour. The poem does not tell us whether Pierrot eventually comes. But the text reads, "The moon, the wicked mocker, / Now mimics with light rays", and Schoenberg converted this literary idea into musical terms by structuring the piece first as a three-part strict canon and then as a four-part double canon with piano accompaniment. And doubtless to make his intentions absolutely clear, he noted at the beginning "the clarinet imitates the viola exactly". The satirical aim extends as far as the instructions for performance and articulation.

Not only Berg and Webern, but Stravinsky and Ravel were also inspired by the melodramas of *Pierrot lunaire*: Stravinsky in his *Poèmes de la lyrique japonaise* (1913) and Ravel in the *Trois poèmes de Stéphane Mallarmé* (1913) and *Chansons madécasses* (1925-26). A performance of *Pierrot* in Berlin in December 1912 made a strong impression on Stravinsky.

[music example 3]
Schoenberg, *Pierrot lunaire* Nr. 14, *Die Kreuze*, Opening

## "God's Eternity Opposes the Transience of Idols"
## On Schoenberg's *Moses und Aron*

History and art are often woven together in mysterious ways. One instructive example of this is Schoenberg's return to the faith of his Jewish forbears: provoked by the spread of anti-Semitism in Germany and Austria –four years after his conversion to Lutheranism – this was immortalised in a series of works.

In June 1921 Schoenberg took a trip with his family and some of his pupils to Mattsee, a holiday resort in the Salzburg state. When an Aryan holidaymaker gave him to understand that as a Jew he was not welcome there, Schoenberg made a hurried retreat from the town. The experience had traumatic consequences for him, forcing him to think about his Jewishness, and discover his national and religious identity. In 1925 he composed the four-part chorus *Du sollst nicht, du mußt*, op.27 no.2, on a self-penned text which formulates some fundamental thoughts on the Jewish faith: the prohibition of images (Thou shalt not make any graven image), the inalienable belief in the "spirit" and the idea of the "chosen people". At this time he took an interest in Zionist ideas, and was clearly familiar with Theodor Herzl's now famous essay *Der Judenstaat*.[1]

In 1925 and 1926 Schoenberg worked on the three-act drama *Der biblische Weg*, on the theme of the foundation of a Jewish homeland, a modern Jewish state ("New Palestine"). A charismatic leader, Max Aruns, does his utmost to unite the Jewish people in the new state, but is killed by a raging horde of Jewish emigrants. Naturally his sacrificial death breathes new life into the founding New Palestine project.

After Schoenberg was obliged to give up his composition class at the Berlin Hochschule für Musik in 1933 and leave Germany, he re-entered the community of the Jewish faith in Paris. From there he wrote to his pupil Alban Berg on 16 October 1933, "As you have surely observed, my return to the Jewish faith took place long ago, and is even discernible in the published portions of my work ("Du sollst nicht... du musst...) [Not, you should, [but] you must] and in *Moses and Aron*, which you've known about since 1928, but which goes back at least another five years; most especially in my drama *Der biblische Weg*, which was also conceived in 1922 or '23 at the latest.[2]

The three-act opera *Moses und Aron* that was written between 1928 and 1932 and was originally conceived as an oratorio, counts as one of Schoenberg's major works. As a *Gesamtkunstwerk* it marks the high point of his long years grappling with music theatre. It treats an unusual subject with unique religious and philosophical depth. And its music continues to make an impression today for its novelty, evocative power and diversity.

The biblical material (Leviticus, chapters 3, 4 and 7, 20-31, 32 and 34) is treated by Schoenberg with remarkable freedom and independence, as well as rigorous logic. Three interrelated ideas stand at the heart of the drama: the idea of one, eternal, ever-present, invisible and unimaginable God, and the inability of "capturing the infinite in an image", the idea of the chosen people ("This people is chosen before all peoples to be the people of the one God") and its tragedy, and lastly the idea of the leader of a people.

The central dialectic of thought and word is personified by the adversaries Moses and Aron. Moses is characterised by Schoenberg as having nothing human about him, and represents the notion of God. He can think but not speak. That is why the lively, nimble and charismatic Aron is his mouthpiece. He is able to guess at the people's wishes and yearnings, and can sympathise with them. The drama of the action stems from Moses's thoughts being are falsified in Aron's words: monotheism becomes polytheism, the Word of God becomes magic, the pure idea becomes idolatry. Eternity and temporality, remoteness from and proximity to real life, mind and soul, thought and form are opposed in the opera as irreconcilable opposites.[3]

Schoenberg brings this duality sharply into focus. Aron recognises the urge for representation of the unimaginable, that the people crave visible miracles, and allows the golden calf to be built for adoration, as an "image of God". The powerfully dramatic scene "The Golden Calf and the Altar" (Act Two, Scene 3) demonstrates the renunciation of God. In Act Two, Scene 4, Moses comes down from the mountain of revelation where he has spent 40 days, carrying the tablets of the law in his hands. One word from him is enough to make the graven image vanish. He proudly proclaims, "God's eternity opposes the transience of idols". At the end of the fifth scene, however, he despairs when he recognises that God's thoughts are ambiguous and that the image that Aron – his mouth – made of God was a false image, one that he fundamentally made himself.

*So bin ich geschlagen!*
*So war alles Wahnsinn, was ich gedacht habe,*
*und kann und darf nicht gesagt werden!*
*O Wort, du Wort, das mir fehlt!*

[Thus I am defeated!
So everything I believed was madness,
and can and must not be said!
O word, you word that I lack!]

Schoenberg's Biblical opera remained a fragment.[4] It is true that the text of the third act (consisting of a single scene) is complete, but Schoenberg did not set it, although he had enough time to do so. There are indications that difficulties in the content prevented him from completing his great work.

The third act confronts us with a new situation. Moses regains his power and takes over the leadership. He accuses Aron, who appears as a captive, of having betrayed "God to the gods, the idea to images, this chosen people to others". When he commands the soldiers to release him, Aron stands up and then falls down dead. Moses's words to the Israelites, cautionary and prophetic in equal measure, are immensely significant for the conception of the opera and Schoenberg's political thinking: "Always, when you go forth among people" and use your gifts for false and negative ends", he rebukes, "always, when you abandon the renunciation of the wilderness and your gifts lead you to the highest peak, you are always thrust back down into the wilderness as a result of that misuse".

The sequence of static and dramatically lively sections is characteristic of the plot, and the music consequently juxtaposes closed forms with more loosely structured sections. There is no doubt that the score of *Moses und Aron* is one of the most complex that Schoenberg ever wrote. Monologues, dialogues and great choral sections follow in sequence, recitative often flows into arioso, and the structure is often characterised by enormous density. The result is a sequence of music of the utmost variety, with sometimes the most heterogeneous elements merged together. In Act One, Scene 4, it is the mixture of martial music from the orchestra, whispering from the chorus and a contrapuntal piece using cantus firmus technique for the reaction of the people to Aron's three miracles that gives the music its special character. There is also the relatively brief interlude that links the two acts together, which is a strictly worked-out double fugue.

*Moses und Aron* is based on a single tone-row that is treated with astonishing ingenuity. Every element in the opera – themes, motifs, lines and entire movements – are developed from it.[5] The mastery with which Schoenberg manipulates twelve-note technique is astonishing. Tonal echoes are quite rare, but where they appear, they are deliberate. The theme of the chorus of the old believers thus begins with a triad: the diehards have nothing to do with the almighty God whom Aron proclaims in the Act One, Scene 4.

The treatment of the voices is equally original and engaging. The strong dichotomy between Moses and Aron is also expressed through the fact that Moses speaks and Aron sings. Moses is denied song. Certainly, his "speech" always means *Sprechgesang*: not just the rhythm, but the speech-melody is fixed. In contrast, Aron's part has a remarkable cantabile quality, and highly expressive melodic arcs are part and parcel of his role. This striking division into spoken and sung words is also assumed by the chorus. The voice of God (the voice from the burning bush) is articulated by both sung solo and spoken choral voices. And the simultaneity of sung and spoken words sets the character of large stretches of the second scene of the first act, and through it the opposition between Aron and Moses acquires its force.

Thomas Mann said that Wagner was a poet as a musician and a musician as a poet. Something similar could be said of Schoenberg. On 8 August 1931 he wrote to Berg about his work on *Moses und Aron* saying that the text would only reach its final state during the composition of the music.[6] It is possible that the music of his sacred opera would not prove so closed if he had not used Wagnerian leitmotif technique. The further one explores this complex score, the clearer it becomes that Schoenberg cast a dense web of musical leitmotifs over his Biblical drama, endowing it with deep conceptual connections. God and His will, the chosen people and Moses and Aron are all personified in this way. Even God's imperative proclamation and the people's demand for a blood sacrifice are underscored by leitmotifs. The opera opens with a characteristic sequence of hexachords, sung by six solo voices, that stand for the notion of God. The wealth of allusions and references is revealed only after repeated hearings.

Yet no attentive listener can miss that fact that most scenes in *Moses und Aron* are really quite static: another indication that the work was originally planned as an oratorio. The "Golden Calf" scene stands as an exception to this, being both dramatically and musically a climactic moment. The action on stage at this point is positively hectic. Schoenberg used every means possible to portray the excess this scene represents. He wrote about this scene in a letter of 15 March 1933 to the author Walter Eidlitz, who had also tackled the subject: "For me too this signifies a sacrifice made by the masses, trying to break loose from a 'soulless' belief. In the treatment of this scene, which actually represents the very core of my thought, I went pretty much to the limit, and this too is probably where my piece is most *operatic*; as indeed it must be."[7]

Some light is shed on Schoenberg's intentions by a long-overlooked sketch that seems likely to relate to the "Golden Calf" scene, Act Two, Scene 3.[8] The key words Schoenberg noted down in it clarify the conceptual basis of the scene. The central words for him were "gold", "senses" and "soul". The "rapture" that they trigger takes various forms. Just as Wagner before him, in the *Ring*, here too Schoenberg associates domination, servitude and might with gold. There is a psychological depth to both extremes which articulate this fascination. "Wildness" is expressed in fire, slaughter, eating and drunkenness. The "human virtues" of bravery, defiance of death and righteousness, in contrast, are associated with the terms sacrifice, healing, belief in miracles and devotion. The word "love", underlined in the sketch, is also central for the composer. To it he ascribes both passion and adoration of potency, of fertility and virginity as perversion, as well priestly love, blood sacrifice and suicide. The "Golden Calf" scene thus presents the "human" in all its shades, in contrast to which Moses – as Schoenberg himself explained in his letter to Walter Eidlitz – is not human at all.[9]

If the German musical tradition, the Jewish faith and a fundamental humanism formed the spiritual foundation of Schoenberg's work, then the composer stood in clear opposition to another important current in new music in the first half of the twentieth century, which served as the basis for the composition of modern art music: folk music. The following chapter will deal with the attitude Schoenberg and other composers took toward this subject.

## Nationalism and Folklorism

As is well known, nationalism, as an artistic movement, left a particular mark on European music in the 19th century. As well as an awakening of national awareness among many peoples, political, social, spiritual and psychological factors also played a significant role in the emergence of the movement. A number of composers in several European countries sought to emancipate themselves from the dominance of the leading musical cultures of Italy, Germany and France. They felt they had discovered in their native folksong an untapped source for the creation of an indigenous national art. Nationalism and folklore are not merely closely connected in music, they are actually two different aspects of the same thing. In the 19th century it was the Spanish, Danes, Norwegians, Swedes, Russians, Hungarians, Bohemians and Czechs who came to the fore with their own national music, and these aspirations continued in the first half of the 20th century, albeit in sometimes different terms. Edvard Grieg in Norway, Jean Sibelius in Finland, Stravinsky in Russia, Isaac and Manuel de Falla in Spain, Respighi in Italy, Bartók and Kodály in Hungary, and Manolis Kalomiris and Emilios Riadis in Greece looked at their national legacy and in a variety of ways sought to inject new blood by including folkloristic elements of their countries' national music.

There is every indication that these attempts were regarded with a great deal of scepticism in German and Austria. Certainly, Mahler did not display the least understanding of them. At the end of October 1907 he stayed for a time in the Finnish city of Helsingfors (modern-day Helsinki) and attended a concert conducted by Robert Kajanus that included two works by Sibelius: the symphonic poem *Vårsång* (Spring Song), op.16, and the famous *Valse triste*. Afterwards he wrote to his wife, "During the concert I also heard some pieces by Sibelius, the Finnish national composer, who is creating quite a stir not just here but in the wider musical world. In one I heard the usual kitsch, served up with "Nordic" harmonisation as a kind of national sauce. […] These national geniuses are the same everywhere. In Russian and Sweden it's the same – and in Italy even more, these whores and their pimps".[1] A little later Mahler got to know Sibelius personally, and found him extremely likeable.

Several of the composers mentioned above were intensively engaged with folk music and folklore, but in many respects Béla Bartók is a special case. He stands apart from most of his fellow-composers for the seriousness and passion with which he undertook his ethnomusicological studies. As is well known, he systematically collected and transcribed hundreds of Hungarian, Romanian and Slovakian folk-songs, analysing and assessing them and then making fruitful use of them for his own compositions. He was a composer, ethnomusicologist, artist and scientist all in one. His colleague Zoltán Kodály expressed it beautifully: "His creative and performing work was accomplished with the precision and fastidious care of the scientist. His scientific work, apart from the necessary precision and thoroughness, is brought to life by artistic intuition. The folklorist offered the artist knowledge of a rich musical life from outside the ramparts of art music. On the other hand, the folklorist received from the artist superior musical knowledge and perception".[2]

Bartók himself made no secret of the fact that his devotion to folklore was linked to the national political current that was generally felt in the arts in Hungary at the start of the 20th century. "The aim was set to create something specifically Hungarian".[3] Through intensive study of Hungarian peasant music, until then unknown and unexplored, he hoped to bring about a renewal of art music, on one hand by emancipating it completely from the "tyrannical rule of the major and minor keys" and on the other by liberating music from the law of strict tempo. "The greater part of the collected treasure, and the more valuable part, was in old ecclesiastical or old Greek modes, or based on more primitive (pentatonic) scales, and the melodies were full of the most free and varied rhythmic phrases and changes of tempi, played both *rubato* and *giusto*.[4]

In various papers Bartók laid ou his many thoughts on the question of how peasant music could influence so-called "higher" art music, and pointed to three principal ways: firstly, the appropriate harmonisation and adaptation of peasant melodies; secondly, the free invention of melodies that show similar traits to peasant music, and thirdly, the composition of works whose music "is pervaded by the atmosphere of peasant music".[5] Bartók was firmly convinced that a composer who has learned and mastered the peasant musical idiom completely, must be able to make free use of it in his art music, just as a poet uses his mother tongue.[6] In this context, his unshakeable conviction that no art music based on folk music could in any circumstances be atonal is particularly significant. He articulated this viewpoint in an essay that appeared in America in 1928.[7]

Only a few years before Bartók's article – at the end of 1925 – Schoenberg had completed his famous, and notorious *Drei Satiren*, op.28. This was a work that earned him nothing but hostility, and can only be understood as a break with every other avant-garde movement of the day.[8] Not only did he here make a personal attack on Stravinsky, but he also turned his fire on the then fashionable "neo-classicism". In his scathing preface he explicitly stated that he was targeting four groups of his fellow-composers: firstly, the representatives of the moderate modernists ("apparent tonal composers" and others "who nibble at dissonance but want to pass for modernists"), secondly, the classicists in the broadest sense of the word, thirdly, folklorists, and fourthly all "-ists", in whom he could see only "mannerists". Clearly Schoenberg was then unwavering in his belief that only his path of twelve-note composition led to Rome.

Many years later – on 13 May 1949 – he told Amadeo de Filippi that he had written the *Satires* when he was very much under attack from some of his younger colleagues, and wanted to warn them that it was not a good thing to "pick a fight" with him.[9] Certainly, it is not possible to understand the *Drei Satiren* unless we examine Schoenberg's philosophical, musical and aesthetic thinking in depth. Fortunately, there is some information to be found in a number of recently published documents and some as yet unpublished texts.[10]

Like Wagner, Schoenberg spent his life railing against fashion, and fashionable musical taste. Art that submitted to the vagaries of fashion was, as he saw it, not genuine art. He was concerned with writing music that would endure, music that would outlast time. In a biting commentary entitled *Der Restaurateur*, he accused Stravinsky of having a great fondness for the fashionable, and even stated that it seemed to him (Schoenberg) that Stravinsky found it outmoded "to allow an artistic creation a relevance beyond that of its time".[11] If Wagner had once accused his counterpart Brahms of taking refuge in stylistic masquerades,[12] now Schoenberg accused Stravinsky – his most influential rival – of being a master of disguise, who had put on Bach's wig to look like "Papa Bach". It seems that Schoenberg numbered Stravinsky among those artists who trim their sails to the wind and are ready to make any concession to popular taste. The commentary referred to above ends with the scathing suggestion that "Maybe for Stravinsky art falls not into this last category, but among the fashionable materials and neckties. In that case, he is right in trying merely to satisfy the customers".

If we focus on Schoenberg's polemic against "folklorism" and attempt to grasp it fully, then we have to take into consideration his opinions on the question of national music, the relationship between folk music and art music, and his unshakeable conviction of the legitimacy of twelve-note composition. He was able to understand that nations with no unbroken musical tradition were anxious to create a national music, given that peoples inevitably compete with one another in the cultural sphere. Yet he doubted that this could succeed simply by hitching on to folk music. As he wrote, "No national music has ever been generated in response to a formula devised by historians. In contrast, the higher levels of a people's genius have developed from the lower, in that they have refined the mode of expression, extended the range of ideas and deepened them".[13] Art music could consequently only come into being through deepening and the unifying of ideas.

Schoenberg showed no appreciation of those of his fellow German and Austrian composers whose heads were turned by the "way of the world" and joined the folklorists.[14] For he took the view that a talented composer could never disown his national identity even when he tried to mimic the local colour of a foreign country. He gave the examples of the *thème russe* in Beethoven's first Razumovsky Quartet, op.59, no.1, Haydn's *alla ongarese*, Mozart's "Turkish" music, Brahms's supposed "gypsy" music and Hugo Wolf's *Spanisches Liederbuch*. In his opinion, Dvořák's "New World" Symphony was for connoisseurs unmistakably Czech, Verdi's *Aida* not remotely Egyptian, Goldmark's *Die*

*Königin von Saba* in no way Jewish and that Spain contained no music like that of *Carmen*.[15]

There was an element of principle to Schoenberg's categorical objection to folklore in music. He saw something contradictory in "wishing to use the naturally primitive ideas of folk music for a technique which suits only complex thought" – as expressed it in the preface to the *Drei Satiren*. Some time before, in a hitherto unpublished article, he had laid out his main considerations on the difference between folk music and art music, assuming "a difference in mindset". Here he writes, "Just as only that which can be grasped by everyone can become popular, so what is either thought or said in this way can be understood by everyone: it is an essential indicator of superior thinking that it can hardly be understood without a certain level of education".[16]

As mentioned before, during a walk in Traunkirchen at the end of July 1921, Schoenberg said to Josef Ruter, the man who would later be his assistant, "Today I have discovered something that will ensure the supremacy of German music for the next one hundred years". What he was referring to was composing with twelve notes related only to each other. Schoenberg was fully aware of the importance of his discovery, and was firmly convinced that the future of music lay in twelve-note composition.

Schoenberg's steadfast belief in the supremacy of Germany music dated back to the days of his youth. In February 1931, around the time he was working on *Moses und Aron*, he wrote the article *National Music*, which culminates in a solemn profession of faith in German music. In another short statement (*A German no longer*) we read: "I am challenged as a German composer, and German art, which people would like to topple from its position of supremacy, is attacked in my person".[17]

There is no doubt that Schoenberg's utter rejection of folklorism was connected with his conviction of the supremacy of German music, and his twelve-note method. He categorically rejected folk music as a source of art music, since he considered that it was incompatible with atonality and twelve-note composition. The position he took was thus diametrically opposed to that of Béla Bartók.

It was not just Schoenberg and Stravinsky but Schoenberg and Bartók too who were polar opposites. They were opposites even in the way they argued. Where Schoenberg rather resembles a prophet who will allow no doubt to be cast on the truth of his assertions, Bartók made more careful, sophisticated and balanced judgements. In his article *On the Significance of Folk Music*, he writes, "Far be it from me to maintain that to base his music on folk music is the only way to salvation for a composer in our days".[18] He was fully aware that in the case of his own creative work it depended on how it was done, and concluded, "And thus we may say: folk music will become a source of inspiration for a country's music only if the transplantation of its motives is the work of a great creative talent".[19]

Arnold Schoenberg, the "conservative revolutionary" as he has been described, championed the view that a truly creative composer composes only "if he has something to say which has not yet been said and which he feels must be said".[20] Schoenberg's music stands as a model of expressive and sophisticated through-composed music. It is also considered the absolute opposite of popular music, so it must seem all the more remarkable that Schoenberg regarded the music of Johann Strauss II highly, and made arrangements of three of his waltzes. There is, however, no reason to see in that a contradiction: Schoenberg made absolutely no concessions to the taste of the general public, and poured scorn on his colleagues who felt they had to write "broadly understandable" and "popular" music. But he was not fundamentally opposed to what was popular, as long as he considered it "genuine". So he spoke in respectful terms about Offenbach, Johann Strauss and later Gershwin, believing that they were "natural" and genuinely popular, and that they possessed the ability to express "popular feelings in popular terms".[21]

There is no doubt that Schoenberg was the most unswerving opponent of folklorism. But it cannot be claimed that he looked down on folk song. In July 1928, when he was composing exclusively using the twelve-note method, he was asked to arrange some German folk songs by the State Commission for the Folk-Song Book for young people. He accepted the assignment and worked up to the beginning of the following year making tonal arrangements for voice and piano of folk songs from the 15th and 16th centuries. He considered it important that these were not "folk songs" but "art songs".[22] Nineteen years later, in 1948, he adapted three of these songs on his own initiative for *a cappella* mixed chorus. These sophisticated arrangements, published in New York as op.49, stand out for both their modal harmonies and rich contrapuntal writing, and are, naturally, completely tonal.[23]

In Schoenberg's instrumental works, particularly his atonal and twelve-note pieces, there are very few folk references or folk tunes. The most striking are the quotation of the Viennese folk song "O, du lieber Augustin" in the second movement of the Second String Quartet, op.10, and the tune by Friedrich Silcher to "Ännchen von Tharau" in the variation movement of the Suite, op.29. The question of the function of this melody must be approached with caution.

The first thing to stress is that from a biographical point of view, the two works are linked. Both are based on secret programmes, and both should be seen in an autobiographical context. The Second String Quartet has the outwardly striking inclusion of a soprano voice in the last two movements, singing settings of two poems by Stefan George, "Litanei" and "Entrückung". Schoenberg started work on the piece in March 1907 and completed it in August 1908, dedicating it to his first wife, Mathilde. The summer of 1908 was overshadowed by a serious marital crisis, when Mathilde left Schoenberg for Richard Gerstl, a gifted painter, whom she was in love with. In a so-called "Testaments-Entwurf" Schoenberg admitted to being extremely affected by Mathilde's infidelity. He wrote that he wept, behaved like a man in despair, and had contemplated and almost attempted suicide.[24] The Viennese popular song "O du lieber Augustin" is quoted note for note in the Trio of the quirky second movement (bars 165-171) by the second violin and viola. Dika Newlin, a pupil of Schoenberg's in America noted down in the course of lesson in which his passage was being discussed that Schoenberg stated, "It's all over, not ironically, but in its true sense!".[25] The folk-song quotation at this point is therefore to be taken for its semantic meaning and was intended as a fairly clear signal to those who knew about his private catastrophe. The cello also plays no fewer than six times in direct connection with the quotation the sequence B-E-E-A-D-D – seemingly a cryptogram, since the four notes B (written H in German notation)-E-A-D are the only note-names in *Mathilde*:

[music example 4]
Schoenberg, Second Quartet op. 10, Trio (bars 171 ff), Cryptogramm for the name Mathilde

On 28 August 1924, shortly after Mathilde's death, Schoenberg married Gertrud Kolisch, daughter of the famous violinist. It is possible that it was at this very time that he decided to dedicate his next work, the Suite, op.29, for 3 woodwind instruments, 3 strings and piano, to her. In any case, the score bears the heartfelt dedication "To my beloved wife". Some programmatic key words in a typewritten page stuck to the sketches and numerous later observations give an unambiguous indication that the work is based on a secret autobiographical programme that has Schoenberg's relationship with his young wife as its subject. And in this regard it is by no means a coincidence that Schoenberg used the song "Ännchen von Tharau ist's, die mir gefällt" as the basis of the piece's third movement. This tonal melody serves as a kind of cantus firmus, completely integrated into the twelve-note movement, and undergoes four elaborate variations. Hartmut Krones convincingly argued that the movement's four variations should be taken as musical interpretations of the four strophes of the song.[26] It should have become clear from all this that Schoenberg incorporated the tune of the song into his suite for its semantic meaning, and it appears as if the hidden lines of the poem should also have a resonance when we hear the variation movement.

When it comes to the controversial question of whether art music can receive a new impulse from folk music, Schoenberg argues from an extreme position. He categorically rejected folklorism and considered folk music incompatible with art music. The quotations from folk songs that appear in many of his instrumental works are there principally to give the music a semantic meaning. But Schoenberg's is not the only answer to the question. Several 20th-century composers (Bartók and Stravinsky at their head) were able to create works of art that were equally expressive and sophisticated by building on folklore.

That what Schoenberg considered the contradictory elements of atonality and/or dodecaphony on one side, and folk and dance music and jazz on the other could achieve a fruitful symbiosis is demonstrated in the work of one his pupils, Nikos Skalkottas. Independently of that, the way Skalkottas developed as a composer is an as yet little noticed example of how Schoenberg's pupils adopted their teacher's rigorous and exclusive twelve-note technique, and by modifying it, made it their own.

## Nikos Skalkottas – A Schoenberg Pupil in Berlin

When Nikos Skalkottas died in Athens on 20 September 1949 at the age of only 45, very few people were aware that his death also marked the passing of one of the most original compositional voices of the 20th century. In Athens, where he spent the last fifteen years of his life, he was considered a misfit, a modernist, an apostle of the reviled style of twelve-note music. His works were barely performed. And yet this highly gifted Greek musician's artistic career had got off to a promising start. He chalked up his first successes in Berlin, where he lived from 1921 to 1933 and attended Schoenberg's composition master classes. It was only after his untimely death that the musical world began to recognise the stature of his multi-faceted output. Thanks to the intervention of some of his friends (most notably Walter Goehr) around 25 of his works were published by Universal Edition. The musicologist Yiannis Papaioannou founded the Skalkottas Archive in Athens, and in the 1950s, the pianist George Hadjinikos tracked down in Berlin manuscripts of his that had long been considered lost. In Newton Centre, near Boston, in the United States, Gunther Schuller created the Margun Music company to bring out unpublished works by Skalkottas. And seminal dissertations appeared in Germany, Greece, the United Kingdom and Austria.[1]

The more one investigates Skalkottas and his works, the more one is struck by how prolific, original and versatile he was as a composer. Conservative estimates put his output at more than 170 works, of which 110 are held in the Athens Archive.[2] His output embraces works in almost every genre, with the exception of opera and church music, and includes orchestral works, numerous concertos, concertante works, string quartets, piano trios and duos for various instruments, piano music, a cycle of sixteen songs, individual songs and choral works, Greek dances for various ensembles, ballet music and the pantomime *Mayday Spell* – altogether an enormous output – ostensibly wider than that of Berg and Webern, although that does not, of course, imply any kind of value judgement.

Skalkottas's astounding productivity seems all the more puzzling when we consider that during his lifetime Athens gave him no encouragement as a composer, but he was actually treated with a fair amount of hostility by the city's predominantly conservative musical culture because of his avant-garde style. The reports that we have suggest that he lived in complete isolation, "in an almost imaginary world".[3] He had no desire to talk about his compositions, firmly convinced that no one in Athens would be able to understand his music. The impression he made on the famous Greek musicologist Minos Dounias was of a man who was psychologically deeply wounded, and who had to work under the pressure of a relentless struggle to survive.[4] Where he found the strength and inspiration to compose under these circumstances remains a mystery.

His level of creativity is therefore well-nigh miraculous. He had an obvious facility for composing and constructing music quickly, as well as a phenomenal memory. Yiannis Papaioannou, who knew him well, relates the amazing feat that many years after their manuscripts had gone missing, Skalkottas was able to write down early works from his Berlin days entirely from memory!

It would be doing Nikos Skalkottas a great disservice to describe him as an imitator of Schoenberg. He had a remarkably individual voice and an unmistakable personality. It is true that he was indebted to Schoenberg for pointing him decisively in a particular direction. He took from him the method of composing with twelve notes related only to each other, but developed it further on his own, and unlike his teacher, was happy to base a composition on more than one tone-row. He did not in any way consider tonality, atonality and dodecaphony to be entirely separate entities, and could write in tonal, atonal or twelve-note idioms either simultaneously or in alternation. To give two examples: 1938 saw the appearance of his first ballet score *The Maiden and Death*, one of his more important tonal works, composed around the same time as three atonal scores, the Piano Concerto No.2, Violin Concerto and the Variations on a Greek folk song for piano trio. Then, in 1943-44 he composed his wonderful pantomime *Mayday Spell*, a work that is mostly written in a free atonal idiom, but nevertheless also contains four short tonal interludes composed in such a way that the listener is never aware of a difference.[5]

There is no doubt that the co-existence of tonality, atonality and dodecaphony is a defining characteristic of Skalkottas, and in a way it links him to Alban Berg. During his Berlin years Schoenberg advocated a radical, intransigent attitude, and created twelve-note works exclusively.

One further aspect also separates Skalkottas fundamentally from his teacher. Schoenberg's *Drei Satiren*, op.28 of 1925 basically amount to a declaration of war against not just Stravinsky but also the "apparently tonal composers" in thrall to historicism, and folklorists as well. Schoenberg therefore considered folk music and art music to be incompatible and was unshakeable in the belief that no symphonies could be created from folk songs.[6] Skalkottas, on the other hand, had a close, lifelong relationship with Greek folklore. Like Bartók, he devoted himself intensely to the study of folklore, made sophisticated adaptations of Greek folk songs and often included folk material in his atonal works.

After successfully completing his violin studies at the Athens Conservatory, Skalkottas came to Berlin at the age of seventeen in 1921 with the intention of continuing them there. Here he was accepted into Willy Hess's violin master classes and took the courses in music theory given by Paul Juon and Robert Kahn. In the summer of 1923 he made the decision to remain in Berlin, and from 1925 onwards strove to make a career as a composer rather than a soloist. In the 1920s Berlin was an artistic hub and the contemporary music mecca, a city with a teeming cultural life, where many creative musicians had gathered.

In 1920 Ferruccio Busoni took over a composition master class at the Prussian Academy of Arts, and in the same year Franz Schreker was appointed director of the Hochschule für Musik. Many gifted young composers gathered around both men. In the autumn of 1922, Edgard Varèse stayed in Berlin, and established the German branch of his International Composers Guild (a precursor of the later International Society for Contemporary Music). Berlin saw the first performances of numerous masterworks of new music, such as Berg's *Wozzeck* and Chamber Concerto. After Busoni's death, Schoenberg took over his master classes in composition at the Prussian Academy of Arts and was a mentor to a whole series of major young talents. And finally, Berlin was where Busoni's pupils Philipp Jarnach and Kurt Weill were working.

The thirteen years that Skalkottas spent in Berlin were crucial for his artistic development, partly because he came into contact with a host of brilliant musicians. It appears that his earliest compositions date from between 1923 and 1925, when he was attending Paul Juon and Robert Kahn's classes at the Hochschule für Musik. From 1925 to 1927 he studied with Philipp Jarnach and from September 1927 to 1931 with Schoenberg. At the same time, he took lessons from Kurt Weill for a certain period after 1924.[7] It can be argued that his originality and versatility is linked to his openness to different artistic trends and influences.

What is the extent of Skalkottas's connections to the Busoni School? There are a number of indications that emerge from a close examination of his solo violin sonata of 1925 that help to answer this question. According to Kostis Demertzis, this is Skalkottas's first unmistakably mature work to have survived, and at the same time the first to be written systematically in a modern idiom.[8] On 24 June 1925 Skalkottas wrote to his friend Nelly Askitopoulos, to whom the sonata is dedicated, "I am only going to describe what today was like. It was lovely, because I was almost entirely alone and was able to work. I held my violin lovingly, immersed myself in chamber music and played Bach for hours on end. Then I longingly took up my pencil and began to compose. To add something to the sonata that belongs to you".[9] This interesting, original and perfectly-structured work consists of four movements: an *Allegro furioso*, an *Adagietto*, an *Allegro ritmato* and a Finale. In terms of structure and tonal system it is characterised equally by free atonality and a linear style. Both the second and third movements are clearly tripartite, and in the Finale two slow-moving recitative sections frame a fugue imbued with the spirit of J.S. Bach. Is the Sonata therefore to be taken as a homage to Bach? To answer to this question decisively, we have to take account of the musical-historical situation of the time.

From 1920 onwards Busoni preached the ideal of "young classicism",[10] a term he used principally to signify stripping away of the sensual, renouncing the subjective, rejecting programme music and lastly realigning with the music of the Baroque and Classical periods. Concertante music, which had long been neglected, Baroque polyphonic forms and techniques and the theory of "linear counterpoint" became surprisingly current. As is well known, Busoni was devoted to Bach, and made elaborate transcriptions of several of his works. In 1921 Busoni's pupil Philipp Jarnach published an essay entitled "The stylistic problem of the new Classicism in Busoni's work", in which he defined the return "to the linear conception of style" as the goal of this development.[11] Jarnach also composed a three-movement Sonata for solo violin, op.13 published by Schott in 1922 entirely in a free atonal style. It may be that Skalkottas knew Jarnach's op.13, and was inspired by it, but whatever the truth, his sonata has nothing to fear from comparison with Jarnach's work.

[Music example 5]
Nikos Skalkottas, Sonata for solo Violin (1925), Opening

Skalkottas's connections with Weill were long shrouded in obscurity. At least from the time of the scandal-ridden Baden-Baden premiere of his "Singspiel" *Mahagonny* in 1927, Weill was one of the best-known and controversial composers in Berlin. In 1928 he scored a sensational success in the city with *Die Dreigroschenoper*, which Skalkottas must have been aware of. In any case, the

Greek composer's penchant for jazz-style music and American dances such as the Tango can be ascribed to the example of Weill. It is interesting to note that in the *Andantino* of the Sonatina for Violin and Piano of 1929 there are blues-like rhythms and harmonies.[12] The famous 32 Piano pieces written in the summer of 1940 are particularly significant in this regard.[13] They can be described as both a *Gradus ad Parnassum* for pianists as well as a kind of comprehensive compendium of current character pieces. They include several highly stylized versions of light-music styles of the day – a Tango (no.14), Foxtrot (no.18), Ragtime (no.25), Slow Foxtrot (no.26), a *Galop* (no.27) and a Blues (no.28). Not only that, but the second quartet for piano and wind consists of a Tango and a Foxtrot. And in the ballet score *The Maiden and Death* of 1938 we find moments when the brass come to the fore and sounds distinctly like Weill.[14] As far as Skalkottas's relationship with jazz and sophisticated light music is concerned, it should also be remembered that he played the piano to accompany silent films in various Berlin cinemas. He was also familiar with film music.

Peter Gradenwitz's excellent book provides a wealth of information on Skalkottas's studies with Schoenberg.[15] It is no secret that Schoenberg held the young Greek composer in high regard (on many occasions he spoke of him in glowing terms) and was very pleased with his progress. As a member of the jury that awarded the Felix-Mendelssohn-Bartholdy bursary, he recommended him to Norbert von Hannenheim as the best candidate for the prize in 1932. Schoenberg's influence on Skalkottas is sometimes quite palpable, as in the 32 Piano pieces mentioned above, almost all of which are punchy character pieces in the Schoenberghian sense. The Gavotte (no.22, see music example 7, p. 90) and the Menuetto (no.23) offer direct parallels with the corresponding pieces in Schoenberg's Piano Suite, op.25 which possibly also served Skalkottas as the classic primer of twelve-note technique. Skalkottas must have learned a great deal from Schoenberg, not simply the rules of twelve-note technique, which he modified according to his own requirements, but also the art of thematic and structural development, the art of variation and varying, the art of "being shamelessly long, or heartlessly brief, as the situation demands", and much more.[16] It is my opinion that, like Schoenberg, Skalkottas also subscribed to subjectivity rather than Busonian objectivity.

One aspect should be stressed: Skalkottas had a particularly penchant for concertante music, concerto form and virtuosity. Of all the composers of the Second Viennese School he was the one who produced the most instrumental concertos and concertante works. He composed no fewer than eleven instrumental concertos of which only nine have survived. These include the first ever atonal double-bass concerto. The defining features of all his concertante works are musical logic, an airiness and musical flow, and a clear intention to bring the solo instrument to the fore.[17] For Skalkottas, concertante music embraces the playful, the characterful, dance-like and expressive. The frequent occurrence of the markings *scherzando*, *leggiero*, *dolce* and *espressivo* and *molto espressivo* give an impression of the character of the music. The last two are found not only in the expressive slow movements, but also in the virtuoso fast movements. In almost all his dodecaphonic works Skalkottas achieves Webern's principle of comprehensibility.

Throughout his life, Schoenberg declared that the greatest thing that art should strive towards was self-expression.[18] His most important pupils were true to this notion, and Nikos Skalkottas will one day be counted among their number.

# Beyond Schoenberg and Debussy
# Nikos Skalkottas's 32 Piano Pieces

Nikos Skalkottas, who ranks with Iannis Xenakis as the most original Greek composer of the 20th century, was once asked why he did not write any music for piano solo, and is said to have replied, "When composing for the piano today you could follow either Debussy's style or Schoenberg's, and since they did it best themselves, it is preferable not to bother". This statement from 1938 refers exclusively to solo piano music, since by then Skalkottas had written such major works as the first two piano concertos and the Concertino for two pianos. The idea of writing music for piano solo seems, however, not to have left him, and as early as the summer of 1940 he produced the 32 piano pieces under discussion here in the space of a few weeks. Skalkottas was not just a first-rate violinist, but a fine pianist as well, and he wrote these pieces for his Athens friends Marika and Yiannis Papaioannou, although they were in fact never performed in his lifetime (he died in 1949).[1]

Since at least the time of the Athens premiere of the complete cycle, given by the Australian pianist Geoffrey Madge in September 1979, the stature of the 32 piano pieces has gradually come to be recognised. Many authoritative commentators have unhesitatingly placed the pieces among the most significant piano works of the 20th century. The works have been examined in depth by Yiannis Papaioannou and Kostis Demertzis, but they continue to prompt many important questions:[2] what was Skalkottas's intention in writing them? What is the standpoint for their design, structure and arrangement? What music do they take a lead from, and how do they relate to the music of Arnold Schoenberg?

The choice of the number 32 is unquestionably not accidental, and prompts thoughts of a major work by Beethoven, the 32 variations, WoO 80 of 1806. Skalkottas prefaced his manuscript with a two-page foreword, first in German and then in Greek. Clearly he was thinking ahead to future publication abroad. Although his German is clumsy and awkward, his commentary shows that he was fully aware of the inordinate technical difficulties posed by the pieces, and also that he wished for a "better", by which he meant a more sophisticated, audience.

He writes, "This music has quite exceptional goals, aimed at solo concert performance, and at creating a new character and a new musical line of piano virtuosity. The sequence consists of thirty-two piano pieces of quite distinct character, and each one naturally demonstrates utterly different content while remaining formally serious and is not ingeniously tailored to superficial success. Each of the pieces is self-sufficient, whether extended or brief, comprising a short or a longer musical idea or musical domain, and the goal is to come closer to a better audience."[3]

There are 32 character pieces, each with a different physiognomy. Skalkottas set great store by having a contrast of musical content, indicating the rigour (the seriousness he refers to) of the form, and also pointing out that he was not at all interested in creating superficial effects.

All the pieces are given titles, most of them generic terms, although there are also some with "poetic" titles. If we were to classify the pieces according to the titles, they would be clearly divided into five groups: the first comprises pieces in which contrapuntal and variation techniques are applied. In the second, there are Baroque and Classical musical forms and constructions. The character pieces of the large third group have titles familiar from Romantic music. A fourth group brings together stylised dance pieces that derive from the jazz and sophisticated light music of the 1920s. Finally, the last group contains pieces that derive from folklore and other sources. To summarise:

Skalkottas's 32 piano pieces (1940)
Breakdown by techniques and movement types

I. Contrapuntal and variation techniques

*Short variations on a mountain theme of a southern character with sharp dissonance* (No.3)
*Little four-part canon* (No.8)
*Passacaglia* (No.15)

II. Baroque and Classical styles

*Marcia funebre* (No.9)
*Sonatina* (No.10)
*Partita* (No.11)
*Gavotte* (No.22)
*Menuetto* (No.23)

III. Styles from Romantic music

*Andante religioso* (No.1)
*Reverie in the old style* (No.6)
*Reverie in the new style* (No.7)
*Little Serenade* (No.12)
*Intermezzo* (No.13)
*Night piece* (No.16)
*Étude phantastique* (No.19)
*Berceuse* (No.20)

*Romance – Lied* (No.21)
*Italian Serenade* (No.24)
*Rondo brillante* (No.29)
*Capriccio* (No.30)
*Waltz* (No.31)

IV. Jazz and light music

*Tango* (No.14)
*Foxtrot – The Old Policeman* (No.18)
*Ragtime* (Dance) (No.25)
*Slow Foxtrot* (No.26)
*Galop* (No.27)
*Blues* (No.28)

V. Folk-derived and other pieces

*Greek Folkdance* (No.5)
*Little peasant march* (No.32)
*Children's Dance* (No.2)
*Disaster in the Jungle (Film music)* (No.4)

The fact that Skalkottas repeatedly turns to the forms and types of movement of Baroque, Classical and Romantic music might at first seem surprising, yet it should not in any way be thought that his intentions were backward-looking. His purpose was much more to bring together all the styles of character piece from his time in one cycle, and in that he was following his former teacher Schoenberg, and the Second Viennese School.

A well-known characteristic of the period of so-called free atonality is the complete avoidance by Schoenberg and his pupils of traditional forms. It was only after 1921 when the system of "composition with twelve notes related only to each other" was formulated that they began to compose movements in sonata, variation and rondo forms, possibly intending to demonstrate that the traditional forms were eminently suited to new, dodecaphonic content. They also reverted to specific Baroque, Classical and Romantic forms and turned them into character pieces. Parallels for several Skalkottas's pieces can be found in the work of Schoenberg and Berg. To name only a few examples: Schoenberg, Berg and Webern all wrote Passacaglias. Schoenberg's Piano Suite, op.25 contains among other things a Gavotte, an Intermezzo and a Menuett. The last of the five Piano Pieces, op.23 is a Waltz. In the Serenade, op.25 we find a March, a Minuet, Variations, a Dance Scene, a Song (without words), and a Finale. And the

Suite, op.29 consists of four movements: an Overture, a second movement entitled "Dance Steps", a Theme and Variations and a Gigue.

However, the question that most concerns us here is where does Skalkottas follow Schoenberg and where does he differ from him? When he wrote the 32 pieces in the space of a few weeks in 1940 he had moved far away from his former teacher in both compositional technique and style, and had long since developed his own unmistakable musical idiom. While Schoenberg applied twelve-note technique in the works of his dodecaphonic period with considerable rigour, and strove to avoid any echo of tonality, Skalkottas was much freer in his use of twelve-note technique and even worked with several rows, which for Schoenberg was taboo. The 32 piano pieces are by all appearances atonal, but in no way strictly dodecaphonic. It is true that it is also rare to find tonal echoes in Skalkottas, but unlike Schoenberg he shows no reserve in using small intervals in his themes and motifs, and his chords are constructed in such a way that they hardly sound markedly "dissonant". There is a further difference: many of Schoenberg's strict dodecaphonic compositions are characterised by their discontinuous nature, while most of Skalkottas's pieces, despite their more frequent contrasts, run along in a much more continuous manner. A third difference lies in the factor of huge structural complexity that was so important to Schoenberg and which, according to Berg, was the reason why his music is so hard to understand; in Schoenberg, it hampers comprehensibility, whereas Skalkottas's music, for all its complexity, is decidedly "comprehensible". There is one other element: Skalkottas's music has a different sonority from Schoenberg's. What Adorno once said of Berg, that he loved a lush, opulent and luxurious sound, can also to some extent be applied to Skalkottas.[4]

A comparison of the Gavotte in Schoenberg's Piano Suite with Skalkottas's Gavotte gives a good demonstration of this. Both pieces are clearly tripartite and both are alla breve. There, however, the similarities end. In line with the Baroque dance, Schoenberg's Gavotte uses an anacrusis throughout. His motifs favour wide intervals and huge leaps, and the rhythms are constantly changing: at the beginning and end no two bars resemble each other, and two interpolated 5/4 bars confuse matters. The central section is markedly more consistent, a sequence of four units to every two bars.

# Gavotte

[Music example 6]
Schoenberg, Suite for Piano op. 25, Opening of *Gavotte*

In Skalkottas's Gavotte we come up against completely different rhythmic, motivic and harmonic relationships. Sometimes the music is all on downbeats, sometimes there is an anacrusis, and the rhythmic movement is consistent. The almost continuous quaver movement at the beginning and end is enlivened by semiquaver figurations in the central section. The fully harmonised four-bar principal theme is made up of two contrasting groups, one proceeding in small steps and the second using larger intervals. Compared with Schoenberg's Gavotte, it is the regularity of Skalkottas's that is striking.

# Gavotte
(No. 22 taken from the 32 Piano Pieces)

[Music example 7]
Skalkottas, 32 Pieces for Piano (1940), Opening of *Gavotte*

With all its stylization, Skalkottas's Gavotte is closer to the Baroque model than Schoenberg's. There is an in-built quality of grace and a hint of the rococo about it. In many respects it is closer to the Musette from Schoenberg's Suite, a delicate piece set in a higher register, in which the lowest line holds to a drone-like G, and whose pronounced rhythmic quality makes it much more regular. It can be argued that Skalkottas was thinking more of this Musette when he composed his Gavotte.

# Musette

[Music example 8]
Schoenberg, Suite for Piano op. 25, Opening of *Musette*

Probably the best known of the 32 piano pieces is the Passacaglia (No.15), which was the first to be published and was premiered as early as November 1952 in London by Marika Papaioannou. As I see it, in conceiving this piece, Skalkottas took a lead from the famous Passacaglia in the fourth scene of Act One of *Wozzeck* – an opera that was famously first performed in Berlin on 14 December 1925 under Erich Kleiber after a legendary number of rehearsals, and which Skalkottas must have studied. Berg's Passacaglia is built on a twelve-note bass theme that undergoes 21 sophisticated variations. In the Skalkottas, there is an eleven-note row which is treated to 20 imaginative variations. In both cases the theme also moves up into a higher register, and both Passacaglias come to a grandiose conclusion with broad, fortissimo columns of sound.

Alban Berg, Zwölftonreihe zu *Wozzeck*, I. Akt, 5. Szene (Passacaglia)

Nikos Skalkottas, Elftonreihe zur *Passacaglia* aus den 32 Klavierstücken

[Music example 9]
Note–rows of Berg's and Skalkottas's Passacaglias

Skalkottas had a predilection for concertante and virtuoso music. Of all the composers of the Second Viennese School, he wrote the most instrumental concertos and concertante works. He composed no fewer than eleven instrumental concertos, of which only nine have survived. Most of the 32 piano pieces also have a pronounced virtuosic element, which takes on different forms. It is in the fast pieces, which make exceptional technical demands on the pianist, that it most comes to the fore. Some of the metronome markings that Skalkottas provided for many pieces are so fast that they cannot possibly be realised. For the Ragtime (No.25), for example, he prescribed minim = 220. Gunther Schuller felt that marking had to be amended to minim = 92.

Several pieces particularly stand out for their virtuoso brilliance: *Disaster in the Jungle* (No.4), Sonatina (No.10), Partita (No.11), Little Serenade (No.12) *Étude phantastique* (No.19) Galop (No. 17), Rondo brillante (No.29), Capriccio (No. 30), as well as the dance pieces, Tango (No.14), Ragtime (No.25), Slow Foxtrot (No.26), Blues (No.28), and Waltz (No.31). A number of pieces are like a *perpetuum mobile*, particularly the Partita, Galop and Capriccio. The semiquaver and quaver movement in the Partita continues with hardly a break. One curious aspect is that the accents on the semiquavers do not follow regular groups of four, but swap between groups of three and five, creating great metrical and rhythmic variety:

# PARTITA

(Nº XI from *32 Piano Pieces*)

[Music example 10]
Opening of the Partita

Skalkottas uses an astonishing range of highly varied and imaginative structures for the pieces. For example, the Blues is divided into three parts, of 14½, 13½ and 18 bars respectively. The third section is no less than an intensified reprise of the first, in which the musical content is enhanced not least by incredibly fast demi-semiquaver and semiquaver figurations, which have no parallel in Schoenberg's work:

# BLUES
(Nº XXVIII from *32 Piano Pieces*)

[Music example 11a]
Opening of the Blues

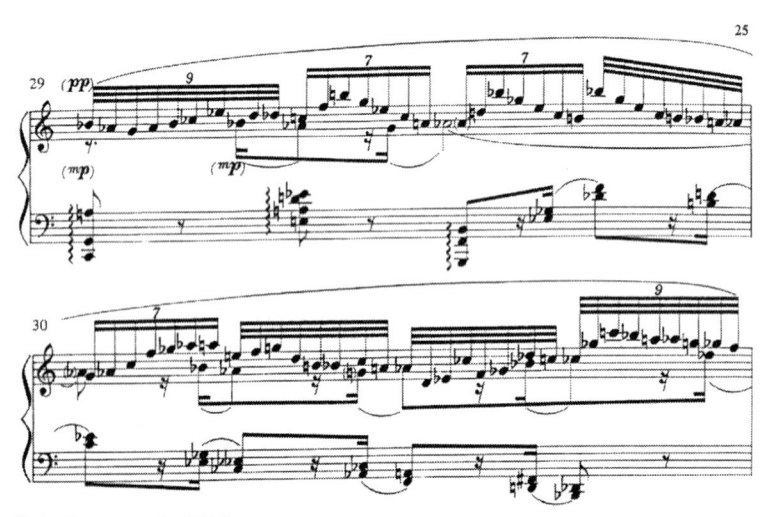

[Music example 11b]
Bars 29-30 of the Blues

Obviously, Schoenberg, who hated every kind of decoration and ornament in music, had very little inclination towards the kind of virtuosity Skalkottas preferred. An oft-described event throws a revealing light on this: Schoenberg raised the objection that in Skalkottas's First Piano Concerto there were "too many notes"; the Greek composer countered equally decisively and confidently that the work contained all the notes required.

In terms of piano writing of extreme virtuosity, a closer comparison for the 32 piano pieces would be with Debussy's *Études*, a work that Skalkottas must have been familiar with. It is true that there are hardly any points of contact between the two works. Skalkottas's sound-world, his sonorities and harmony have nothing in common with Impressionism, apart from a shared preference for dance-like music.

While in the history of piano music in the first half of the 20th century Claude Debussy and Arnold Schoenberg stand as polar opposites, Skalkottas can be said to have struck out on an independent third way. The music of his 32 piano pieces written in complete isolation in the summer of 1940, is not just of its time, but also points towards the future. Through their idiosyncratic sonorities and their extreme virtuosity, the 32 piano piece to a certain extent anticipate the epochal *Études* for piano by György Ligeti.[5]

The following chapters are dedicated to some of the most significant composers of the 20th century, whose work and whose impact essentially belong to the period after the Second World War. Although the influence of Stravinsky or Hindemith was clearly dominant in the immediate post-war period, it can justifiably be said that in the wider span of the 20th century, the Second Viennese School had much greater influence on later generations than any other musical current. This is the reason why most of the chapters up until this point have been devoted to the work of Schoenberg and his school. It will now be shown that the themes covered until now – music as personal expression, as a message and a declaration, the strained relationship between these aspects and musical technique, the relationship between music and language, that of new music to the art and folk-music traditions, as well as the issue of comprehensibility, played a central role after Schoenberg as well. Although there was an increasing tendency in new music to define a musical artwork on purely technical terms, and although public discourse and countless personal communications from composers about their works revolved almost exclusively around technical and formal issues, it can be seen that for many leading representatives of new music the notion that music had, and has to this day a message, continued to be valid.

Arnold Schoenberg: Suite for piano op. 25. First page of the manuscript.
Published with the permission of the Arnold Schoenberg Center (Vienna).

# A Conversation with Luigi Nono

During the 1980s Luigi Nono (1924-1990) was a regular visitor to Freiburg im Breisgau, and it was in the electronic studio there that he worked on his *Prometeo* (1984). Through Annette Kreutziger-Herr, who was in touch with him, I learned that he had taken a keen interest in my research and was eager to make my acquaintance. On 10 March 1985 Hans Zender conducted the Hamburg State Philharmonic Orchestra in the first performance of *A Carlo Scarpa, architetto* (1984), Nono's orchestral work dedicated to the memory of the architect Carlo Scarpa,[1] and it was then that the composer called me to arrange a meeting. After various attempts to find the "right" café (no easy matter, since Nono did not like either up-market or noisy cafés), he came straight to the point. He spoke to me about my publications on Mahler, Brahms and Bruckner which he had read, expressed his agreement with what I had written, and focused on my semantic analysis of Berg's *Lyric Suite*, which he had read in a volume of *Musik-Konzepte*.[2] He then revealed to me – with a mysterious smile – that his String Quartet *Fragmente – Stille, An Diotima* from 1979-80, was based on a secret programme. From the way he said this, I was led to conclude that Berg's *Lyric Suite* had been the inspiration for the work. I also took his message to be a kind of invitation to explore his quartet and analyse it with the possible goal of revealing the secret programme.

The conversation on the *Lyric Suite* led us on to a topic that we both had a keen interest in, that is, the mystery of music. Work on my book on Berg was uppermost in my mind at the time, and I was deep in Berg's sketches. I told Nono how Berg from the time of his String Quartet, op.3 onwards was unable to compose without programmes, but for various reasons did not want to disclose them, partly because of their personal nature, and partly because after the First World War programme music was considered an anachronism, if not frowned upon. He agreed, and stated his opinion that numerous composers had inserted many secret elements into their music. According to him, it was a long-standing tradition dating back to the Gnostics.

Moving on from Berg, we came to talk about Nono's father-in-law, Arnold Schoenberg. Obviously he knew that several of Schoenberg's instrumental works were based on secret programmes that, for personal reasons, could not be disclosed, but he was surprised when I told him there was also a concealed autobiographical programme for Schoenberg's First String Quartet, op.7, that was discovered by Christian Martin Schmidt.[3] If we are to believe this programme, in 1904 or 1905 Schoenberg left his first wife Mathilde for another woman, only to return later. I promised to send him the text, and did so quickly, but received no reply. After some time Annette Kreutziger-Herr, who had spoken to him, explained to me that his silence was due to his profound personal shock.

Around the time of our conversation, Nono's thoughts were revolving around his *Prometeo*. The first performance of the first version of this *Tragedia dell'ascolto* (Tragedy for Listening) took place in the church of San Lorenzo in Venice on 29 September 1984. Nono talked passionately about this work, and about his wonderful collaboration with his librettist, the Venetian philosopher Massimo Cacciari, who had advised him on questions of philosophy and mythology. He mentioned that he had also talked with Cacciari about my volumes on Mahler.[4] When I told him about my book on the myth of Prometheus and Beethoven's Prometheus music, he registered such interest that I promised to send him the book.

The more we talked, the clearer it became to me that historical ideas and music-historical relationships were of great importance for him. With his knowledge of the history of early music, he enjoyed drawing historical parallels, making connections between *Ars nova* and the early Flemish composers and Italian Renaissance music, and spoke of his admiration for the bold harmonies and expressive power of the madrigals of Carlo Gesualdo, a composer he had a particularly high regard for. When I marvelled at the extent of his knowledge, he modestly referred to his teachers Francesco Malipiero and Bruno Maderna.

Nono's String Quartet is a key work in his output for various reasons: on one hand because of its secret programme and its mysteriousness, and on the other because it marks a turning-point.[5] The many Hölderlin fragments scattered throughout the score, the underlying *scala enigmatica* that Nono took over from Verdi's *Ave Maria* of 1889, the composed silence and not least the Ockeghem quotation (*Malor me bat*) towards the close can all be understood as an invitation to solve the enigma and reveal the secret. Many people have expressed their astonishment that Nono, known until then principally as a politically-engaged composer, suddenly seemed to retreat into the private sphere. Asked how this change might be explained, Nono stated in an interview during the *Musiktage* in Badenweiler in 1980, "I have not changed in any way; the delicate and private also has its collective, political side. For this reason, my String Quartet is not the expression of a new, retrospective direction of mine, but of my current experimental stance. I want the great, incendiary message with the smallest of means".[6] He explained the change in his creative work to me in similar, but more precise terms. He felt that in his earlier works he had explored expressive power in the *forte* range, going from simple *forte* to multiple *forte*. Now he was experimenting in the opposite direction, and was concerned with exploring all the expressive possibilities in the *piano* range, going from simple *piano* to multiple *piano*.

The great sensitivity that is characteristic of many of Nono's works is a mark of the man. Although he spoke calmly and with a friendly tone and smiled a lot, it did not escape me that he could be touchy and easily offended. The impression he made on me was of a man who was often deeply wounded. I sensed something rebellious and subversive about him, and it was easy for me to imagine the extent of his passion for the great political ideas that so moved him.

When we were saying goodbye, I said to him, "Non dire addio alla speranza".[7] He gave me an earnest look and walked away.

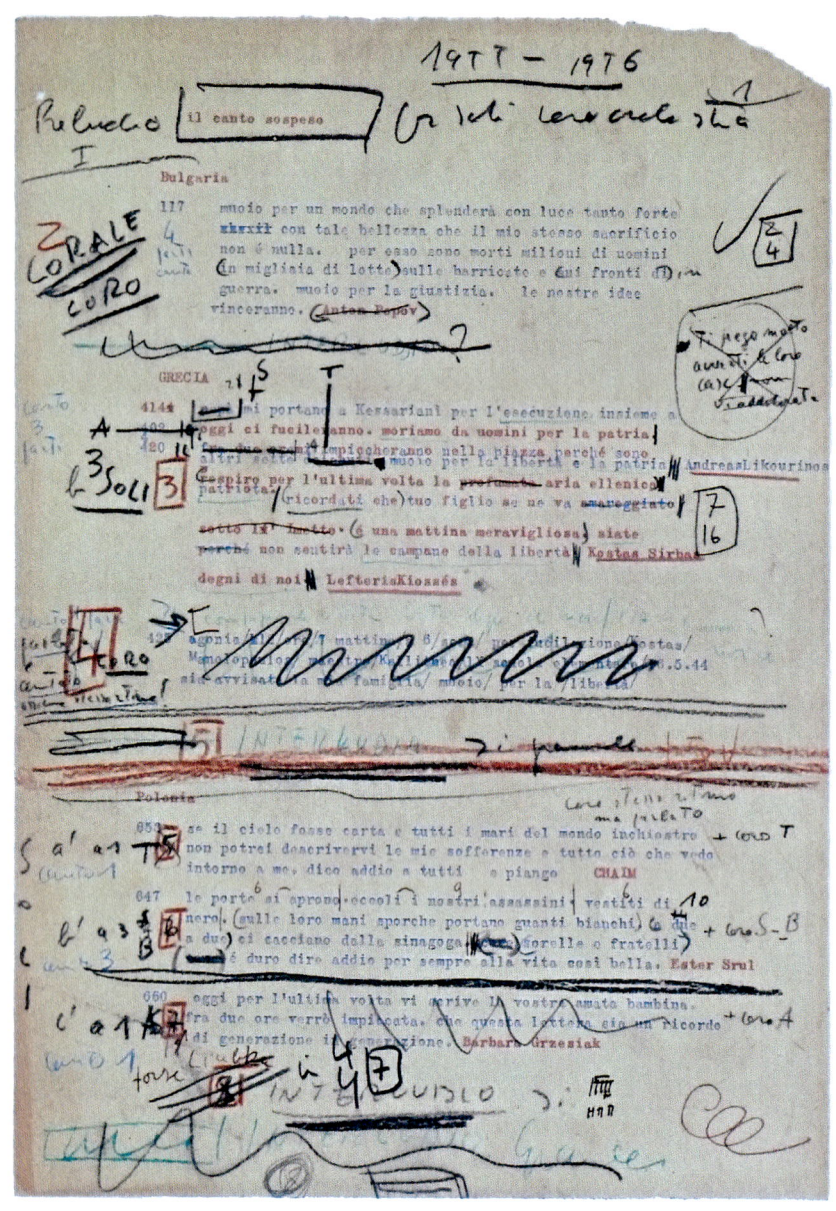

Luigi Nono: Canto sospeso (1955/56). Draft.
Published with the permission of the Archivio Luigi Nono (Venice)

## Olivier Messiaen's "Theological Music"

In the 20th century religious music does not occupy the position it once did. Nevertheless, a number of prominent composers were believers, and wrote significant pieces of religious music. Works that spring to mind include Stravinsky's *Symphony of Psalms*, Hindemith's *Marienleben*, Schoenberg's late works, and many of Bernd Alois Zimmermann's compositions.

The extensive output of Olivier Messiaen (1908-1992), which he himself categorised as "theological music" is a special case. What he understood as such was "contemplative" music that would make "the truth of faith" manifest.[1] "All my works, whether religious or not," he once said, "are an act of faith".[2] He repeatedly expressed an unshakeable faith not only in God, but in the Trinity.

He was firmly convinced that it was within the power of music "to explain things that even mystics and theologians have so far not been able to make comprehensible".[3] In his numerous works he dealt with the central questions of Christian theology: the mysteries of the incarnation, as well as the Eucharist, resurrection and the Trinity. And it was characteristic of him that he did not shy away from putting particularly sensitive subjects such as the transfiguration of the body into music (*Le Corps glorieux*).

How was this unusual synthesis of music and theology realised? Messiaen described his working method in the following way:[4] he would generally concentrate on a subject of meditation – the birth of Christ, the resurrection of the dead, Pentecost, etc. – and would try to find texts in the Bible, in the writings of the Fathers of the Church and in other church texts that were in some way related to the subject. Then he would try to turn this subject into music, not just in notes and rhythms, but also in tone colours and chord colours.

Looking into his work, it soon becomes clear that his thinking is determined by the imaginary, the visionary and poetic. Messiaen deals with the theological subjects in a personal, inventive and vivid manner. It is true that he generally started from theological sources, but he also looked at various commentaries, and physical or surreal concepts and pieces of visual art also had an important role to play.

Messiaen's personal set of beliefs would possibly be less interesting if it were not for the fact that he wrote music that was equally beautiful and original. It can confidently be said that along with Debussy and Ravel he ranks as one of the most important French composers of the 20th century. Graduates of his composition classes in Paris include Boulez and Stockhausen. He was both a Catholic believer and a man with an enquiring mind, one who made many new discoveries in compositional technique. He developed and expanded a new system of "modes", scales of between five and ten notes, and these lie at the root of his chords and melodies. They offer an alternative to the major-minor system as well as every kind of atonality using all twelve semitones, and dodecaphony. He also explored in depth the rhythms of the ancient Greeks and Indians, which he used in his music, and in many pieces laid the foundations for later serial techniques.[5]

A brief examination of his *Vingt Regards sur l'Enfant-Jésus*, his "Twenty contemplations on the baby Jesus", can clarify some of those points. This important work for piano the dates from the time of the Second World War – it was composed in 1944 and was first performed in 1945 by Yvonne Loriod. At that premiere, Messiaen prefaced each piece by reading out a commentary, giving an introduction to the content, form and structure of the twenty compositions.

Messiaen was prompted to write the piece by a work by the Irish theologian Columba Marmion, who had been serving as the abbot of a Benedictine monastery in Belgium since 1909. In his book of 1919, *Christ in His Mysteries*, Marmion speaks of the shepherds, the angels, the Virgin and the Heavenly Father contemplating the baby Jesus. Messiaen took up this idea and treated it in a rather different way, adding sixteen new contemplations to these four. The work begins with that of the Father, and end with the contemplation of the Church of love. Messiaen's personal understanding is particularly evident in those pieces in which intangible or symbolic elements such as time, the heights, silence, the star or the Cross contemplate the baby Jesus. As Aloyse Michaely has demonstrated in a powerfully-argued essay, the work is more easily understood against the backdrop of Thomist theology on the triple birth of Christ, that is, the eternal, the temporal and the mystical.[6]

In line with the highly varied, indeed, contrasting contemplations, each of the twenty pieces has its own distinctive physiognomy and individual expressivity. However, the cyclical nature of the work is maintained in the recurrence of four themes and elaborate variations on them. These are the theme of God, announced in the very first piece, the theme of mystical love, the theme of the star and the Cross, and that of the chords.

Some comments on a few of the pieces can help convey the work's conceptual, intellectual and musical richness: the very first piece, "Contemplation of the Father" refers to Matthew, chapter 3, verse 17 ("This is my Son, the Beloved, my favour rests on him"), and naturally uses the theme of the Father. The sixth piece, "By Him everything was made" is a highly poetic vision of Genesis, the creation story. Messiaen quotes John, chapter 1, verse 3: "Through him all things came to be, not one thing has its being but through him", but this does not prevent him from making reference to modern quantum theory. In his commentary, he speaks explicitly about expansions of spaces and durations, galaxies, photons, reversed spirals and inverted thunderbolts. He fashions the piece as an extremely elaborate fugue – a technique that here undoubtedly has the symbolic meaning of work and creativity. Notions of astronomical magnitudes and large and microphysical particles are expressed in the piece's structure. The seventh piece, "Contemplation of the Cross" is naturally based on the theme of the star and the Cross. This polymodal piece is entwined with expressive, chromatic sighing figures. Messiaen experienced synaesthesia, and the piece is marked by a particular richness of colour. The following piece, "Contemplation of the heights" is a transposition of the idea of *Gloria in excelsis* into instrumental music. The heights, however, are not symbolised by the angels, but by birdsong. Messiaen is well known to have researched birdsong and it was a subject he was exceptionally knowledgeable about. Finally, the tenth piece bears the striking title "Contemplation of the joyful spirit" and is particularly revealing, conveying as it does a quite distinctive view of the Christian religion. As Messiaen writes in his preface "During Christ's earthly life, his soul had the privilege of enjoying an abiding joyful vision. God is happy, and Christ possessed the same happiness, that spiritual intoxication that we convey with the words *tu solus sanctus*." It has to be said that Messiaen here managed to express this idea with equal eloquence and conviction.

Messiaen seems to belong to that group of artists who have no religious doubts. In 1978 he justified his faith in the following terms: "Scientific research, mathematical evidence and the accumulation of biological experiments have increased our uncertainty, in that they have revealed ever more realities under what we believe to be real. In fact, the only reality belongs to another order: it is found in the realm of faith".[7]

Religiously-orientated composers such as Messiaen and Zimmerman were the exception in the second half of the 20th century. Since the Second World War, belief in God has faded and atheism has made greater inroads. Belief in the humanity, justice, freedom and dignity of mankind have therefore been on the rise. So-called politically-engaged music is also inspired by these ideals. The music of Karl Amadeus Hartmann, Hans Werner Henze, Luigi Nono and Helmut Lachenmann – to name only a few composers – belongs to this strain, and in this sense, they can be described as composers of music of a humanitarian "creed". Whether mankind can live without spirit and spirituality is another matter.

## Pierre Boulez's Masterpiece *Le Marteau sans maître*

Of all leading 20th-century musicians, Pierre Boulez (born 1925) is also one of the most versatile, a composer, conductor, essayist and music administrator in one. Many music-lovers know him better as a conductor than a composer. In the latter guise, he found his inspiration not just in Schoenberg, Webern and his teacher Messiaen, but literary figures such as Joyce and Mallarmé as well. In the 1950s he and Karlheinz Stockhausen were the most committed representatives of serial music, and the phrase "Music is as much a science as an art" that appears at the end of the volume *Boulez on Music Today* became a watchword for serialists.[1]

It is well known that at the outset of his artistic career, Boulez reacted against Schoenberg and particular his *Pierrot lunaire*. *Le Marteau sans maître*, the painstakingly-constructed work that he composed between 1952 and 1954 and which Stravinsky made famous, can, in a sense, be seen as the product of this creative conflict. Boulez himself at times pointed to the similarities, but also the differences, between the two works. In his view, both are "of the same duration, almost to the minute; they call for an ensemble of around the same size; both involve a soloist".[2] There is a further point in common: *Pierrot lunaire* is divided into three parts, and consists of three times seven poems. The nine pieces that go to make up *Le Marteau* are similarly constructed from three cycles that draw on poetry by René Char – although three cycles that are elaborately intertwined. Boulez also spoke about further "direct and conscious references" to Schoenberg: the range of instrumentation varies from piece to piece, and in *L'Artisanat furieux* the poem is sung in a highly decorated manner, accompanied by the flute, providing a counterpoint to the vocal line. This is similar to the seventh melodrama of *Pierrot lunaire*, "Der kranke Mond".

Boulez nevertheless also stressed that both works spring from different points of view and arrive at opposite aesthetic positions. One first difference is that while the poems in *Pierrot* are recited in a wholly new manner, Boulez in *Le Marteau* strove for a "great variability in the function of the vowels": the poems are partly sung and sporadically recited, while isolated words are spoken (no.9). There are passages of vocalise, and the voice is actually used like an instrument in the final piece. More importantly, in *Le Marteau*, alongside pieces that use the voice, there are purely instrumental pieces – both continuations of "L'Artisanat furieux" and the three Commentaries on "Bourreaux de solitude".

Precisely to explain the function of these pieces, Boulez has resorted to some unusual formulations. As he explained, *Le Marteau* develops from a "poetic kernel, the centre around which the music crystallizes".[3] He described the text as oscillating between the actual and the potential. As soon as the poetic structure comes to the fore it is "absorbed by the musical context". Of the instrumental pieces he writes, "the poem is at the *centre* of the music, although it is in fact *absent* from the music – just as the shape of an object is preserved by lava even when the object itself has vanished – or like the petrification of an object which is both RE-cognizable and UN-recognizable".[4]

In another essay,[5] Boulez points up a difference – albeit without direct reference to *Le Marteau* – between the poem as "action", taken over by the music, and poem as "reflection", and expressed the opinion that the music takes over responsibility for the active poem. "The poem as reflection, on the other hand, may be submitted to a kind of fragmentation or distortion of its original form, may indeed even absent itself from the music, in which it persists in the form of appended commentary".[6] Thus the poem, which is normally the central point of the music, can be absent from it, and in this way it arrives at the petrification of an object: it is at the same time no longer recognisable and recognisable again. In Boulez's view a genuine encounter between poetry and music can only take place on the structural level. It is the structural notion that he espouses, while ascribing no or at most a secondary importance to the other levels where the two come together, as outlined above. Boulez disputes the ability of music to convey the meaning of a poem. In his opinion music can assert no claim on the precise semantics of spoken language. It possesses its own semantics, that depend on independent structures, that themselves follow special laws. Poetry and music come together on the levels of description and expression too, but on the most imprecise and vague terms.[7]

What Boulez valued in the poetry of René Char on which *Le Marteau* was based was the fact that density of the poetic material had made it possible to "graft on to it musical structures that are to burgeon and proliferate, so that there is no place for the descriptive element as such".[8] What Boulez is stating is that, in complete contrast to Schoenberg, he did not start from imagery when conceiving and composing the cycle. In any case, that would not be possible, since the surrealistic tangle of images in Char's poetry could not be reproduced in music. The poetic images derive from vastly different levels of reality. Yet André Breton, the theorist of Surrealism, had stated that the supreme goal of poetry was to "compare two things as far apart from each other as possible, or – a completely different method – to juxtapose them in a surprising way".[9]
The first poem reads:

*L'artisanat furieux*
*La roulotte rouge au bord du clou*
*Et cadavre dans le panier*
*Et chevaux de labours dans le fer à cheval*
*Je rêve la tête sur la pointe de mon couteau le Pérou*

In English:

*Furious craftsmanship*
*The red caravan on the edge of the nail*
*And corpse in the basket*
*And workhorses in the horseshoe*
*I dream of the head on the point of my knife Peru*

It nevertheless seems to me that Boulez has attached a personal meaning to his work, one that, on closer acquaintance, can be put into words. In the double of "Bel édifice et les pressentiments" that constitutes the finale of the work, the voice first speaks the words of the poem in Sprechgesang style, but then joins the instrumental ensemble, humming, without articulating the words. As Boulez has said, "It sinks back into anonymity," while the alto flute "now steps into the foreground and as it were takes over the role of the vocal element". Shortly afterwards, from bar 100 onwards, the three idiophones that appear only in this number, a gong and two tam-tams, are heard for the first time. They are heard at various points, mostly as a background to the alto flute's expressive monodic phrases. The tempo indication is mostly *Modéré, sans rigueur* (Moderato, not in strict tempo, crotchet = 84). Considering that in 19th and 20th-century music the sheer sound of the gong and tam-tam, independent of characteristic motifs or harmonies, serves to denote death, fear and eternity, then the thought arises that here Boulez has deployed them with a similar semantic meaning,[10] like a commentary on the first line of "Bourreaux de solitude": "Le pas s'est éloigné, le marcheur s'est tu..." (The footstep has moved away, the walker has fallen silent).

## Fascinated by the Music of Ligeti

How can we account for a composer's popularity? The reasons are never easy to arrive at. For many, fame and success are *a priori* suspect terms, and it should not be forgotten that the work of many prominent artists gained recognition only after their deaths. On the other hand, it cannot be denied that many avant-garde works have a very short life-span. Only a very few pieces are permitted to join the standard repertoire. Most fall into oblivion.

Of all leading contemporary composers, György Ligeti, who died on 12 June 2006 at the age of 83, was probably the most showered with awards: he received the highest honours that the cultural world could confer, and there is no doubt that, given the inspired quality of his music, he fully deserved them. These accolades could also be taken as the tardy rehabilitation of an artist who in his prime had at times to endure bitter hardship. After he fled from Hungary in December 1956, Ligeti lived for several years on tiny grants and lectureships. He taught and composed in Italy, in Aix-en-Provence, Denmark, Sweden and the United States – little wonder, then, that he became a cosmopolitan.

Today, Ligeti is one of the most-performed composers in the world. Many of his works – *Atmosphères*, the Requiem, Horn Trio and the concertos for piano and for violin, to name only a few – are without question classics of the modern repertoire. His anti-opera *Le grand Macabre* has been and continues to be given in the main musical centres, and the number of pianists who perform his piano *Études* seems to grow with every passing day. One sometimes has the impression that the extreme technical difficulties of his studies constitute a special challenge for ambitious pianists. Volker Banfield was however the first to smooth their path into the concert hall.

György Ligeti today is almost a popular composer, and many of his works could be said to have a special aura. What is the explanation for the spell cast by his music?

In any discussion of the most significant innovators in recent music history, the first names to come up would be Wagner and Schoenberg. To Wagner we owe the astute observation that reflection has a considerable part to play in artistic creativity. Reflection, speculation, innovation and experimentation all run like a thread through the history of 20th-century music. Almost every prominent composer of this time struck out on new paths, exploring every corner of the acoustic universe, and developing new areas of sound and expression.

Ligeti, the "intelligent musician" *par excellence*, shared this tendency, and in his work too innovation occupies a central place. What he wrote was new music, *ars nova*, yet the path he followed took him quite some distance from the musical avant-garde of the 1960s. His critique of Boulez's Third Piano Sonata shook the fundamental principles of serialism, and ushered in a new period of musical creativity. His conviction that musical logic was not automatically to be equated with mathematical logic was a significant and valuable insight, and at the same time one that clearly differentiates his work from that of a Iannis Xenakis or Clarence Barlow.

His tireless efforts to regenerate music were often focused on the fundamental elements, and he had a keen interest in tuning and temperament in both European and non-European music. He experimented with pure tuning and microtones, as well as quarter-tones and even smaller intervals, with new forms of sound, and new types of melody, harmony, metre, rhythm and polyphony. The study of historical composition techniques of *ars nova* and *ars subtilior*, that is the rhythmically and polyphonically highly sophisticated music of the 14th century, as well as the polyphony and polyrhythm of central-African music inspired his own creativity in all sorts of ways, and he had a wonderful ability to blend it all together. After many experiments, he arrived in his Piano Concerto at a point between microtonality and equal temperament that was utterly original. What he said he was aiming for in this extremely complex work was "quasi-equidistance", that is, that the music should give the illusion of equidistance: that it should arise from equal temperament, yet not belong to it. Some explanation is in order for this apparently complex question: "Equal temperament", which we are generally familiar with, divides the octave into twelve equal semitones, in other words, it is "equidistant". But the octave can also be divided into five or six equal notes – the Javanese Slendro, for instance, is a five-note, tempered, approximately equidistant scale (each interval being of around 240 cents). In his Piano Concerto Ligeti achieved his idea of quasi-equidistance in various ways: by combining two whole-tone scales, using diatonic and pentatonic scales simultaneously, and so on.

The new sonorities that Ligeti developed captivate the listener. In his early works he frequently favoured his ideal of a shimmering, iridescent, oscillating sound. In later works he aspired to undermining the tempered system, and *scordatura*, the tightening or loosening of the strings on a string instrument to vary the standard tuning; microtonal divergences, "mistuned" instruments and natural harmonics all played a key role.

The special fascination of Ligeti's music, however, cannot be ascribed merely to its tuning and sonority, but to its great imaginative qualities and associative power as well. Ligeti was known to experience synaesthesia. He regularly referred to the fact that his music was not "pure" but "loaded with associations". "When I hear music," he once stated, "I also see colours and shapes".[1] As he stated, his sources of inspiration were frequently extra-musical. Lines of verse, poems and texts that affected him, colours, images, paintings and artistic objects – all provided a creative impulse. The associative element is sometimes indicated in the titles of his works – in *Apparitions*, *Atmosphères*, *Continuum*, *Monument*, and especially in the titles of the piano *Études*, in which poetic elements appear alongside purely technical or musical terms.

Ligeti's music, with its "burden of associations" makes special demands on listeners, asking for them to be synaesthetically in agreement. Ligeti's ideal would be the sort of educated listener who is able to recognise the music's in-built allusions and is also sensitive to their associative qualities. In this respect his music prompts comparisons with that of Debussy, Ravel, Scriabin and above all Messiaen, a type of art that without a matching synaesthetic response one can neither properly perceive nor fully enjoy.

There are two further characteristics of Ligeti's music that relate to his strong visual imagination: the quasi-stereometric, or spatially graphic sound-form of many pieces, and his aesthetic of illusion. The notion of music as "frozen" time was a favourite idea of Ligeti's. He never let an opportunity pass to stress the importance of the aspect of "imaginary space", of spatial thinking, in his music. Again and again spatial notions set the course for his compositions, and many works suggest spatial ideas to the listener, creating spatial illusions: an imaginary perspective of closeness and distance, depth and height, breadth and narrowness. These spatial effects are brought out mostly through differing levels of volume, the weight of the sound, the simultaneous use of very high and very low notes as well as unison octave doublings across multiple registers. The listener often has the impression of perceiving elements of movement within the imaginary space, rising up from the bottom to the top. In other cases, one has the impression that the music is expanding out from a particular point to gradually occupy the entire musical space.

The first piano study, *Désordre*, gives a striking example of a quasi-stereometric sound-form. The piece opens in the central register and then gradually opens outward in both directions. While the right hand occupies the space right up to the extreme top register, the left hand dominates the lower area, down to the lowest point. This is accompanied by an intensification of the volume. A second, shorter musical element is introduced later, and here again the two hands move apart. It is only in the last two bars, when the music is on the point of vanishing, that they move in parallel.

The timbre of Ligeti's music exerts a powerful fascination: he demonstrated a highly-developed sense of sound and created many utterly distinctive and quite unforgettable sonorities. The "cystoscopic" sound, an accumulation of slowly changing, extremely dissonant clusters in the high register that sounds so piercing as to be almost painful, is one such. "Cystoscopy" is a medical term for a painful bladder endoscopy. Another of Ligeti's striking sounds is the thin two-part texture that evokes a vacuum by combining a very slowly unfolding melodic line in the very top register with held pedal notes in the very lowest register. Between the two there is no other sound, and the immediate impression is of a void. Ligeti had a special fondness for ethereal flageolet tones. Many of his works contain entire sections that are exclusively or predominantly made out of flageolet tones and glissandos. They often prompt associations with the music of the spheres, as at the beginning of the fourth scene of *Le grand Macabre*, where the music depicts Piet and Astramadors floating freely in space. The ethereal background to the music of the spheres in this scene is provided by string harmonic clusters, while the sounds of a harmonica, horns and organ give a rather sweet tone to the music.

Ligeti had at his disposal a unique wealth of associations that enabled him to combine seemingly distant or disparate themes and areas in a single context. His astonishing power of association could also be productive in the conception of his works. The most varied things inspired him, and all sorts of elements were amalgamated in his unmistakable musical idiom. His "sources of inspiration" in the broadest sense came not just from Western art music, European folklore and non-European music, but also dance-music, jazz, works of literature and visual art as well as various other visual images.

As far as dance-music is concerned, Ligeti had a keen interest in both jazz and dance from all sorts of places: Balkan, northern European, Caribbean and South American. A close look at his Piano Concerto and Violin Concerto reveals jazz-like moments that are also marked by distinctive rhythms, syncopations and instrumentation. In 1978 he composed a Chaconne for harpsichord entitled *Hungarian Rock*. His later works often have dance-like moments, or even movements: the second movement of his Horn Trio is a fast, polymetric dance. Ligeti said the piece was inspired by various types of folk music of non-existent peoples, "as if Hungary, Romania and the whole of the Balkans lay somewhere between Africa and the Caribbean". And similarly, the finale of his Violin Concerto consists, according to an early draft, of a series of "Romanian-Caribbean" dances.[2]

Ligeti's wide-ranging output bucked the fashionable trends in new music. Positioned beyond the avant-garde and the post-modern, it is certainly modern, and even represents the modern where it affects to be bound to tradition.

# Ligeti's *Hölderlin-Phantasien*
# A Letter from the Composer

In the autumn of 1975 the Free and Hanseatic city of Hamburg awarded its prestigious Bach Prize to György Ligeti. I was asked to deliver the speech in his honour, which was subsequently published in the journal *Musik und Bildung* in 1978.[1] Shortly afterwards, the Swedish journal *Nutida Musik* (New Music) offered to print a Swedish translation of the text.[2] This marked the beginning of a closer collaboration with the journal, which involved me providing articles to introduce a number of works by Ligeti in advance of their first performances.

Early in 1983 I was asked by the journal's editor to write an introduction to Ligeti's recently-completed *Drei Phantasien nach Hölderlin*, a work that the highly-regarded Swedish Radio Chorus was due to premiere in Stockholm on 26 September 1983 under conductor Eric Ericson. After extensive study of the manuscript score, I informed Ligeti of the editorial deadline for the article (1 August 1983) and asked him for some brief comments on his choruses. After I had sent my text to Stockholm, I received the following letter from Ligeti, which I here reproduce in full:

*Vienna, 2 August 1983*

*Dear Professor Floros,*

*Your letter of 18 July was forwarded to me in Vienna, where I am now, having left Hamburg in the middle of July.*
*And I have to thank you* over and over again *from the bottom of my heart, not just for your (personal) letter, but also for your first, printed letter marking my birthday!*[3] *I should have said thank you long before now... but I have only recently learned about the existence of this letter! You enclosed it by sending the programme that it was printed in, but a little earlier, on 6 July, I had already received it from Professor Rauhe, who gave me the programme (before then I knew nothing about it, and you can imagine what pleasure it gave me!).*
*So* once again *a* huge, heartfelt *thank you!*[4]
*I found it deeply affecting.*

*I should have known about the concerts back in May, but I only heard about them later. I did not receive any news at all, either from Mr Ceccato or the Philharmonic Orchestra. I would actually have liked to attend a rehearsal (because if a composer is still alive, and also, as it happens, present in the city where the performance is taking place, it's nice if he's told and invited to a rehearsal and concert). But nothing happened. I didn't see any poster or anything*

113

*in the paper, since I was (as usual) working and struggling with a deadline, and I was already due to travel to Bonn (obviously I would have postponed that if I had known beforehand about the concert....). I only learned at the last minute, and indirectly, because Herr Rauhe rang me on 28 May and said that there was a concert that included* Atmosphères *the following day, but by then I was already packing my suitcases and couldn't put off my trip at such short notice. So because of this I also didn't have any knowledge of the programme and the fact that you had published such a lovely, wonderful "letter" in it. And* very special, heartfelt, enormous thanks *for your fantastic understanding of what I'm trying to "say" secretly in my music! Now, on the* Drei Phantasien nach Hölderlin: *I'm distraught – you want to write the article by the 1st of August – and thank you for writing about my works again for* Nutida Musik *– and today is the 2nd of August, and I wasn't in Hamburg when you wrote to me, and now it's too late. I couldn't say very much about it anyway – you can see the polyphonic structure and harmonic combinations from the score. The fact that I chose Hölderlin: it is not just that he is one of my favourite poets.*[5] *For the "setting" I actually chose those poetic fragments for their marvellous imagery and emotional aura. (In the past I have written choruses on Hungarian texts, on poetry by Sándor Weöres, where the element of verbal imagination is the most important element, while in the Hölderlin poems the field of imagery had greater resonance for me).*[6] *I took a madrigal approach to some turns of phrase, for example the imitation of the wind in* Hälfte des Lebens. *In the* Abendphantasie *the association of Altdorfer's* The Battle of Alexander at Issus, *the vast scenery of cloud formations pierced by rays of sunlight plays a role: that could be quite random on my part – I don't know if Hölderlin saw* The Battle of Alexander.

Lux aeterna *and the* Drei Phantasien: *the only thing they have in common is the number of voices, 4 x 4 = 16, so only a surface connection, although the number of voices in* Lux aeterna *serves the imperceptible harmonic transformation (by way of supersaturated canon formations), while in the* Phantasien *imperceptible transformation has a lesser role to play (and my style too has changed somewhat since 1966, when I wrote* Lux aeterna*). In the* Phantasien, *dramatic outbursts, cumulative movement and harsh harmonic contrasts play much more of a role.*

*I would be very pleased if you could send me a copy of your text (I don't receive* Nutida Musik *automatically and won't be able to attend the first performance).*[7]

*I'm very happy and touched to know that you write about my music.*

*You can reach me by post in Vienna until around the 25th of August (the address is at the top of the letter) and after that I will be in hospital, where I won't be able to receive any post, and around the end of September (after a trip to Berlin) I'll be back in Hamburg.*

*It would be a great pleasure for me to meet you in person! Incidentally, have you had an invitation from Mr Zimmermann (in the Faculty of Philosophy) to the Wednesday afternoon get-togethers? I asked Mr Zimmermann to invite you without fail! I hope very much that he has done so (he organises the event). It would be wonderful if you could attend a couple of these discussions! (I won't be able to be there on a regular basis, but do so occasionally). I would also be very keen to meet you privately, if you have time, and we can discuss that in the autumn.*
A huge thank-you
*and very best wishes,*
*Yours sincerely,*
*György Ligeti*

## Iridescent Sound

The history of musical aesthetics, as much as music theory, is unimaginable without the notion of purity. It is, nevertheless, a notion that has, over the course of time, undergone some ebb and flow. In 1825 the legal expert Anton Friedrich Justus Thibaut, whose Heidelberg lectures the young Schumann attended, published his short but widely-read book *Über Reinheit der Tonkunst* (Purity in Music) in which he attacked the liturgical music of his time and argued passionately in favour of Palestrina's vocal polyphony. From the beginning of the 19th century, music theory considered certain intervals (unison, fourth, fifth and octave) to be pure. The term took its bearings from mathematics and acoustics, tunings and tonal systems. What is termed mean temperament, used by musicians in the 16th and 17th centuries, was, as is generally known, based on pure thirds.[1] In contrast, the twelve semitones of equal temperament – the work of Andreas Werckmeister and J.S. Bach – abandoned the acoustically pure system and used the melodic principle of equal intervals as a musical basis. The tempered intervals were now considered to be pure, and the music of the 18th and 19th centuries can be said to belong to a culture of pure sound according to those terms.

In the 20th century, the undisputed primacy of equal temperament was challenged as microtonality gained ground, noise-like structures entered music, and the invention of electronic music in the 1950s led the establishment of new standards.

After he fled to the West in December 1956, Ligeti pursued a whole host of new ways to move beyond the tempered system. He felt that it was exhausted, that chromaticism was spent.[2] What he aimed to do was move on from both tonality and atonality. Although he was leaning towards microtonality and experimented with it in many ways, he had as yet not written any rigorously structured microtonal works. After many attempts, he found within equal temperament a way to create sonorities that give the impression that alien, exotic tonal systems are being used (see page 110).

In his earliest works, Ligeti created a new kind of dodecaphony. The listener to Ligeti's music often has the impression that they are hearing constantly changing twelve-note fields and sounds. The soundscape, however, is fundamentally different from that of Schoenberghian dodecaphony and serial music alike.

The world of pure tuning held a strong fascination for Ligeti. He enthused about the musical culture of the Chokwe, based on pure fifths and major thirds, Georgian polyphony, which equally has only natural fifths and natural major thirds, and the yodelling of pygmies as well. As early as the Horn Trio, and later in the Piano Concerto and Violin Concerto, he makes frequent use of natural, pure intervals. He was particularly attached to the natural seventh and natural eleventh, which are considerably flatter than their tempered equivalents (minus 15 and minus 49 cents): at certain points in the last movement of the Piano Concerto the music asks for a natural horn and natural trombone. Manfred Stahnke's opinion that microtonality was part and parcel of Ligeti's overall thinking, even where he was writing with tempered intervals, seems irrefutable.[3]

In an interview with Louise Duchesneau in October 1992, Ligeti described his attempts to realise new concepts of sound: "When I look back it becomes clear to me that whether consciously or not, I was always looking for an alternative to the tuning of twelve equal intervals. I think the idea actually arose with my piece *Atmosphères* (1961). The first time I heard the shimmering sound that previously I had only been able to imagine, I understood that what I was looking for lay between noise and musical sound. The next step on in the development from the tempered system was taken in the *Requiem*, correct intonation from the choral voices being impossible, because the piece is far too difficult. In fact, the shimmering effect depends on the spontaneous variations in pitch of a sufficiently large number of singers and instrumentalists. The idea of writing *Ramifications* in quarter-tones came to me after I had heard the *Requiem* in 1965 although I wasn't setting out to write quarter-tone music. Once again I was seeking the iridescent, impure sound in the shimmering manner of *Atmosphères* and *Requiem*".[4]

The first works where Ligeti was able to realise his new ideas on sound were *Apparitions* and *Atmosphères*, first performed in 1960 and 1961 respectively. Ligeti would have been unable to write the two works in their existing form confidently if he had not previously been extensively involved with electronic music in the Cologne studio. His experiences with this medium were key to his compositional development.[5] *Atmosphères* is an astonishingly original piece of cluster writing. Divided into 22 sections of varying length, it is based on dense chromatic clusters, generally made up of four, eight or twelve notes. It is important that the partials or "partial sounds" are completely absorbed in the overall sound, so that they lose almost all of their individual tone colour. Ligeti described this phenomenon in a hitherto unpublished commentary: "The individual harmonic spectrums of the instrumental sounds, superimposed and telescoped non-harmonically, give rise to a confusion of beats through the interference of numerous spectral components. These beats themselves lead not just to a blurring of the total sound, but also to a fluctuation in the colouring, to a constant *iridescence* – an impression that could not have been achieved with the tone colour mixtures hitherto available".[6]

To indicate these new types of sound, standing halfway between sound and noise, Ligeti made use of the word "sonority", a term that belongs to French music theory[7] – Debussy uses it, for example, in his Prelude *La Cathédrale engloutie*.[8] Mauricio Kagel also uses the term with a similar meaning to Ligeti's in an article on tone-clusters.[9]

On various occasions Ligeti described the ideal sound he had in mind as being iridescent, shimmering, fluctuating and also "impure". In prismatic colours, iridescent means shimmering – the term also applies to the spectrum and, particularly, refraction. Shimmering itself means changing or fluctuating at the greatest possible rate. How does the iridescent sound in *Atmosphères* come about?

In a conversation with Josef Häusler in 1968, Ligeti gave two explanations for this impression.[10] The broad bands of sound that follow one another in *Atmosphères* were, in his opinion, not always completely chromatically filled in. In fact, little gaps appear in the clusters where the lines are constantly changing. Consequently, there are places where many notes are doubled, and others where, in contrast, they are missing. The iridescent sound-effect also arises from the change in bowing by the string-players. The piece begins *sul tasto* (bowed on the fingerboard), changes to normal bowing position, and later moves on to *sul ponticello* (on the bridge) and then, with a crescendo, reverts to normal style.

Further explanations for the iridescent sound emerge from a closer examination of the score. Analysis shows that the individual sections that the composition is divided into are considerably differentiated from each other in terms of frequency band, register, tone colour combinations, dynamics and playing style. This gives rise to three basic types of sound plane: flat plane, vibrating plane and mosaic-like textures.[11] The term "flat plane" essentially means an unchanging cluster: static, stationary sounds that can nevertheless have nuances of colour and dynamic. "Vibrating planes" are realised through a trill, tremolo or oscillating figurations or through internal movement within a broad range of texture, and mosaic-like textures are characterised by the lines dissolving into individual components.

It is clear from this that the "vibrating" sound-planes play a fundamental part in creating the shimmering sound-effect. The same applies to the vast differentiation in string playing styles in the 18th and 19th sections (bars 79-84). It is stipulated here that the various instrumental groups should play simultaneously with and without mutes, on the fingerboard and bridge, *sul tasto* and *col legno* (with the reverse side of the bow), *gettato* (ricochet off the string) and *legato*. In this way, and through the frequent tremolos the listener has the impression that the surface of the sound is trembling.

There is a further, highly important factor that should not be overlooked when attempting to account for the iridescent sound, one that is only partly conveyed by the terms density and redundancy. Sections 9 and 10 of *Atmosphères* (bars 44-53, rehearsal letters H and I) demonstrate an archetypal example of Ligeti's now celebrated technique of micropolyphony. Here the micropolyphonic texture consists of 48 lines (14 first violins, 14 seconds, 10 violas and 10 cellos), and is clearly structured as a canon and mirror canon: while the violins play a 28-voice strict canon, the violins and cellos play a 20-voice mirror canon in inversion. That is, the mirror canon is a precise reflection of the canon, the underlying melodic line proceeding in exactly the opposite direction (see music example 12, p. 123. The violins' "theme" is ascending, that in the violas and cellos is descending).

One begins to understand the special nature of the highly complex make-up of the music when one realises that all the voices of the micropolyphonic texture are used simultaneously, not on the same note, but on every step of the chromatic scale. The intervallic relationships of the cantus firmus-like melody are preserved in all the voices of the giant canon, but the rhythmic relationships undergo significant modifications, and are organised according to a different principle. At the same time, the complexity of the rhythmic organisation defies description. Suffice it to say that the strings play at three different speeds: while the second violins and violas play at a normal speed, as it were (4 units per half-bar), the cellos play slower (3 units per half-bar) and the first violins faster (5 units).

In his essay *Music and Technique* Ligeti explains the effect these procedures have on perception, referring to the phenomenon of blending.[12] If individual optical or acoustic events occur in quick succession, we perceive them as a blur. If the sequence of images, notes or sounds exceeds a given amount then we no longer perceive the individual events, but instead have an impression of continual movement. If more than 20 individual notes sound in succession in the space of a second, then the notes become merged. We reach the "blending limit". It is characteristic of the melodic and rhythmic procedures described in the micropolyphonic texture of *Atmosphères* that they – as Ligeti would say – "dip into the area below the blending limit".

The experiments carried out by Jan Kasem-Bek are informative in this context.[13] As he was able to demonstrate, some passages in *Atmosphères* have as many as around 200 different sequences of notes within the space of a second. The flow of information derived from that of around 719 bits per second is almost four times higher than the speed that can be perceived by the listener. In other words, too much information changes into a loss of information.

The new kind of sound is the product of the special density of this micropolyphonic texture. In the essay referred to above, Ligeti differentiates between three qualities of tone colour. The first is the instrumental colour of the individual voices, the second the compound tone colour of the combined voices, and third – the new quality – is the so-called "moving or blurring colour". He refers to a "global" sound that results from the superimposition of the 48 voices. The aural impression one receives is in his opinion only slightly different from that produced by electronic music.

Significant advances in the area of sound analysis have been made in recent years, and new methods have been developed. Digital processes have made it possible to map precisely the sound construction of a given composition. Andreas E. Beurmann and Albrecht Schneider compiled an amplitude diagram of *Atmosphères* that gives an impressive illustration of the overall form of the piece.[14] The two writers describe the progression of the work as "...a delicate oscillation, a coming out of nothing, five areas of an extremely slow dynamic surging and ebbing and vanishing into nothing, symbolising the title of the music – atmospheres.

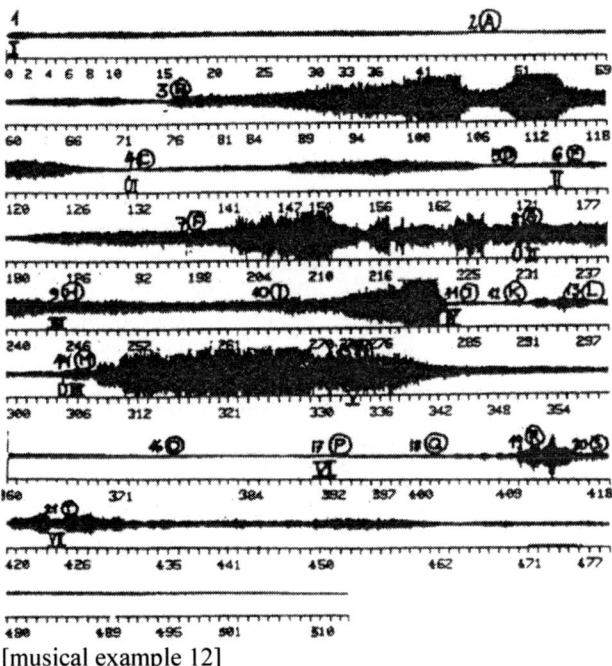

[musical example 12]
Amplitude diagram of Ligeti's *Atmosphères*

The diagram makes it possible to see how the music progresses, and provides a visualisation of the individual agglomerations of sound.[15] The dark patch at M indicates the brass areas of section 14 (bars 58-65, rehearsal letter M) – a twelve-note cluster field that in terms of dynamic compactness constitutes the climax of the piece. The permanently jagged edges of the envelope curve are an another striking element. They give an image of what the listener perceives as oscillation, fluctuation and flickering.

*Atmosphères* was first performed in Donaueschingen on 22 October 1961, by the Südwestfunk Sinfonieorchester under Hans Rosbaud. The piece was so enthusiastically received that it had to be repeated immediately.[16]

In his now famous study *The Work of Art in the Age of Mechanical Reproduction*, Walter Benjamin developed his theory of the "auratic" existence of an art-work, with reference to works of visual art.[17] He drew an important distinction between an original and its reproduction. In his view, what was lost in the age of mechanical reproduction of a work of art was its "aura", a term he used to mean "the unique appearance of distance, however close it may be". Admittedly, it is difficult to define the term "aura" with any precision. It is generally take to cover the allure, the effectiveness, the outer casing and particular expressivity of an art-work.

Theodor Adorno took up Benjamin's theory in his *Aesthetic Theory* and developed it dialectically.[18] He was interested in the dichotomy of the auratic and technological art-work. His criticism of Benjamins's theory was that the aura was not just the here and now of an art-work but what transcended its reality, its "substance" (*Gehalt*). What Adorno meant by "substance" was the "truthful content of the arts", above all, the "human content". This "human content" was for him a way of measuring the value of works of art.

Our focus here, however, is on the duality of the auratic and technological art-work, which it seems to me can usefully be applied to music. It could to a certain extent help to explain why many exceptional works of art live on and make an impact on people decades, even centuries after their creation, while most sink into oblivion. The quality of a musical art-work is not just related to compositional logic or mastery of compositional technique, but also depends on factors that the words "tone", "gesture", "character" "idiom", "expression" and even "aura" can only approximately convey. No one can deny that many compositions are surrounded by a particular "aura". Wagner's music dramas, Bruckner's and Mahler's symphonies, for example, are highly "auratic". *Neue Sachlichkeit*, on the other hand, which was opposed to expressiveness, had a marked antipathy to the "auratic".

The same sort of thing could be said of the serial music of the 1950s and 1960s. A work such as Boulez's *Le Marteau sans maître* is undoubtedly auratic. In other serial works that emphasise the element of construction, the aura – as Benjamin would have it – is quite lost. But the works of Ligeti are extremely auratic. Construction does indeed play an absolutely key role, but not everything can be reduced to it. (Ligeti himself once said that one could hear his pieces as construction, but then one would not hear them properly).[19] The person listening to *Atmosphères*, for example, does not perceive the complexity of the construction, as we have seen. They are fascinated by the new type of sound, one that magically draws the listener in. Ligeti's extremely synaesthetic disposition opens a new way into his music, one that demands the listener's synaesthetic response, creating allusions and illusions and making them audible in sound With works such as *Atmosphères* Ligeti showed a new way into the future, which is often prophesied will bring about the end of art.

[Music example 13]
György Ligeti, *Atmosphères*, full score (bars 45 ff.)

## "Folklore in Serious Music is a Lie"
## Ligeti's Relationship with Béla Bartók

György Ligeti complained bitterly on many occasions about the cultural policies of the post-1945 communist regime in Hungary. He would relate, not without indignation, that most of the major works of Béla Bartók as well as of many other leading composers (not only Schoenberg, Berg and Webern, but Debussy and Ravel too) were considered "new" and "decadent" and were not to be performed. Exceptions were the Concerto for Orchestra, Third Piano Concerto, the First and Sixth string quartets and the folk-song arrangements. The enforcement of "socialist realism" led all non-conformist musicians into internal exile. Much of what Ligeti composed during his time in Budapest was intended only for his desk drawer. "Composing for your drawer was like a badge of honour".[1]

At the beginning of the 1990s Ligeti told me that during this time he had a quite ambivalent relationship with Bartók. On one hand he felt a deep devotion to the leading representative of modern Hungarian music. On the other, he was trying to free himself from his influence, having felt that he recognised Bartók's affinity with Beethoven and that the occasional strong element of pathos in his music was essentially alien to him. On closer examination, the impression emerges that the nature of Ligeti's relationship to Bartók did not remain constant. It seems to have undergone considerable fluctuations, and there were times when it was close and others when it was so distant that Ligeti was completely alienated from the older composer.

A considerable part of Ligeti's early work remains unexplored. If Ove Nordwall's work list is complete, Ligeti must have composed no fewer than 74 works between 1944 and 1956, of which only a few have so far been published.[2] In any case, the few known pieces indicate that he started out on his artistic career as a folklorist in the wake of Bartók and Kodály. According to the ideas prevalent in Hungary at the time, a composer also had to be an ethnomusicologist. As a young man, Ligeti had devoted himself to both Hungarian peasant music and Romanian folklore. In 1949 he received a grant to pursue ethnomusicological studies at the renowned European Folklore Institute in Budapest. In villages near Cluj he assiduously collected Hungarian folksongs. In addition, he transcribed Romanian folksongs that Bartók had recorded on wax cylinders at the Ethnographic Museum in Bucharest in August and September 1950. He did not find this pursuit fulfilling, however, and gave it up. Nevertheless, his experiences with Romanian folk music found expression in the Romanian Concerto, a four-movement work from 1951 that later appeared on CD, and which Ligeti thought would ruin his reputation, since it had nothing in common with the Ligeti style.[3]

The next major work, *Musica ricercata* for piano, written between 1951 and 1953, consists of eleven character pieces, and its main point of interest lies in its compositional technique. Just like Bartók in his *Mikrokosmos*, so too Ligeti here works with a specific set of notes. The first piece is based on a single note, the second on two, and later three notes, and in the subsequent pieces the number increases until finally the entire set of notes is in use. The final piece is a fugue on a thirteen-note theme by Frescobaldi.[4] Each of the eleven pieces has its own physiognomy, and the expressive range extends from *Mesto* (Nos.2 and 9) and *Lamentoso* (No.5) to *Allegro con spirito* (No.3) and *Capriccioso* (Nos.6 and 10).

In at least four pieces the Bartók model is impossible to miss. No.5 is an invention on rubato – the free relaxation and speeding-up of the tempo – one of the great composer's specialities. No.8, a piece in 7/8, has a pronounced folk character, a tempo indication *Presto energico* and the familiar Bartókian expression mark *ruvido* (roughly). No.9 is explicitly dedicated to the memory of Bartók, and could be seen as an invention on the heavily-accented Lombard rhythm, or "Scotch snap". In No.10, *Vivace, capriccioso*, a theme based on a chromatic idea with a changing time signature, is subjected to an endless series of variations, repeatedly alternating with sequences of triplets marked *grazioso*. Shortly before the end, a sforzatissimo (*sff*) gesture is repeated again and again, easily creating a dissonant sound. Parallels in Bartók for chromatic themes can be found in the second movement of the Fourth String Quartet, and for the model of triplet sequences in the Scherzo of the Fifth.

Ligeti's First String Quartet, which bears the poetic subtitle *Métamorphoses nocturnes*, was composed in 1953 and 1954, and is undoubtedly one of the most significant instrumental works of this early period. It could be said to be Janus-like: together with more backward-looking traits, it contains seeds that would only germinate some time later. One aspect that looks to the future is the use of glissando harmonics by all four strings in the penultimate section (from letter UU on), but here we are more concerned with aspects that point to Bartók. At the basis of the work is an intervallic idea, a configuration of two major seconds separated by a semitone that undergoes all sorts of transformations (metamorphoses) as the work progresses.[5] An early version of this intervallic cell (G – A, G sharp – A sharp) can be found in the *Adagio molto* of Bartók's Fifth String Quartet, where it appears in the configurations E flat – F – F sharp – E or F – G – G sharp – F sharp. All the indicators of Bartókian vitality and folklore are present in the 7/8 section *Subito prestissimo*, bars 600-654, which is predominantly rhythmic. In addition Ligeti makes much use of what is known as the Bartók pizzicato, a powerful pizzicato where the string hits the fingerboard, and of distinctly Bartókian glissandos. Even more indicative is the fact that Ligeti's expressive manner in the First String Quartet is very close to Bartók's. This calls for some specific examples.

Bartók's string quartets have hitherto been analysed principally in terms of their compositional technique. Many performers have been profoundly impressed by their rigour and originality, the logic of their construction, the structural elements, the linear voice-leading in many sections, but also by their amazingly tough sound.[6] Another hugely important factor – their expressive world, the character, gestures and tone of the music – has been considered marginal, if taken into account at all. This aspect deserves our attention.

Generally speaking, Bartók's string quartets can be divided into four expressive fields that can be characterised as "soft", "hard", "expressive" and "light" music. The "soft" music belongs to the *piano* and *pianissimo* domain. As a rule, it is distinguished by polyphonic, imitative writing, and a preference for *legato* lines. It occasionally comes with the expression mark *dolce*. It has its counterpart in the wild gestures and aggressive, hard music that Bartók was particularly attached to, at least from the time of his *Allegro barbaro* of 1911. It belongs to the *forte* and *fortissimo* domain, and comes with expression marks like *ruvido* (roughly) and *marcato, marcatissimo* and *martellato*. This wild gestural style favours rhythmic accentuation, homophonic blocks, dissonant chords and syncopations. In the second movement, *Allegro molto capriccioso* of the Second String Quartet, composed between 1915 and 1917, Bartók transferred this style from the keyboard into chamber music for the first time. The first part of the Third String Quartet is an eloquent example of repeated alternation between "hard" and "soft" music.

The "expressive" music, for which Bartók occasionally used the marking *espressivo* itself, constitutes a separate area of expression. The second (*Adagio molto*) and fourth (*Andante*) movements of the Fifth String Quartet provide good examples of this type, as do all the sections in the Sixth String Quartet marked *mesto*. Finally, there is a playful element of the category of "light" music, which characteristically uses markings such as *leggero, leggerissimo, grazioso* and *scherzando*. There are good examples of this type in the mainly dance-like second part of the Third and the Finale of the Fourth String Quartets.

Anyone reasonably familiar with Ligeti's early work will find all these expressive domains in his First String Quartet. The very first section, *Allegro grazioso*, represents the "soft" type, while the second *Vivace capriccioso* is capricious, and the third, with the characteristic expression mark *sempre feroce*, is particularly wild.

After his flight to the West in December 1956, Ligeti did not just leave behind all his belongings, but also a part of his artistic identity. The new intellectual world and mentality that he encountered in the West presented him with new challenges. Serialism had spread like a doctrine, and exerted its power over countless young composers. Both Schoenberg's dodecaphonic method and folklorism were considered completely outdated. It is significant that in Cologne Ligeti did not dare show Herbert Eimert – a master of the avant-garde – his First

String Quartet. In the Cologne studio for electronic music he gained experience with the new medium that was later to have a positive impact on his instrumental works. He immersed himself in the scores of Stockhausen and Boulez, and through his highly detailed analysis of Boulez's *Structure 1a* called the axioms of serial music into question. Boulez based this composition on three rows of twelve elements that determined the pitches ("note qualities") as well as durations and levels of intensity, while there was a row of ten different kinds of attack. Ligeti caused a sensation when he demonstrated that despite this apparent total organisation, irregularities and deviations from the strictly applied serial principle arose. His deduction was that the composer's decision and automatism were interdependent. Ligeti's formulation was that "the mutually affecting decisions lead inescapably to automatism, determination creates the unpredictable; and vice versa: neither the automatic nor the chance can be engendered without decision and determination".[7]

The works that he composed in the West at the end of the 1950s and into the 1960s, and that quickly established his fame, represent Ligeti's unmistakable style and are not in any way related to Bartók's music. Micro-polyphony, his technique for creating the surface sound, and the stereophonic form of many of his "sound sculptures" represent something entirely new in the history of 20th-century music. It is all the more remarkable, then, that his Second String Quartet, composed in 1968, is so reminiscent of Bartók. In a conversation with Josef Häusler Ligeti himself spoke of "more or less clear allusions to Bartók's string quartet style" and stated that his quartet contained "quite consciously a little homage to Bartók".[8] It is not that the music is quoted, but much more that its spirit, its aura are present within a quite different context.

There is a world of difference between Bartók and Ligeti's Second String Quartet in terms of compositional technique. Three differences tip the balance: all six of Bartók's quartets are characterised by extended tonality; in each one there are dominant notes, what might be called central notes. In contrast, Ligeti's string quartet occupies a position beyond tonality and atonality. Secondly, Bartók's string quartets are consistently tied to metrical pulse, while Ligeti's work is entirely free of it. And there is a third, no less significant difference: while Bartók works principally with themes and motifs, developing and elaborating them in a logical manner, Ligeti's quartet is strictly a-motivic and athematic. Themes, in the traditional sense, do not appear at all. Ligeti favours mesh-like textures and web-like structures; on one hand there are cluster-like sounds, and on the other extremely virtuoso parts with a decidedly concertante quality.

It is true that there are subliminal, hidden connections with Bartók. Ligeti shares the contrast between "soft" and "hard" music. "Soft" music covers the static, diffuse, blurred and hazy, and occupies the *piano* and *pianissimo* domain. "Hard" music, in contrast, is typically abrupt and fragmented, at times wild and untamed, so that the listener can have the impression that the music is going completely out of control.

These types of motion found in Ligeti's music of the 1960s appear in various forms in the Second String Quartet. Ligeti said of the five movements of the work that he was anxious "to realise a musical idea that would return in every movement, but quite differently each time".[9] To put it another way, the five movements contain the same musical and formal ideas but the perspective and colour is different in each "so that the overall musical form only emerges when all five movements are heard and considered in relation to each other.

Looking more closely at the five movements, we can see that the first – *Allegro nervoso* – gains its momentum from the abrupt switch between restrained sections and extremely wild ones. Long, sustained, shimmering and ethereal sounds alternate with extremely agitated, virtuoso passages. The principle of contrast, it could be said, is taken to its furthest extreme. The point is made by the fact that the indication *Sostenuto calmo* repeatedly swaps with *Prestissimo sfrenato* or *Ferocissimo, tutta la forza, wie verrückt* (as if demented). The mood at the close is one of exhaustion and silence, and the movement ends *morendo al niente*.

In the second movement, the idea of sudden change is realised in a completely different manner. The basic mood of the movement, characterised by sustained, cluster-like sounds, is peaceful. But that almost static quality is broken by increasing sudden fortissimo outbursts, which irritate the listener. Ligeti understood the movement as a "long variant" of the first, and spoke about numerous "subterranean connections". The most striking of these comes at the end: this movement too closes in a mood of exhaustion and silence.

As he himself stated, the technological world was a significant source of inspiration for Ligeti. Clocks, clockwork and regular patterns had always fascinated him. He had, as he once declared, composed pieces that represented "mechanical processes". One characteristic type makes regular appearances in several works, whose inflexible, clockwork-like rhythmic structure is reminiscent of precision machines. (It would seem that Ligeti was inspired by the hurdy-gurdy sound of the *meccanico* passage in the finale of Bartók's Fifth Quartet). It is no coincidence that the indication "like a precision mechanism" appears on many occasions. It is also found at the beginning of the third movement – a pizzicato piece that leaves the listener with the impression of knocking and hammering. Ligeti, who mentioned "mechanical ticking" pictured "the imaginary machine breaking down and splintering into its component parts".

The movement is likewise a kind of homage to Bartók – the allusion to the *Allegro pizzicato* in the composer's Fourth Quartet is unmistakable. But Ligeti has in the meantime moved on a considerable distance from Bartók.

The fourth movement is marked *Presto furioso, brutale, tumultuoso*, and can be characterised as a kind of negative version of the second movement.

Where that movement was calm, this one is built on wild gestures, although several pianissimo passages are interpolated. Ligeti adds an informative note in the score: "This movement is to be played with enormous haste, as if demented (except for some *pp* moments) and always with the greatest force: press the bow down hard on the string (scratchy noise). If some of the hairs have come away from the bow by the end then it will have been played correctly".

For the finale, Ligeti provides the following commentary: "The fifth movement is like a memory, seen through a mist: the whole progression of the piece up until now is recapitulated, but muted – the music sounds as if it is being heard from a great distance". There is an extraordinary quality to the sound when the music plunges into the *pianissimo* domain and at times becomes barely perceptible. There are hardly any *fortissimo* moments, apart from two short interjections. The aural image is one of vibrating sounds, ethereal sonorities and scurrying figures. One often seems to hear whispering. At the end, the music suddenly disappears as if into nothingness.

At the beginning of the 1980s Ligeti felt he could perceive a change in the art and music of the time – one that inspired a great period of creativity. He was convinced that his path lay beyond the post-modern and the avant-garde, and his striving to start afresh ultimately led him to re-orientate his style. The key impulses came from his interest in the music of the Mexican composer Conlon Nancarrow, from his study of central African music, whose polyphony and polyrhythms made a strong impression on him, and from close observation of fractal structures, in which he discovered a beauty he found both fascinating and stimulating.[10]

There is considerable evidence to suggest that at precisely this time of re-orientation, Ligeti was looking back on his youth, his home and his artistic past. In any case, both in the Horn Trio – the first work in the new style – and in the piano Études there are clues to support this hypothesis. The second study has the distinctive title *Cordes vides* ("Empty Strings") and is a strict invention on the interval of a fifth: it forms the basis of the piece from the first note to the last, and the music sounds reminiscent of both *Musica ricercata* and Bartók's *Mikrokosmos*. The fourth study, entitled *Fanfares*, was originally – as the sketches reveal – conceived as a homage to Bartók. A draft notated in 7/8 has the explicit designation *Bartoque*, and among the most striking elements in the music is the use of "grating seconds", one of the great Hungarian composer's stylistic markers.[11] For whatever reason, this draft was discarded and the homage to Bartók omitted. In the final version, the study is based on an eight-note figure on the Bulgarian rhythm of 3 + 2 + 3 quavers which runs throughout the piece like an ostinato. Ligeti bases the second movement of the Horn Trio on a similar eight-note ostinato figure. Ligeti wrote in his informative programme note for the first performance, "The second movement is a fast, polymetric dance, inspired by various kinds of folk music of a non-existent people, as if

Hungary, Romania and the whole of the Balkans lay somewhere between Africa and the Caribbean".[12] The statement suggests that he wanted to forestall any comparison with Bartók's compositions in Bulgarian rhythm. One last significant element is that Ligeti discarded the first movement he wrote of his Violin Concerto, not least because it reminded him of Hungarian folk music, and because a Hungarian folksong was concealed within it.[13]

Ligeti was well versed in European folk music and non-European music alike, and he loved to talk about and discuss both. Just like Bartók with Hungarian peasant music, so too Ligeti found inspiration for his many different works in the freshness of the material of various ethnic groups. References to places of ethnomusicological significance in the sketches for his later works are particularly revealing in this context: numerous references to Hungarian, Transdanubian, Transylvanian, Romanian and gypsy music, to music from Shetland and Norway, and on to parts of Africa and the Far East. He undoubtedly found a stimulus in both European folklore and non-European music in the early stages of composing his later works, but he did not want this to be read as either an amalgam or "eclectic combination of various elements", but rather as a "structural way of thinking".[14] It is this point that marks out the fundamental difference between his method and Bartók's. However much he may owe to the study of ethnic music, his later output is not remotely folkloristic. The Africa and Far East, and the countries that his music seems to suggest are more like constructs and dreams. His protracted artistic development finally brought him to the same conclusion that, paradoxically, Schoenberg – a composer he had many reservations about – had so vehemently maintained: that is, that folklore in serious music is a "lie".[15]

Many composers have nevertheless found and continue to find an important source of inspiration in their involvement with folklore and national traditions – sometimes even an intellectual basis for their work. Debussy's response to the gamelan music of Java and Bali that he heard at the 1889 Paris World Exhibition could be said to mark the point where folklore first started to be used in European art music in a way that went beyond mere exotic colouring. Since that time other composers have sought to enrich their work, set out in new directions or arrive at their personal musical identity by using European and non-European musical traditions and their intellectual content creatively. Folklore and nationalism have certainly received considerable critical attention, from the beginnings of new music up until the present. In the following chapters, works by Messiaen, Stockhausen, Isang Yun and György Kurtág will be examined to demonstrate four quite different ways of tackling native or foreign national musical cultures.

# Multicultural Phenomena in the New Music

> "A hundred year ago, Nietzsche already prophesied that the future worth and meaning of culture would lie 'in a mutual melting-together and crossfertilization.'"
> WOLFGANG WELSCH (1992)[1]

*A Musical World Language?*

The gigantic upheavals as a result of World War II have radically transformed the cultural landscape of the world. Thanks to the new mobility, a flourishing international traffic and the spread of the media, an unexampled cultural exchange has developed. Intellectually and culturally, the continents come ever closer together. Western science, technology and ways of life penetrate deeper and deeper into Asia and Africa. Conversely, Asiatic mentalities, art and culture are becoming acclimatized in Europe as well.

Multiculturalism creates special problems for many countries, especially the so-called immigration societies, and is a phenomenon that occupies a number of disciplines intensively: anthropology, sociology, psychology and political science. Sociologists point out that all societies are becoming at once increasingly multicultural and more porous.[2]

These developments have consequences for music as well. Musical life today is marked in many ways by international traits. European and American symphony orchestras, as well as certain ensembles of ethnic music, concertize all over the world. Our musical horizon has never been as wide as it is today. Many European composers transcend the narrower national borderlines and become cosmopolites. Conversely, American and Asiatic composers receive vital impulses from Europe. Often they are trained there.

Three aspects are gaining increasingly in importance in this connection:

1. Since 1945, a number of European composers evince a lively interest in non-European and ethnic musical cultures. Thanks to the progress made by musical ethnology, Chinese, Indonesian, Japanese, Middle Eastern and African music is more familiar to us than ever before. Conversely, the European major-minor music has spread practically over the entire globe and represents a danger to the indigenous ethnic music cultures.

2. Since 1945, a kind of musical *lingua communis* has developed, which is widely "spoken." Its grammar and syntax are dictated by the rules that Arnold Schönberg and his disciples established: I am referring to the maxims of the "composition with 12 notes related solely to each other." Much of the spread of this basic language of the New Music was due to

the Darmstadt summer courses attended by composers from many nations. After 1946, Darmstadt became the Mecca of the New Music and, after 1953, Anton Webern the idol of many young composers.

3. Since the 'seventies, at the latest, some speculative heads have been occupied with the idea of a "world music." Karlheinz Stockhausen let himself be guided by the conviction that developments would inevitably led to a mingling and integration of musical cultures and published his draft of a "world music," i.e., a "music of the whole earth, all countries and races." In a similar sense, the Chinese musicologist Naixiong Liao thought in 1988 that in our time, when the inhabitants of all parts of the world are much closer to each other than before and international understanding is growing, the musical forms of the continents were bound to get ever closer to each other and were increasingly merging. For Liao, music is "national art and at the same time world language": he regards the "commingling of diverse musical cultures" as an indisputable fact and concludes his argument with the (apologetic) sentence: "We are marching toward world music so that our national music tradition will radiate in new pomp and splendor."[3]

These theses raise many questions requiring detailed discussion. In what follows I shall try to describe and interpret a few multicultural phenomena of the New Music since 1945 with reference to four composers – one French, one German, one Korean and one Hungarian.

*Olivier Messiaen and non-European Music*

If one keeps in mind that France was in the past one of the foremost colonial powers, it becomes clearer why French culture has always had a special affinity with exoticism. In the 19th century, not only poets and painters but musicians as well felt drawn as if by magic to Spain, Africa, the Near East, as well as the Far East. One need only cite the Goncourt Brothers, Prosper Merimée, Eugène Delacroix, Edouard Manet, Georges Bizet and Félicien David. The Paris World's Fair of 1889 was an event of considerable importance to French art. There Claude Debussy encountered Annamitic theater and Javanese music. How strong the impression was he received from the latter is demonstrated by his piano piece *Pagodes*, which transfers principles of the Gamelan orchestra to piano composition. Maurice Ravel, too, was greatly interested not only in Spanish folklore but also in non-European music.

Olivier Messiaen belongs to this tradition. Already during his apprenticeship years he was interested in the rhythms of the ancient Greeks, Hindus and Indians. He closely studied both Indian and Javanese music and engrossed himself in detail in non-European folklore. His affinity with extra-European music manifests itself most fully in three connected works composed between 1945 and 1949: *Harawi*, a "song of love and death," the Turangalîla Symphony and the *Cinq Rechants* for 12 mixed voices a cappella.

Messiaen himself called this triptych his trilogy of Tristan and Isolde. The subject of the work is human love, which "transcends, overtakes everything" – in contrast to divine love, the subject of most of his works.[4]

The Turangalîla Symphony, composed between 1946 and 1948, is no doubt one of Maessiaen's most important works. On first hearing it, one can only marvel at its originality, glowing color and splendor of sound. The title *Turangalîla* derives from Sanskrit and is richly significant. Messiaen explicates it as follows: "*Lîla* literally means play. But play is used in the sense of the divine working in cosmic events, that is, the play of creation, destruction, recreation: the play of life and death. *Lîla* also means love. *Turanga* is time running off like a galloping horse, time, that is, that dissipates like the sands of an hourglass. *Turanga* means movement and rhythm. *Turangalîla* thus comprises the meanings at once of love song, hymn of joy, time, motion, rhythm, life and death."[5]

In what does the exotic in the Turangalîla Symphony consist? As in other works, Messiaen here works at times with Indian rhythms. These determine the structure of the music, though they may remain virtually unregistered by the listener. More audible is the exotic coloration of the music.

The score calls for an entire series of exotic instruments, such as the tamtam, Chinese cymbals, Turkish cymbals, maracas, wood blocks, bells, etc. Even more significant is that the piano, glockenspiel, celesta, vibraphone and metallic percussion instruments in many passages form a small, nearly independent orchestra in the midst of the big orchestral apparatus, one that reminds of Gamela ensembles from Java or Bali in terms of sound character and task to be performed, as Messiaen himself pointed out.

One characteristic of the Turangalîla Symphony is its composition in layers. The complexity of the music results from the fact that in many of its movements differently structured layers have been superimposed upon each other. This is especially noticeable in the seventh movement (*Turangalîla 2*), where the actual Gamelan formulation is combined partly with chromatic lines, partly with a layer of an entirely different cast, formed by the cello solo. Here Messiaen achieves a remarkable amalgamation of European sound conceptions and Far Eastern tonality.

The case is quite different in the ninth movement (*Turangalîla 3*). Here the so-called Gamelan formation commands the center of the composition. The coloration here is hardly European any longer, but properly Far Eastern.

# "A Music of the Whole Earth, All Countries and Races": Karlheinz Stockhausen's Utopia of World Music

> "We are becoming more and more aware of the fact that the entire globe is one village."
> KARLHEINZ STOCKHAUSEN[1]

The term *Weltmusik* appears to have been coined in 1906 by the German music theoretician Georg Capellen.[2] Karlheinz Stockhausen's equally bold and prognostic thoughts on this subject have numerous implications and are large in scope. To understand it better one needs to know how it came about.

In 1966, Stockhausen resided in Japan. Profoundly impressed by the Japanese mentality and reality, he realized his composition *Telemusik* in the electronic studio of the Japanese Broadcasting Corporation between January and April. With this work, he thought he had come closer to "an old and ever-recurring dream" of his, namely to compose not "his" music but "a music of the whole earth, all countries and races."[3]

His endeavor was to amalgamate, by modern electronic means, acoustically existing "objects" from Japan, Bali, the southern Sahara, a Spanish village festival, Hungary, the Shipitos of the Amazonas, China, Vietnam and elsewhere in such a way as to obtain "a higher unity." His intention was to bring into close relation folklore and cultic music from diverse parts of the world, with the aid of diverse processes of so-called "modulation." Thus he modulates an event with another, e.g., the rhythm of one event with the volume curve of another, or self-produced electronic chords with the volume curve of a priests' chant, etc., understanding *Telemusik* not as a collage, but as a kind of metacollage.[4]

A year later Stockhausen realized his work *Hymnen* – an electronic and concrete music with soloists, based on tape recordings of the national anthems of every country on earth and likewise not to be understood as a mere collage. He regarded this new composition as "a further project of integrating all races, all religions, all nations" and frankly admitted to having yielded to a utopia – the utopia of the creation of a musical world that "reflects not simply today's human world as it is" but the vision of a better world, in which "the tones, the fragments, the 'found objects' get along and together realize the *one* world as it grows together and its divinely destined purpose."[5]

Questioned, in an interview, what possibilities he saw of translating his humanitarian ideals into music, he replied that he did not want the music he was making to be understood as a mere "humanitarian gesture" or "humanitarian concern." He regarded as especially important the breakthrough "to a consciousness of the whole." What mattered to him was that "the diverse characteristic elements of the world, which had largely fallen apart," would come together through consciousness.[6]

In his essay *Weltmusik*, published in 1973, Stockhausen prognosticated that at a time when many people had opportunities to experience the music of other nations at first hand, the individual cultures were in a process of dissolution and "would all issue into a more unified earth culture."

He held that this confidence was based on the belief that every human individual had "all of humanity within him." Stockhausen regarded the "process of the mingling and integration of all music cultures" as inevitable and predicted that this process would occur in two stages. The first stage, he thought, would be one of "uniformity and leveling," but in the second stage "a strong contrary tendency against the trend toward uniformity" would set in.[7]

What is one to make of these ruminations? The notion of a world music contains problems that begins to emerge once one considers the anthropological, ethnological, psychological and culture-philosophical implications of the idea. Thus one may wonder whether at a time when the supposedly exploded nationalism and separatism begin to flourish again, the cultures will mingle as rapidly as Stockhausen postulates. Secondly, it is questionable whether humanity will overcome its traditional, national and cultural conditions readily enough to be able to identify with an entirely different spirituality and culture. And, finally, will a European who is moved by a certain Indian music really discover the Indian within him, as Stockhausen assumes? There is reason to doubt these premises.

*The Music of Isang Yun as a Multicultural Phenomenon*

It can be said of East Asians that they frequently experience their first encounter with Western music as a greatly stirring event. This becomes understandable once one recalls that Chinese and Japanese music knows heterophonic methods but not polyphony. Grown up in the Korean music tradition, Isang Yun first received Western-style musical instruction at school.

Many years later he spoke of it having put him in a daze. He had not regarded this music as beautiful, yet definitely as surprising and exciting – "so loud and so many notes at once, so massive."[8]

Yun was already a respected, prize-winning composer when he decided, in 1956, to travel to Europe to extend his studies. After a one-year stay in Paris, he went to West Berlin in August of 1957 to study, at the Academy of Music, music theory with Reinhard Schwarz-Schilling, twelve-tone technique with Josef Rufer and composition with Boris Blacher.

In 1958 he took part in the Darmstadt Summer Courses. Fascinated as he was by the experimental music he encountered, he nonetheless asked himself the question where he himself was standing and where he should go from there – whether he should compose equally radically and thus find his place in the Avant-garde, or go his own way. He remembered his East Asian origins and began, once he had mastered the new techniques, to transmute Korean sound conceptions with the aid of Western techniques.

Whenever one hears Yun's music, its pronounced character is unmistakable. Although for the most part it speaks in a timely atonal idiom, it differs essentially from the music of Nono, Stockhausen, Boulez, Maderna or Cage – the composers who most impressed Yun in Darmstadt. Its principal characteristic is, according to Yun's own admission, its flowing or streaming.[9]

If one considers what is Korean about it, six main points present themselves for inspection.

1. In some of his works, Yun applied dodecaphonic techniques, which he modified in an individual way. As a rule he worked with the twelve notes of the chromatic scale, but combined this modern method with the so-called main-tone or main-sound technique he derived from the Korean music of his past. As main tones his works often employ diverse held notes, which at times are also united into chords. In the *Gasa*, for example, a piece for violin and piano, the violin during the first forty measures plays only the main tones c sharp and d sharp.[10]

2. In many of Yun's works, intonation and articulation are frequently regulated according to principles derived from Korean music, including 88 glissandi, vibrati, grace notes, quarter-tone fluctuations, changes in tonal color and similar effects.

3. The inclusion of Asiatic instruments into the European orchestra further adds to the Far Eastern character of Yun's music.

4. The unique sound atmosphere in Yun's operas results in large part from the original treatment of the singers' voices, characterized by constant switches from speech to singing and singing to speech.[11]

5. Josef Häusler described Yun's compositional method as an expansion of heterophonic techniques into polyphony[12], which the composer agreed with.[13]

6. Many of Yun's earlier compositions have Korean titles, such as *Riul, Piri, Bara, Nore, Shao Yang Yin, Gagok, Namo, Réak*. The titles suggest that the works were inspired partly by secular Chinese court music and partly by ritualistic temple music.[14] *Réak*, for example means something like solemn, festive music, evoking the music played at the court of the Korean king.[15] The score of this important work prescribes, besides strings and winds, numerous non-Western instruments: not only tamtam and tomtom,

but also Thai boss gongs, temple blocks and so-called Baks, i.e., Korean multi-sound whips.[16]

One critic once tried to describe Yun's tightrope walk between East and West by calling it an "Esperanto of music." To which the composer replied that that was just what he never wanted, Esperanto being an artificial language. His music, he said, had, on the contrary, grown quite naturally from his native Korean soil, and although he included also modern Western compositional techniques, that was "no alienation, no turning away" from his native tradition, "and nothing artificial, only something added on."[17]

*György Kurtág and the Hungarian Musical Tradition*

Present-day composers can be divided into groups according to, among other things, their relation to tradition. Whereas some are altogether disinterested in tradition, even want to break with it altogether, others respect and reflect it. Karlheinz Stockhausen and Iannis Xenakis, for example, belong to the former category. The latter is represented by composers like Krzysztof Penderecki, Witold Lutoslavski and Hans Werner Henze.

György Ligeti's position vis-à-vis this question is very characteristic. On the one hand, he negates tradition, he once remarked, by creating something new. On the other hand, tradition is present subliminally even in his most advanced works.[18]

A similar standpoint is taken by another Hungarian composer, György Kurtág, who has undergone a remarkable development and whose work constitutes an illuminating special case.

Born in 1926 in then Hungarian Lugos, Kurtág grew up with the Hungarian musical tradition. He studied piano in Budapest with Pál Kadosa after the end of World War II, chamber music with Leó Weiner and composition with Sándor Veress and Ferenc Farkas. His great model at the time was Béla Bartók. He received important new impulses during his stay in Paris in 1957/58, where he attended the composition course of Darius Milhaud and Olivier Messiaen and closely studied Pierre Boulez's *Pli selon pli*. Somewhat later he visited Karlheinz Stockhausen in Cologne, who made him a present of the score of his *Gruppen für drei Orchester* (Groups for three Orchestras).

A major influence on Kurtág has been the thought and music of Anton Webern. He shared with Webern the preference for concise statements, for implacable severity of construction and an unequalled concentration of expression. At the same time he must not by any means be included in the Webern succession. His music impresses by its originality, its unmistakable personal idiom.

Kurtág makes new music, yet does not burn the bridges to past works: on the contrary, he favors tradition, the continuity of culture, and fears that European civilization is in danger, threatened by decay, dissolution and eclecticism.[19] Well versed in music history, he has let himself be inspired by composers like Monteverdi, Heinrich Schütz and Johann Sebastian Bach.[20] It is symptomatic for him, however, that he neither quotes nor paraphrases but rather projects certain older compositional problem formulations onto today's compositional situation. With all its newness and originality, his music is deeply immersed in tradition, especially in the Hungarian one. Listening closely to the *Messages of the Deceased R. W. Trussova*, one of his central works, reveals his distaste for dogmatism. Thus the organization of pitch in this work obeys neither serial technique nor any other rigid system. What is characteristic is rather the juxtaposition of chromaticism and centering, of whole-tone technique and tonality.[21] Each of the 21 pieces of the cycle contains, besides frequent twelve-tone areas, also central tones.

In his *Harvard Lectures IV*, Béla Bartók distinguished between three different rhythmic formations predominant in the rural music of Eastern Europe, i.e., the *parlando-rubato* type, strict rhythms (also called *tempo giusto*) and dotted rhythms in diverse constellations.[22] Significantly, all three of these formations can be traced also in the *Messages from Trussova*.

Above all, the top-heavy Lombardic rhythm demonstrates Kurtág's proximity to Bartók.

Especially characteristic for the Hungarian tone color of many passages in Kurtág's music, finally, is that of the cimbalom, an instrument used in several works, including the *Trussova*.

Let us attempt to summarize the results of our observations. In the Turangalîla Symphony, Olivier Messiaen succeeded in creating an impressive, artistically convincing amalgamation of European musical thinking and Far Eastern sound. Equally remarkable and convincing is Isang Yun's attempt to express Korean conceptions and Korean spirituality with the means of Western European music. The music of György Kurtág presents us with the case of an original composer who discovered and speaks a modern idiom of his own and yet remains committed to the regional musical culture of his native country.

What is and remains problematic is the notion of a "world music," if that music is defined as one resulting from the cross-breeding of diverse cultures. For this idea presupposes not only openness, but an actual fall of all borders between nations, races and cultures and could become reality only if a true cosmopolitanism had actually established itself, if the globe had actually become a single village. We have not reached that point. Only a distant future will show whether history will develop in that direction.

# The Philosophy of Time and Pluralistic Thought of Bernd Alois Zimmermann

> "Schoenberg once spoke of the music as having the character of a draft. In fact, the composer is the reporter, the performer."
> BERND ALOIS ZIMMERMANN[1]

The music of Bernd Alois Zimmermann (1918-1970) is far less "music for music's sake" than that of other avant-garde composers, in that it almost always has some intellectual foundation. Zimmermann not only had an affinity with philosophy, theology, literature and the visual arts, but, like Mahler, he was also a philosopher-composer. The subjects of his major works were often related to existential questions: the contradictions of existence, human freedom, transience and death, last things. There is every evidence to suggest that he was more attracted to the time-transcending than the temporal. He certainly took a keen interest in the political problems of his time, but he was even more affected by eternal questions. He saw it as his task as a composer to comment on situations that paradoxically have always existed, and which he thought would return in the future.

He himself considered his compositional development to be on-going, and his work divides into three phases: the pre-serial, serial and post-serial.[2] After following Hindemith, Stravinsky and Schoenberg in his first period, he immersed himself in serialism in the second, further developing the method's techniques. In his third phase he was able to move beyond serialism, and he devised a new method, known as pluralistic composition. The beginning of this phase is marked by the keynote essay *Intervall und Zeit* ("Interval and Time") that he wrote in 1957 and in which for the first time he set out the basis of his intriguing philosophy of time.[3]

One of its premises is the difference between "objective" and "internal" time, or, in other words, between the "cosmically measurable" and "experienced time". He distanced himself unequivocally from the philosophical notion of time as being unrepeatable, irreversible and directed towards a purpose, and declared the idea of a "unity of time" as the "unity of present, past and future". As he saw it, past, present and future all merge into one in humanity's stream of experience and consciousness – an original proposition, for which he coined the engaging term "the spherical nature of time" (Kugelgestalt der Zeit). The way to understand this is by considering that the past actually only becomes such in the present, and that it is only in the present that we can articulate future desires and plans.

Without overstating the case, it could be said that Zimmermann was drawn to the idea of a "perpetual present", a notion that he felt was equally modern and age-old. He was also inspired by writers as much as philosophers, his principal sources of inspiration being St Augustine, Ezra Pound and James Joyce, followed by Henri Bergson, Edmund Husserl and Martin Heidegger. His writings contain many references to Pound, whose notion of the perpetual present he expressed in such poetic formulations as "Dawn breaks over Jerusalem while the pillars of Hercules are still shrouded in midnight. All ages are present... the future stirs in the mind of the few... that applies above all to literature, where real time is independent of the apparent, and many of the dead are the contemporaries of our grandchildren".[4]

A philosophy of time and pluralistic thinking are united and interdependent in Zimmermann. He was completely convinced that a pluralist way of thinking about the complexity of our intellectual, cultural and musical reality was intrinsically more appropriate than other philosophical notions. It was his belief that the cultural life of the present was permanently inhabited by "witnesses of the past".[5]

This conviction had significant consequences for his creative work. He strove to synthesize all (or at least several) fields of intellectual life, and it cannot be denied that he did actually succeed in integrating words and art music, jazz, *musique concrète* as well as other elements in his ambitious works It is indicative that what he had in mind for his opera *Die Soldaten* was a kind of modern *Gesamtkunstwerk* – a multimedia art form that would bring together architecture, sculpture, painting, music theatre, straight theatre, ballet, film, amplification, television, tape and audio engineering, electronic music, *musique concrète*, circus, musical and every kind of dance theatre.[6]

In several of his works, the listener initially finds the conscious collage-like assembling of texts from different periods disconcerting. The method's deeper meaning only starts to emerge when the listener becomes aware that specific circumstances of grief, love and prayer are at the centre of the work in question (Zimmermann was a practising Catholic) – situations that people have given expression to at various points in the history of ideas. However strange it may seem, what begins to take place is a conversation, an imaginary dialogue between epochs. In *Requiem für einen jungen Dichter*, for example, Ludwig Wittgenstein refers directly to St Augustine, and the freedom slogans of the Greek politician Andreas Papandreou spontaneously appear in the voices of the ancient Greek tragedians. The call to freedom echoes down all the years of human history.

Zimmermann's philosophy of time is most clearly expressed in the simultaneous scenes of *Die Soldaten*. The first scene of the fourth act, conceived by Zimmermann as the presentation of a dream, has rightly been seen as the summit of pluralistic simultaneity.[7] As the composer writes in the score, "Several scenes occur detached from their space and time, simultaneously anticipating and returning to the time when they happened on stage, in three films, and from the loudspeakers. [...] Flashing fragments of the most varied scenes light up the stage, from top to bottom and from side to side, flickering here and there as in a dream. The scene as a whole presents the rape of Marie as an allegory of the rape of all those bound together in the action: physically brutal, psychological and spiritual rape".

Just as Berg in *Wozzeck*, so too Zimmermann uses the forms of absolute music in his "pluralistic opera". In the first scene of the fourth act, during the *Toccata III*, segments and fragments from fourteen scenes in Jakob Michael Reinhold Lenz's drama are overlaid on each other.[8] The scene is dominated by the "iron rhythm" (*in ritmo ferreo*) that symbolises all things martial, and refers back to the *Preludio* to the opera.

Fortunately, Zimmermann discussed the semantics of many of his works on a number of occasions. It is clear from his commentaries on the opera, on his *Requiem für einem jungen Dichter* and on the *Antiphonen* for viola and small orchestra that he composed between 1961 and 1962, that various existential questions are central to his thinking. In the fourth of the *Antiphonen* the players surprisingly recite short texts in a total of eight languages. Zimmermann said that the texts were chosen for their semantic connections to aspects of human existence and love.[9]

Zimmermann also wrote about the semantics of many of his works in letters to various recipients. He wrote to Karl Amadeus Hartmann telling him that the well-known spiritual *Nobody knows the trouble I've seen* formed the basis of his trumpet concerto: "In my opinion, the moment that binds all together, despite divided stylistic tendencies, lies in the shared roots of deep, emotional expression, as in the negro spiritual unaffected by 'commercial jazz'. This is the fear and hope, grief and joy of a human heart that leaps from despair and confusion into the open arms of the divine redeemer with childlike trust."[10] He spoke in similar terms about his Sonata for solo viola in a letter to the viola-player Albert Dietrich: "The solo sonata expresses musical thoughts that consider the basic facts of human life: birth and death, coming into being and vanishing, love, and everything that moves a human heart."[11] The solo sonata is based on the chorale melody *Gelobet seist du Jesu Christ* and is an instrumental requiem for the composer's daughter Barbara, who died shortly after her birth. The large number of chorale quotations in many of his works lend his music a religious connotation.

The *Requiem für einem jungen Dichter* stands as one of Zimmermann's most important works.[12] It is, at the same time, one of his most personal. It was originally conceived for the Russian poet Sergei Yesenin, who committed suicide. The texts that stand out of the many that Zimmermann collected and assembled in his "Lingual" (spoken piece) are those by Vladimir Mayakovsky and Konrad Bayer – two poets who also took their own lives. The piece was conceived as an oratorio, radio play, feature and mystery play in one, and was composed between 1967 and 1969. After completing the score, the composer declared that he had not been thinking of a specific poet, but "in a sense, of young poets per se".[13]

Nevertheless, the work has an unmistakable autobiographical connotation. The young poet, to whose memory the Requiem is dedicated and whom he wanted to show "in his multifarious connections" to the situation in Europe between 1920 and 1970, was fundamentally himself.[14] Zimmermann, born in 1918, experienced the Second World War at the front, and chose to end his life in August 1970. The moving passage that he quotes in his Requiem from the autobiographical novel *Niederschrift des Gustav Anaias Horn*, feels as if it had been written expressly for him. It reads, "The question of who I really am is still today not silenced within me. I look back, and it is easy to count up the facts. Fifty of my compositions have been printed. Many chamber and symphony orchestras have turned to my scores. Every so often large works have been performed.

A couple of organists slave away at my preludes and fugues. Journalists have praised and criticised me. In recent textbooks my name appears as an important, if headstrong composer.

For many years I have been almost dumb, and I don't know if I am battling with a kind of fatigue, with rampant, incomprehensible death".

## Alfred Schnittke and Polystylism

Alfred Schnittke owes his position among the most prominent composers of our day to three factors: the enormous scale of his output, the huge popularity his works enjoy, and the captivating emotional quality of his music.

His astonishingly vast catalogue of works embraces music in every genre, from orchestral pieces to chamber music and numerous vocal works. In an age when we see many composers having a troubled relationship with the symphony, he had the courage to write no fewer than nine such works.[1]

He was one of the most successful composers of our time. His 60th birthday was celebrated with concerts and festivals in Hamburg, Stockholm, London and Utrecht. When three festivals devoted to his music were held in Sweden in 1990, no fewer than forty of his works were performed. There is already a complete edition of his works on CD. Tragically, he died at the relatively early age of 63 in Hamburg on 3 August 1998.

In looking into the reasons for his enormous popularity, there are several factors to be taken into consideration: Schnittke was by no means an avant-garde composer, if we take the term to denote an artist who loves experimenting with sound above all else. He offers the listener a way in, and that listener hears something familiar in his music. Schnittke's sound is understood by countless people all over the world, because his music – expressive, evocative and full of associations – has huge emotional power.

More than ever before, there is a widespread feeling of homelessness in the troubled times we live in. Schnittke shared the fate of those who have roots in several national groups and yet find themselves caught between different worlds. His father was a German Jew, his mother a Volga German. He grew up in the Soviet Union, and as a young man already had the feeling of being a stranger in his own land. Later he began to view himself as a cosmopolitan, someone whose feelings crossed national boundaries. And yet in 1986 he felt like a stranger in Poland: as a Jew and as someone who came from the Soviet Union. The situation is reminiscent of that of Mahler, who considered himself homeless three times over.

There is no trace of a cosmopolitan outlook in Schnittke's music. It is based on the solid pillars of the Russian and German musical traditions. His development as a composer stemmed from his engagement with the work of Scriabin, Stravinsky and Prokofiev, and Shostakovich – to name only these four great Russians. At the same time, he felt a link with the German tradition: J.S. Bach was for him the alpha and omega of music. He loved the music of Mahler and Berg – undoubtedly for its expressive qualities. And for a long period he immersed himself in the study of Webern's work. Schnittke's Third Symphony is a tribute to German music: amazingly, the musical material is all developed from the initials of more than 30 German composers, from Bach, Handel and

Mozart to Schoenberg, Berg, Webern, Eisler, Dessau, Weill, Stockhausen, Bernd Alois Zimmermann and Hans Werner Henze.

When one thinks of Schnittke's originality and the narrow-mindedness of Soviet cultural politics, it is no surprise that he received hardly any support in the Soviet Union. For a long time his work was considered mannered, experimental and directed towards the western European avant-garde. His compositions were not among those works thought properly representative of Soviet art. And since he was not remotely ready to compromise, he was unable to travel abroad for many years. Bizarre and grotesque reports on the desperate attempts of Soviet cultural functionaries to block performances abroad of his works continue to circulate. It was, in fact, outside the Soviet Union that Schnittke first came to attention. Increasing numbers of performances at international festivals from 1966 onwards prompted curiosity about the hitherto little-known Soviet composer.

The key period in Schnittke's development as a composer came between 1963 and 1968. During this time he grappled with various contemporary avant-garde musical trends, and with the rules of twelve-note technique and the principles of serialism alike – a trend that he did not manage to get on with at all. He objected to the idea of automatism inherent in the method. Many years later he spoke about his decision to turn his back on serialism and follow his own path: "When I reached the final station I decided to get out of the already overcrowded train. [...] So I looked for an opportunity to give my music back a richer content of associations. I tried to abandon myself romantically to my feelings, and also take up literary and visual subjects".[2]

In 1968 Schnittke formulated his later famous concept of polystylism.[3] What he meant by the term was composing in various different layers, and communicating with the musical past. To gain a better understanding of Schnittke's train of thought, we have to look at the odd situation of art in our time. Contemporary art occupies a relatively small patch in the cultural life of today. We are surrounded by the cultural artefacts of the past, those that make a marked impression on our consciousness. The past is ever present, and there is a definite museum-like quality to cultural affairs. The power of tradition has never been so oppressive as it is in our time, and that applies particularly to music. Even in the 1960s the German composer Bernd Alois Zimmermann rightly drew attention to the fact that in the music we consume many works from earlier periods are more contemporary than so-called contemporary pieces. As he put it, we live today in peaceful co-existence with a tremendous range of cultural wares that date from every period imaginable: "Gregorian chant, jazz, so-called serious music [...], opera, beat and the top twenty surround us on a daily basis, together with literary products, cinema, theatre and so on".[4]

Schnittke's thoughts were similar in principle to Zimmermann's: "Our time," he once declared, "is different from earlier times in the reception of music. Once there was only the music of the last hundred years. For us what happened in the past is more current than for earlier generations. We enter into a dialogue with the past, as if it were a dialogue with folklore. [...] The composer of today cannot pass by the music of the past that is present every day. [...] It is possible for us to live in different times."[5]

Alfred Schnittke was guided by the conviction that there has never been a time in the history of music when reference has not been made to earlier music. He pointed to Guillaume de Machaut, Charles Ives, Mahler and Berg, who integrated a Bach chorale into his Violin Concerto. He discovered polystylistic tendencies in many piece of new music too, and listed the prominent examples of Stockhausen's *Hymne*, the *Stabat Mater* in Penderecki's *St Luke Passion*, Stravinsky's *Pulcinella* and *Canticum sacrum*, Berio's *Sinfonia* and Zimmermann's *Die Soldaten*, a work that he regarded particularly highly on account of its humanitarian sympathies.

I should insist on the fact that Schnittke's "polystylism", his stylistic plurality and composing in layers, has nothing to do with eclecticism. Nor should it be confused with the sort of stylistic masquerading so beloved of Stravinsky. Even the catchy phrase "music about music" does not do it justice. The crucial aspect for Schnittke was that the music of the past that many of his works quote or evoke is always confronted by the musical idiom of today. It was important for him for there to be a conversation between the past and the present, as experienced, understood and reflected by him. One example is his piece *(K)ein Sommernachtstraum* ("Not) a Midsummer Night's Dream") of 1985. The ambivalence of the title is significant. Schnittke wrote that this piece should be performed as part of concert of Shakespeare settings, even though it had no direct connection with Shakespeare, and added that all the "antiques" in it had not been "stolen", but "forged". Two diametrically opposed sound-worlds are pitted against each other in this piece: the allusions to Mozart and Schubert represent an idyllic, fairy-tale, almost childlike realm. Something demonic suddenly erupts into this healthy world with indescribable brutality. If Schnittke's method is to be compared with anything, then it would be not so much Stravinsky as Mahler and Shostakovich.

Schnittke was a man of great perspicacity. He loved balance, and thought in genuinely dialectical terms. An examination of his statements on the fundamental questions of art and on his own music reveals a striking "on one hand, and on the other" pattern. Scepticism, questioning, neither one nor the other, caveats – all these are part and parcel of this thinking. In 1968 he composed *Quasi una sonata* – a piece that expresses "much Slavic gloom" about the then enforced cultural partitioning of Europe. As he explained, "The piece is a borderline case of sonata form. It is simultaneously called into question and seems not to be working out – and then the sonata is already over. It is like Fellini's film that is actually only a story about how difficult and impossible it is to make the film. And it doesn't even get made, but in the meantime the film has already been finished."[6]

Every work by Schnittke is an intellectual adventure in the sense that the listener cannot guess how the piece is going to turn out, but is kept in a permanent state of suspense, with no idea of what is coming, of where the piece is going. It seems typical of Schnittke that conflicts are mostly not resolved – many pieces end undecided. An example can be found in *Quasi una sonata* – one of the most anarchic pieces he ever wrote – where an extremely hard-edged sound-world collides with a soft one. The dynamic of the composition, a witty and profound invention on the B-A-C-H motif, arises from this conflict. The soloist desperately attempts to break out of a rigid regime, and repeatedly rebels against the merciless, unchanging chords of the chamber orchestra. The ending is unresolved.

Dread, danger, horror, grief and imminent death are all written into Schnittke's music. It is significant that several of his works have a Requiem-like character. Between 1972 and 1976 he wrote *In memoriam* on the death of his beloved mother, and this event is connected with the creation of his Requiem of 1975. This was followed in 1984-85 by *Ritual* for orchestra – a memorial for the victims of the Second World War, and at the same time a sombre evocation of terror. *In memoriam* is one of his most personal works, marked by the experience of grief, although it flows into a *Moderato pastorale* movement that combines a peaceful mood with dark shadows.

In my opinion, Schnittke's most striking movements are those that express obsession, such as the middle movement of the Viola Concerto, and most of all the second movement of the Cello Sonata, which works itself up into a frenzy. Music is rarely as close to madness as here.

Schnittke was very interested in expanding the acoustic space and developing new sonorities, but for all his strong attachment to technological artistic progress, it was never for him an end in itself, but only a means to an end. His principal concern was with making a statement, and his criticism of many trends in new music was that they concentrated solely on the rational and overlooked the emotional. He favoured art that balanced the rational with the emotional, a parity that was at the same time his way of measuring a piece's impact. "The audience," he once declared, "is not interested solely in the external qualities of a piece of music, but in the psychological content of the subject and action as well, and if this content is thin, then the audience loses interest. [...] I am convinced that music finds its audience when it is written with conviction and contains an idea".[7]

What is the secret of Alfred Schnittke's global appeal? My feeling is that it lies in the fact that his music has marked similarities with language. It is an expressive idiom with a wealth of associations that many people can understand, since it conveys experiences common to us all. There is something expressed in this music that we today find deeply moving.

# And Always for a Better World –
# Approaches to Hans Werner Henze

> "For it is time to acknowledge the voice of humanity, the voice of a captured creature that is not quite capable of speaking its suffering, nor singing the measures of its heights and depths."
> INGEBORG BACHMANN[1]

In his autobiography, Hans Werner Henze (1926-2012) gives a rather cursory account of his experiences with the Darmstadt avant-garde in the 1950s. In the early summer of 1955 he, together with Boulez and Maderna, was invited to give a course in composition at Darmstadt. He was not at all amused – as he wrote – that young composers who chose to "express themselves in a pre-Webern musical idiom" would not even be asked to attend.[2] By then at the latest he was aware that he no longer belonged, if indeed he ever had, and he was happy to make the decision never to return to Darmstadt. Then, in October 1957, his *Nachtstücke und Arien* was given its first performance in Donaueschingen, and he was taken aback to see after only the first few bars, Boulez, Nono and Stockhausen noisily leaving their seats and the hall.[3] Even as a young man, Henze had the feeling that he "had no travelling companions".[4] He was aware that he had to pursue his artistic path alone, and felt that he knew precisely what his goal was.

Henze could not and would not conform: his defining characteristics were self-reliance and independence, and every kind of dogmatism was alien to him. For a long time he viewed himself as an outsider and maverick. As a young man he had a distrust of every kind of restricting system, doctrinaire theories on music and composition technique, and group thinking. "Freedom, wild and beautiful new sounds," he once wrote, "can only emerge from the feeling of being alone and free. The genuinely new does not appear ready-polished, ready to be established, but vigorous, generous and unclassifiable".[5] On another occasion, he said that music was not written by groups, but by individuals, "who are all the more effective the fewer traces there are in their work of conformism".[6] And in 1964 his answer to the question, "Where are we now?" was "Everyone is at a different place. Alone".[7]

It should be clear from the above that Henze cannot be pigeon-holed in any specific category of new music trends. The closer one looks at his output, the more a picture emerges of individuality and uniqueness. For that reason, this will be no more than an attempt to get closer to his work, to grasp and clarify his distinctive features as an artist.

Several ideas spring to mind when considering the reasons why he distanced himself from Darmstadt and the avant-garde of his time. As is well known, there was a period when the serialists invoked the theories of Adorno, particularly his concept of the "tendency of musical material"[8] (see the Introduction, p. 9), a partisan concept that angered Henze and which he battled against.[9] They also advocated the total through-construction of the musical artwork, and venerated the ideal of "pure" music, free of every associative connection. These notions ran counter to Henze's artistic experiences. The ideal that he had in mind was in no way the vaunted model of absolute, abstract "pure" music, but instead what, referring to the poetry of Pablo Neruda, he called *musica impura*, that is, music that embraces the human, allegorical, literary and political as well.[10]

Political Engagement

One first point of entry into Henze's hugely varied work can be found in his politically engaged music. Between 1967 and 1975 he wrote several works that belong explicitly to this category, including the oratorio *Das Floß der Medusa* (1968), *Versuch über Schweine* (also 1968), the "Cuban" Sixth Symphony (1969), then *El Cimarrón*, a recital for four musicians (1969-70), the show *Der langwierige Weg in die Wohnung der Natascha Ungeheuer* (1971), the allegory *Heliogabalus Imperator* (1971-72), the song-cycle *Voices* (1973)[11] and the "musical actions" *We Come to the River* (1974-76). All these works, with which he engaged with the extra-parliamentary opposition, the Third World and world revolution, have an appellative character.[12] They continue on a path that many artists (musicians, writers, poets and visual artists) have pursued since the Second World War. As early as 1948, in his book *What is Literature?* ("Qu'est-ce que la littérature?"), Jean-Paul Sartre encouraged contemporary writers to convey political messages and protest against man's oppression of man.[13] He had made a decisive step toward embracing the conviction that in art as elsewhere, the aesthetic imperative cannot be separated from the moral.[14]

From at least the time of his experiences of fascism, Henze's thoughts were moving in a similar direction. He took comfort from the fact that in the 1950s, Nono and Maderna, two composers he valued highly, thought and worked in much the same way. Much later he spoke of this: "We were thinking of the possibility, aided by music, and in music, to bring about intellectual and moral change, of making things human, freedom, creative humanistic freedom, returning to the old forms and reshaping them".[15]

In the meantime, Henze had got to know two German musicians whom he had a profound admiration for, not least for their views: Paul Dessau and Karl Amadeus Hartmann. A photo of 1952 showing Henze with Hartmann conveys an impression of seriousness, determination, close affinity and total accord.[16] Hartmann was an avowed opponent of National Socialism and no advocate of art for art's sake. He put his music at the service of ethical ideas, and was a firm believer in the notion that the artist had to express the attitude toward life of their time. All through his life he seems to have considered music to be a public matter, something that "concerns all".[17] It is understandable, then, that Henze felt drawn to Hartmann, and the two were linked by a "brotherly friendship".[18] The extensive eulogy that he wrote several years after Hartmann's death is one of the most important things ever to have been written about this eminent Bavarian composer. What Henze had to say about Hartmann's Sixth Symphony – a work inspired by Zola's novel *L'Oeuvre* – matches his own artistic position exactly: "The *Oeuvre* symphony is a declaration of faith through music. Its writer declares his belief in the ostracized, the outcast, the beaten and the captive. His music emerges from underground, in solidarity with the victims, he weeps over them and with them, he gathers round them, battles creatively for them, works, like Zola, for the humanist ideal of a world freed from injustice and reaction".[19]

The key to a deeper understanding of his compositions can be found in Henze's original way of thinking about music. His view of existence, and of the communicative power and function of music were markedly different from the ideas of his time. One widely-held opinion, especially in German-speaking areas, is that music is nothing but sound, "sonically moving form", a kaleidoscope and sound texture. Henze was fiercely critical of this self-evident proposition, and took the opposing view that music cannot be "abstract" as a language. He was not arguing against the fact that because of its specific nature, music was semantically vague. But he was firmly convinced that a composer, through musical markers that he himself puts in place, can convey such aspects as love, yearning for death or the message of freedom in a way that is precise and unambiguous.[20]

Music does not flourish either in sterile spaces or in ivory towers. For Henze, art and music were part and parcel of life. No engaged artist could shut themselves off from the world. "It forces its way into the workroom" and "establishes the character of the work".[21] And Henze had a high regard for Mahler and Berg partly because more than other composers they tied music and life intimately together. Both had looked at the times they lived in with open minds, and observantly and sensitively reflected the intellectual and political movements of their day.[22] As early as 1975, Henze recognised that Mahler's music was increasingly having an influence on his own, and that he was "indebted" to its realism.[23] Monteverdi, Mozart and Mahler were for him "the greatest realists in music".[24]

The fundamental theme of confrontation between opposing worlds

Henze was one of the many thousands of people who were profoundly traumatized by the events of the Second World War. Well before he reached the age of eighteen he was "conscripted" first into paramilitary labour service and then military service.[25] At military barracks he was trained as a tank radio operator.[26] He was later taken prisoner and must generally have had horrific experiences. Many years later – as he himself admitted – he suffered from a "Nazi-trauma" and experienced a panic fear of the police state.

All this helps to explain why he quickly saw himself as an outsider and "segregated" artist, and also why he left Germany in search of a new start, which he found in Italy. In a thoughtful essay he examined the psychology of the segregated artist and argued convincingly that that type of artist's innate desire for integration leaned toward a social form that corresponded to their nature, that is, "to whichever form of minority that warranted their compassion and fired their emotions and intellect".[27]

A considerable part of Henze's output convincingly expresses this outlook in artistic terms, and it is particularly characteristic of him that he preferred subjects to do with conflict and lives on the margin. A leitmotif that runs through his work is the collision of two heterogeneous, irreconcilable worlds: one inhumane, powerful and violent, and one humane and suffering. Many of his stage works, and many of his instrumental compositions as well, are about menace and might, the persecuted, disenfranchised, the condemned and oppressed, and the fate of victims. It is particularly characteristic of him to identify with the victims. His sympathies are always with minorities and all those who live in the shadows. His music always takes sides and accuses.

One of Henze's fundamental maxims is the initially odd-seeming view "that art belongs to the world of the persecuted: to people whose emotions and characteristics are too odd, and will always remain a closed book to the majority, to so-called normal people". This statement comes from Henze's autobiography of 1996,[28] but the composer was even clearer on the subject in an interview from 1986 with Ian Strasfogel. Here he made the analogous statement that " my music is on the side of the suffering. They get the best and most beautiful music. In contrast, horrible people like murderers, collaborators and traitors get ugly music. I make them ridiculous, I denounce them. In my opinion, it is important for the audience to grasp the emotional intent of the score".[29]

These ideas seem quite new. There is no comparable differentiation between "beautiful" and "ugly" music in opera and music drama in the 19th century and into the 20th. In Beethoven's *Fidelio*, the vengeance aria sung by Pizarro, who is a proper villain, is a character piece, but could not be described as ugly. The same is true of Jago's "Credo" aria in Verdi's *Otello*. The music that Wagner composed for Hagen in *Götterdämmerung* has sinister but not markedly ugly features. And the vocal lines that Nick Shadow sings in Stravinsky's *The Rake's Progress* are, for all their demonic nature, utterly singable.

The linguistic nature of music

One specific, key concern of Henze's was the linguistic nature of music, its ability to be perceived as a language.[30] For the best part of fifty years he did his utmost to turn it into a linguistic medium, developing a system of signs that allowed the enlightened listener to understand what he wanted to say in music. The tenacity, consistency and passion with which he strove for this goal had no equivalent in contemporary music.

Debates on music as a language lead nowhere if history and significant factors such as tradition and continuity are not taken into account. In a discussion from as early as 1975, Henze advocated looking to the parallel situation in literature in order to clarify any issues. He referred to the fact that in a specific literary tradition, ideas, sentences and even verbal formulations by poets from the past can be transferred into the present "where they re-emerge in new light and create new connections". In this regard he regretted the fact that in new music this continuity, "this kind of historical thinking" had hitherto been "vehemently" battled against.[31] Much of his battle, as he explained, had been about "conveying the language of music as such", even one "that arises from the history of our civilisation, that finds itself in a process that has an origin, a present and a past, and will also have a future", for which composers themselves are responsible.[32]

Over the course of fifty years Henze worked ceaselessly to create semantics for his musical language, and displayed astonishing ingenuity in doing so, following a variety of directions. A first semantic possibility lay in contrasting the opposing worlds of tonality and atonality, or dodecaphony. He put this idea into practice in his opera *Boulevard Solitude* (1951), for example. Starting from the notion that dodecaphony could represent a "free, bohemian world", Henze composed the love scenes using the twelve-note system, while reserving tonality for the "old, corrupt" world.[33]

In the music of Wagner and his successors, the most obvious way of creating musical semantics is of course by using leitmotifs. It was with them that Wagner was able to create the astonishing "magical connections" that so captivated Thomas Mann.[34] Leitmotifs and similar indicators can also at times be found in Henze, but they are not the most important aspect. Henze creates musical semantics principally through tone colour, quotations, musical idioms and musical gestures.

Firstly, musical symbols play a prominent part. The confrontation of opposing worlds found in several stage works is principally expressed through the use of different instrumental groups. In *Orpheus* (1978), for example, the conflict is between the human world of Orpheus and Eurydice on one hand, and on the other, the implacable counter-world of Apollo, which represents the divine, law and authority. Henze assigns the strings to Orpheus and Eurydice, and the woodwind to Apollo.[35] In several of his operas he assigned specific instruments to the protagonists: in *Elegy for Young Lovers* (1959-61), for example, Mittenhofer is characterised by the brass, Elisabeth the first violin, Toni the viola, and so on.[36]

Henze applied this procedure of instrumental identification in his instrumental music as well. In *Le Miracle de la rose* (1981), a clarinet concerto based on a novel by Jean Genet, the presenter of this "imaginary theatre" is identified with an instrument.[37] The sixteen year-old double murderer Harcomone, in prison awaiting execution, is characterised by the cor anglais and solo clarinet. The four men in black who enter his death cell are, in contrast, matched to other instruments: trumpet for the judge, horn for the chaplain, trombone for the lawyer and heckelphone for the executioner. The instruments are also treated to a certain extent as characters who act, and a listener who consciously picks up their timbre and inflection is able to follow the action in this "imaginary theatre" through listening rather than seeing.

A further way in which Henze gave his music a semantic meaning was by quoting significant moments in his own compositions or in works by other composers, starting with medieval music (the *Lamento di Tristano*), and music by Hans Leo Haßler, Monteverdi and J.S. Bach, through Mozart, Beethoven, Chopin, Wagner, Brahms and Mahler and on to Karl Amadeus Hartmann, Paul Dessau and Pierre Boulez. As one looks in more detail at his scores and becomes more familiar with his work, one starts to recognise more and more quotations and allusions. Quoting, as he once explained, was an element in his working strategy. The quotations function as "signposts", in the sense of "thinking signposts" and should help the listener to hear and think in the intended way.[38] For example, a listener who perceives a Tristan chord in a work by Henze is able to associate it with the polarity of day and night, and the configuration wound/death.

Music – the all-knowing, wise woman

Wagner understood music as the voice of emotion. It was, for him, the epitome of the "womanly".[39] For Henze it was more than that: the "all-knowing, wise woman" who expresses convictions, bemoans the fate of the characters on stage, and conveys her sympathy for the protagonists. Henze once stated that when he quotes from Mozart or Monteverdi, he expects the listener to be aware of and remember what is happening in the music.[40] Through sounds and symbols, the instruments help him to relate to the listener the story concealed behind the action. In his view, the music always knows more than the words being sung. To illustrate his point, he referred to Minette's entrance aria in *The English Cat* (1980-83), where individual chord changes already reveal that everything is going to end badly.[41]

Henze's bid to make music into a language is bound up with his preference for instrumental music related to a subject. Many of his instrumental works were inspired by poems, epics, dramas or works of visual art. In some cases he revealed the source of inspiration, but not in others. While this may sound close to programme music, it would be inaccurate to associate the two, since the historic genre of programme music comes burdened with preconceptions. What Henze sought was to grasp a poem or a drama's specific mood and atmosphere, and convey it musically. The advantage of music created in this way is that it can be flexible, clear and vivid, and the idea of modelling the structure on that of the extra-musical source is something quite new. There are historical precedents for this way of composing, in Mendelssohn's famous *Songs Without Words*, Schumann's attachment to the idea of "operas without texts", and the "instrumental drama" and "musical epic" of Berlioz and Liszt.[42] In Henze's multi-faceted output these notions acquired an unprecedented topicality and relevance.

For the ancient Greeks the art of music was not just for enjoyment, but for people's moral education as well. From the time of the French Revolution at the latest, music's utopian potential began to be widely discussed. While E.T.A. Hoffmann sought to establish this potential more in metaphysical terms, and spoke of the "miraculous realm of the infinite",[43] Beethoven, in his Ninth Symphony looked forward to a real social utopia, a brotherhood of man in a humanitarian spirit. Many 20th-century composers make a connection, whether directly or indirectly, with Beethoven's vision. Henze supported the idea that Beethoven considered his life's work as a contribution to human progress[44], and thought that music could in some way signal "the utopia of human freedom".[45] As I see it, a considerable part of Henze's output can be understood as an optimistic pointer to a better world, free from violence and aggression. Many of his works do not just evoke visions of horror, but also conclude with "beautiful", harmonious and peaceful music. A comparison of the *Rex tremendae majestatis* and *Sanctus* from his *Requiem* of 1990-92 provides an illuminating example of this. This is a piece that in Peter Petersen's inspired formulation does not have otherworldly, but "this-worldly" transcendence".[46] While the *Rex tremendae majestatis* exudes an atmosphere of violence, menace, danger and hardship (the concertante trumpets here give a matchless impersonation of the inflections and gestures of a commander, the *Sanctus* ends with the evocative sounds of bells, harps, celesta and piano.

I consider Hans Werner Henze, a naturally communicative musician and former *enfant terrible*, to have been the most significant representative of humane music of his time. He was able to express through the medium of music the human problems, passions, conflicts and above all agonies of our time in a way that is both gripping and convincing. His music is like a seismograph registering the most subtle human, social and political disturbances and tremors. It can be taken as a warning about the collapse of human culture not only in Germany but in the whole world, and this is what makes it topical, because it calls passionately on the community of rational people, to mobilise all their strength to bring about the utopia of a better world on this earth that we dream of.

## So-called Postmodernism

The striking term "postmodernism" has been in the air for a good thirty years, yet for all the discussion it has prompted, the term itself still escapes precise definition. The question of whether it means the negation of the avant-garde or the continuation of the modern by new artistic means has been much debated,[1] yet what is beyond dispute is that the now fashionable term covers a whole range of different trends.

In 1950s America, an artistic movement emerged which had no parallel in Europe, that of minimal art. Both then and now its leaning toward extreme simplicity was found baffling, and it became known as the art of reduction. It stood in opposition to the European concept of art, the notion of art with a message, traditional forms and, above all, complexity. Carl Andre, one of the movement's leading sculptors, made the following comments: "The meaning of art does not lie in its conveying a message like a telegraph. There is no idea behind the artwork, the idea is in the artwork itself".[2] Minimalists question the category of "artwork", the category that for Western artists is absolutely key. Many of them claim to be "anti-art", in protest against Western ways of life and thought.

It is striking that many representatives of minimal art are guided by East-Asian philosophy, and Zen Buddhism, Indian and Chinese philosophy has had a profound effect on their thinking and artistic outlook. John Cage (1912-1992), one of the movement's unquestioned pioneers, used the Chinese book of oracles for his chance procedures in his first aleatoric work, *Music for Changes* of 1952. In 1966 he recollected how he learned from an Indian musician the reason why music is traditionally created in India: to "calm the spirit and make it receptive to divine influences".[3] Terry Riley (*b.* 1935) made a similar comment: "Music should be the expression of more noble, more spiritual aims, those of the philosophy of knowledge and truth – humanity's most precious assets. To give expression to these aims, music has to have the necessary calm and poise".[4]

As he admitted, John Cage had a particular affinity with Erik Satie. He turned to his music repeatedly, and adapted several of his works. He took Satie at his word when the composer ironically said that his short piano piece *Vexations* should be played 840 times, and in 1963 organised a performance lasting around eighteen hours given by six pianists in relay – a spectacular event that many see as marking the birth of minimalist music.

This term is used to denote music that survives on only a few notes and stereotypical patterns, is limited to a few basic rhythmic values, and demonstrates a particular idea of musical form. Those familiar with the style are keen to point out that minimalism does not mean simply repeating identical material, since it comes down to the gradual transformation of the music. According to Ulli Götte, the four leading representatives of the trend – Terry Riley, Steve Reich (*b.*1936), Philip Glass (*b.*1937) and La Monte Young (*b.*1935) – are fundamentally different from each other in approach. What unites them, however, is the emphasis they put on gradual transformation.[5]

In 1974 Terry Riley wrote about his music, "Over the last ten years I have given up the traditional role of the composer in favour of more self-interpreting improvisation. [...] In a certain sense, my music makes reference to the techniques of Indian classical music, where the interpreters can develop endless series from the same theme, specific mode or rhythmic period (10/12/16 beats, and so on). In this concept, the composed sections remain unchanged, but the player has sufficient freedom to carry them as far as his imagination will take him".[6] Glass shares with Riley the fascination with using a complete system to compose work than "has no direct counterpart in Western music".[7] It is undeniable that some of Glass's pieces – his Violin Concerto, for example, have a refinement that gives them a unique appeal. In recent years, the reach of minimalism has expanded enormously, and it now seems to have conquered Hollywood as well.

Minimal music has been and continues to be subject to many misunderstandings. The psychiatrist Peter Oswald accused its "repetitive techniques" of being incapable of presenting "psychological, social or other processes", but of being merely "self-referential play".[8] Ligeti, who became acquainted with Reich and Riley in 1972, was considerably more generous, and dedicated his *Three Pieces for Two Pianos* (1976) to them, with the intentionally self-mocking title *Self-portrait with Reich and Riley (and Chopin is in there too)*. He explained in a note how he had merged techniques that the two minimalists had developed with his own procedures of "overlapping meshes" and "hyper-saturated" canon.[9]

If one takes Postmodernism to mean turning away from experiment, attempting to reconcile the "frightened" larger community of music-lovers to new music, then the names of three prominent Eastern-European composers spring to mind, all of whom started out as members of the avant-garde, and at some time made a decisive change in their writing. The great works that Krzysztof Penderecki (*b.*1933) wrote in the 1960s – the *Threnody* for 52 string instruments of 1960 (dedicated to the victims of Hiroshima) and the famous *St Luke Passion* (1963/65) to name only two – display both a delight in experimentation and great expressive power. Their distinguishing features are noise-like sounds, graphic notation and an alteration in the usual character of the instruments. It is all the more surprising to find that this has all disappeared in his Violin Concerto of 1974-76, a forty-minute single-movement work based on two organically unfolding contrasting motifs, continuing the tradition of the great violin concertos, close in manner to the music of Berg.[10] In subsequent years, Penderecki's intense devotion to late-Romantic music has made his work both even more different and even more expressive.

In a similar way to Penderecki, Henryk Górecki (*b*.1933) also started out as an avant-garde composer. The works that he produced in the 1950s and 1960s, partly based on dodecaphonic and partly on serial techniques, caused a sensation with their tone colours, clusters and sounds. When searching for new expressive possibilities in 1963, he discovered a different way, by reducing the compositional material to the minimum. One famous piece by Górecki is his Third Symphony, op.36, of 1976, known as the *Symphony of Sorrowful Songs* – a work that achieves an urgent expressivity with relatively simple means. The texts used in the symphony (a 15th-century lament, the prayer of an eighteen year-old girl imprisoned by the Gestapo, and a folksong from around Opole) are all religious, and all three are addressed to the Virgin Mary. The astonishing thing is that a few years after its first performance, this symphony became an international hit.

The Estonian Arvo Pärt (*b*.1935) has had quite an unusual development as a composer. After he writing much-criticised avant-garde pieces at the beginning of the 1960s, he ceased composing for a while, and became absorbed in the study of medieval music. In 1976, in the short piano piece *Für Alina* he unveiled a new, plain style that he has since gone on to develop further in many other works. Using the Latin word for bells, he described the style as "tintinnabuli", and explained it in the following terms: "Tintinnabuli style is a route I take at times when I am looking for a solution in my life, my music, my work. At difficult moments I can see quite clearly that everything surrounding a particular thing has no meaning. Abundance and diversity only confuse me, and I have to seek out the one. What is this one, and how can I find the way into it? There are many manifestations of perfection: everything unimportant disappears. Tintinnabuli style is something like this. There I am alone with silence. I have discovered that it is enough for a single note to be played beautifully. This one note, hush or silence move me emotionally. I work with little material, one voice or two voices. My building blocks are the most primitive material, a triad or a specific tonality. The three sounds in a triad sound like bells. That is why I called it tintinnabuli".[11] The techniques that Pärt applies in his later, sacred works (there is an unmistakable affinity with the rapt music of the Orthodox Church) are more refined than the composer's words would suggest, and it is striking how he succeeds in creating a grander impression with relatively simple means. In the area of "meditative" music, the first names to spring to mind would be those of Pärt and Sofia Gubaidulina (*b*.1931), whose works are rooted in mystical experiences.[12]

Toward the end of his life, Ligeti was highly critical of both the avant-garde and Postmodernism. As he saw it, what was once avant-garde was now "conformist" and "obsolete", and he considered the postmodern to be modish.[13] In a similar fashion, Peter Petersen placed Henze's multi-faceted work beyond both the avant-garde and Postmodernism.[14] Yet neither Ligeti nor Henze underestimated the strength of tradition in new music too. "Every cultural activity, from composing to painting and acting," said Henze, "creates a strong link with our traditions".[15] And Hans Zender thought that the appealing term "postmodern" should "not be used in the sense of arbitrariness or even nostalgia, but in the sense of exposure to the total freedom (the lack of constraints) to which we are condemned to live and think in nowadays".[16]

When considering the factors that led to the great turning-point in new music at the beginning of the 1980s, one aspect that should not be overlooked is the astonishing Mahler renaissance that started after 1960. The universal quality of Mahler's symphonies, their vast range, in terms of character, of musical breakthroughs and suspensions, and their astounding expressivity has continued to fascinate countless listeners. Significantly, there is not a single leading composer of our time who does not acknowledge Mahler: Luigi Nono, Luciano Berio, Hans Werner Henze, Alfred Schnittke, György Ligeti, Dieter Schnebel, Helmut Lachenmann, Friedhelm Döhl, and Peter Ruzicka, to name only a few. Mahler is one of those artists who showed the way to the future.[17] In Peter Ruzicka's words, "We are only now gradually grasping that Mahler elevated nature, the everyday, the visionary and simply everything that surrounded and affected him, to the lonely heights of his spirit, and transformed it into music that is more real than the real. And that is why, after all these years, the extraordinary feeling prevails that we are still only at the beginning with Mahler. His time is always far ahead of us".[18]

The term "postmodern" was coined by the French philosopher Jean-François Lyotard and quickly taken up by British architectural theorists. According to Berio, the label can only be applied with any justification to architecture: "Postmodernism is a typical architectural concept".[19] In musical discourse the word is used as an umbrella term covering a variety of directions, but all have one thing in common: the rejection of ideas of progress and the once appealing concept of the "tendency of the material" that, as we know, goes back to Adorno.[20] It should, however, be taken into consideration that this now established term is prone to a number of misconceptions. It does not, as has occasionally been claimed, mean the exclusion of the subject, but exists in dialectical conflict with it.[21] One of Postmodernism's avowed goals is to try to close the deeply-felt gulf between artist and audience that arose in the 1950s and 1960s.

One key aspect of Postmodernism is that it favours pluralism over serialism. Although John Cage did not explicitly identify himself with it, he was co-opted by it and talked up as its leading figure, simply because he opposed structuralism, denied everything that had until then been held as sacrosanct, and espoused chance and aleatorical operations. While many composers since the renaissance have been strongly aware of being creative artists, questioning voices have been raised in recent years about what had long been taken for granted. Roland Barthes spoke about the "death of the author"[22] and Cage never tired of promoting his provocative notion of the non-intentionality of his music. It is no surprise to learn that he was not the least interested in the proper way to understand his music.[23]

Composers of the stature of Krzysztof Penderecki, Alfred Schnittke, Roman Berger, Arvo Pärt and Sofia Gubaidulina belong to another branch of Postmodernism. They have all been keen to reclaim the realm of expressivity and emotionalism that has occasionally been smothered, either through a new simplicity or by falling back on aspects of traditional musical language. In many cases, there have been perceptible spiritual or religious tendencies. At least from the time of Stockhausen's composition *Stimmung for six vocalists* (1968) and *Mantra* (1970), "meditative music" has been in vogue. It would not be wrong to see the way several composers have turned to Indian or Far Eastern philosophy as an attempt to escape from the dictates of our completely rationalised European world.

The last thing to say about Minimalism is that it can be found in a variety of forms. It often accompanies the minimalising of human values, and intellectual and emotional potential as well. Whether it has to be interpreted as an impoverishment remains an open question, but in any case, disorientation is a serious symptom of our times.[24]

# "No Artist Works at a Distance from Humanity" –
# In Praise of Wolfgang Rihm

Wolfgang Rihm has frequently spoken in praise of his fellow composers, but once declared that praise often amounts to arrogance – a statement that makes me nervous – so I would like to start by stating that my intention is to do no more than present a few personal thoughts on his music.

It has rightly been said that artistic creativity is surrounded by mystery. If it does obey any laws, these remain to be discovered and explored. Stefan Zweig laid great emphasis on the fact that creativity was "a permanent struggle between the unconscious and the conscious" and that the formula for the artistic process itself was "inspiration plus perspiration".[1]

Among contemporary composers, Wolfgang Rihm is one of the most versatile and productive, if not the most productive. For forty years he has produced work after work, and his well of invention seems inexhaustible. His output runs to more than two hundred works in almost every genre: music theatre, orchestral, chamber and vocal music, and recently "sacred" music as well. One particularly strong characteristic seems to be a boundless desire for freedom and independence. He studied for a while with Stockhausen, with whom he was on friendly terms, as he has been with Boulez and Helmut Lachenmann, and Luigi Nono was one of his mentors. Yet while he has engaged with the music of all these composers, he has always remained himself. He is associated with no trend and no school of composition – something that his "huge desire for freedom" precludes. When Rihm talks about music, especially his own, the words that come naturally to his lips are freedom, energy, strength, flow, current, "form in movement" unbridled, untamed expression. His desire is to "release music and let it flow."[2]

One observation he has made is that "there is nothing that gives us the same physical experience of power and energy as music, and we forgo its possibilities and wall ourselves up inside anxious, rarefied interiors."[3] Music for him is the other, the counter-world, but at the same time a sensory medium that has a strong physical dimension. Sounds have to be formed in a way that they can be grasped hold of.

The more I explore Rihm's writings on music, the stronger the impression I get that his thinking is genuinely dialectic. Almost everything he says contains its contradiction, its negation. This seems to affect his compositional work as well. "A key aspect in my composing, and in my whole way of thinking as well," he once wrote, "is the principle of almost ridiculously rapid change from one thing to another, the experience of something moving straight – I won't say without a break – from one thing to another".[4]

More than fifty years ago the word "structure" came to acquire magical properties. People rhapsodised over "structural thinking", while for a time the serialists put every element into a composed structure, and in musicology too, so-called structural analysis was highly regarded. It was as if music could not be conceived without structure. But music is in no way simply a matter of structure: it has a hugely significant, deep psychological dimension as well. It is probably for this reason that Wolfgang Rihm called on composers to take a new attitude toward structure. "Musical structure," he has said, "will be recognised as a fact of music, but not as a prerequisite. Through the expansion of the structural idea, the energies in music audibly convey to us that the essence of musical structure is upheaval".[5]

Rihm's music is always about humanity. This is why it affects people, and why it speaks directly to the listener: this is the secret of its success. It is quite different from the sort of music that the listener only begins to get a grasp of when it has been explained how it is structured.

Rihm's music plumbs psychological depths and brings them to the surface. It expresses something subterranean, chthonic. An early orchestral piece by Rihm is entitled *Magma* – a geological term that means hot molten rock created from igneous rocks in the bowels of the earth, and the word prompts associations with eruptions.[6] Rihm associates it with flow and solidification. An informed listener might be aware that there is an element of the archetypal and atavistic in Rihm's early works, and this manifests itself in a preference for drumming, for abrupt contrasts, obsessions and striking, persistent ostinatos. These aspects can be heard in the "poème dansé" *Tutuguri*, after Antonin Artaud, as well as *Die Eroberung von Mexico*. Ritual appears to be a feature of Rihm's music theatre. After all, Artaud labelled his play the "theatre of cruelty", and intended it to "introduce the terribly relevant question of colonisation". As Ivanka Stoianova pointed out, Rihm's work "is based on the eternal opposition of the feminine, vocal, melodic Mexican world of Montezuma that almost completely renounces speech, and the masculine, brutal, often spoken and shouted world of Cortéz's *conquistadores*".[7]

The last thirty years have been dominated by the avant-garde and Postmodernism, and in the sphere of cultural criticism it is significant that the retreat of the avant-garde has been accompanied by the increasing expansion of Postmodernism. Many reasons for the possibly temporary success of the postmodern can be put forward. Undoubtedly, one of these is the desire to win back the broader seam of listeners that the avant-garde had lost.

As Rihm sees it, time has moved on from discussion of avant-garde and postmodern, and he considers the terms to be vague and unenlightening. In his view, Postmodernism is an art on one level.[8] His ideal is music of the highest quality that makes demands on the listener, and through its emotional and expressive qualities directly engages the listener's attention. "I think," he once said, "an audience reacts to a piece when it has been created from a subjective, highly personal situation and stance, and recognisably so".[9]

Is music created in an ivory tower, or is it rooted in a living context? For many years it has been my belief that good music is still about people, which is why people react strongly to it. For that reason I was very pleased to read comments in a text by Rihm that seemed to me to come from the heart. He wrote, "No artist works removed from humanity. That may sound surprising, if one believes that Utopia is something distant from people. Schoenberg's music too, to give a simple example, is a passionate address to men and women. And art never says anything abstract when it is articulated in so-called abstraction, at a distance from habitual realism".[10]

But does music refer to the current social and political problems of a given time? At least since the Second World War many composers have placed their work in the service of humanity, and protested against violence, oppression, brutality and enslavement. Rihm's music is not politically engaged in the same way as that of Karl Amadeus Hartmann, Luigi Nono or Hans Werner Henze. A number of his works do refer to current social problems, but this is never overt, but almost always subtly done.

Textual collages are not uncommon in new music. However, the way that Wolfgang Rihm takes up texts, subjects them to various processes and gives them a new meaning, and an uncanny relevance as well, is something quite original. His musical scene *Andere Schatten* of 1985 is based on the long *Rede des toten Christus vom Weltgebäude herab* from Jean Paul's *Siebenkäs*. By omitting a large number of words, he reduces the text to a fragment that in its concentration is reminiscent of Expressionist prose. In his *Dies* of 1983, he creates an idiosyncratic amalgam of liturgical and Biblical texts mixed with an extract from a treatise by Leonardo da Vinci. Finally, in a recent work, *Deus passus*, premiered in Stuttgart in 2000, he brings together parts of the Good Friday liturgy and the Book of Isaiah with Paul Celan's *Tenebrae*. In all three cases the ancient texts seem to be perfectly suited to the problems of our day, which we take to be the destruction of the environment, the danger of the planet being blown apart, the appalling events and consequences of the Second World War, and humanity's sorrow and guilt. This allows the sacred to be placed in the here and now. The profoundly sorrowful music of *Deus passus* also documents the extent of Rihm's development: here is a composer who is always creating anew, and never repeating himself.

For many great composers since Beethoven's time, composing has not been in any way a purely artistic matter, but also a manifestation and a purpose of life, about seeking, finding and realising oneself, and I think Wolfgang Rihm belongs in their company.

# Afterword

> "For the ordinary descends silently to
> the Underworld"
> FRIEDRICH SCHILLER: *NENIA*

"But I believe much more: the new sound is a symbol discovered spontaneously, one that proclaims the new man who thus declares his individuality". Schoenberg's comment of 1911 provides not just the perfect description of the Expressionist music of his time, but applies to other paths in new music as well, even those that are primarily experimental. As previously mentioned, Schoenberg was opposed to the analysis of his twelve-note works purely in terms of their tone-rows, and asked his pupils to focus on finding the essence of his music. Luigi Nono proposed something similar in 1953 in a short article on Webern, in which he writes:[1] "In Webern I see a new human, one who has the two qualities of serenity and assurance that have made it possible for him imbue his present life with inner tension. The tension in Webern's music is the same that, dialectically, rules nature and life. It would be a grave error and profoundly dangerous to conceive of Webern's creative power purely in terms of technical structures, and choose to understand his technique as a ready reckoner. Instead one must try to fathom why he used this technique. Looking purely at the technical content of music means failing to recognise its meaning and content".

In 1948, only a few years after the end of the Second World War, the literary critic Hans Mayer spoke of a profound cultural crisis that every creative artist was in the grip of, and he attempted to describe its consequences using the terms "historicising, specialising and formalising".[2] He referred to Thomas Mann's *Dr Faustus* and the character of the brilliant German composer Adrian Leverkühn who felt he recognised "that valid, enduring work is no longer possible in our time, that art has become too heavy, operating through artifice and irony, and hence in isolation".[3] In his celebrated novel, which had just appeared, in 1947, Thomas Mann seems amazingly to have foreseen the crisis which serialism was to plunge so-called serious music into in the 1950s and 1960s.

In 1948 Hans Mayer summed the situation up succinctly: "Things are not looking good for the music of our time".[4] What has changed since this statement was made, and how do things look now? Firstly, the gulf that has always existed between so-called light and serious music has grown even wider. In the process, the popular music that the entertainment industry publicises so vigorously, and which ranges widely in terms of quality, is pushing every other type of music to the margins.[5] Even jazz, which used to have such a following, is now a niche genre. Concerts of the traditional Classical and Romantic repertoire are certainly as well attended as they ever were, especially when familiar and much-loved works are on the programme. At the same time, the repertoire has visibly contracted and become standardised. Adorno rightly spoke of a "regression in hearing".[6]

Another aspect that is particularly characteristic of our time is the way the distance that once separated art from commerce has shrunk considerably. It is not just so-called light music that is commercialised, but a sizeable part of serious music as well. It is surely no coincidence that both film music and various types of "crossover" between serious and popular music have such a wide appeal. It would be no exaggeration to say that film music reaches an audience of millions. Successful scores move out of the cinema to become soundtrack albums that are sold in their thousands. In the light of this, has Ligeti's gloomy fear that the future would belong to functional music come true? "PR and marketing and everything that directly brings material gain," thought Ligeti, "are now already far more important than art". Yes, there should be plans to link music production to lemonade production![7]

Busoni had no illusions about the difficulty that the new has always had in establishing itself. Even so, he consoled himself with the thought that "however much attachment to the familiar and laziness are part of human habit and nature, energy and opposition to the established order are equally characteristic of every living thing".[8]

In his late (1888) book *Antichrist*, shockingly subtitled *Curse on Christianity*, Friedrich Nietzsche again proposed his doctrine of the transvaluation of all values. He acknowledged his "inclination for questions that no one has the courage for" and in this connection called for "new eyes for what is most distant" together with "new ears for new music".[9] Nietzsche here perceptively hit upon an essential element, that new music actually required a new way of hearing, and also a readiness to deal with it each time anew. What a new way of hearing means is being impartial, open to what one has never heard before, leaving behind comfortable habits and customs, as well as having aesthetic expertise, a certain level of education and, as with any other kind of music, an awareness of the artist's intentions. We accept that experienced listeners do not now find the music of a number of 20th-century composers at all difficult. Stravinsky, Bartók, Hindemith, Milhaud, Messiaen, Penderecki, Prokofiev, Shostakovich, Ligeti and Henze – to name only these – are today modern classics. The reasons why some experimental trends in new music fell into a profound crisis are to be sought elsewhere. As I see it, they lie in the way music was made completely academic, aligned itself entirely with technology and deliberately marginalised every human element[10] – all trends that Rihm stands against with his perception that "no artist works at a distance from humanity".

# Notes

## Preface

1 György Ligeti: Conversation with Constantin Floros on 15. September 1999 in Hamburg.

2 Iwan Martynow: *Dmitri Schostakowitsch*, Berlin 1947. Quoted from Hans Heinz Stuckenschmidt: *Neue Musik (zwischen den beiden Kriegen*, Vol. 2), Berlin 1951, 329-332.

## From Expressionism to Experiment

1 Ernst H. Gombrich: *The Story of Art*, 16th ed. London 1996, 612.

2 Paul Bekker: *Neue Musik* (1919), in: Bekker: *Neue Musik. Dritter Band der Gesammelten Schriften*, Stuttgart/Berlin 1923, 85-118.

3 Robert Schumann: *Gesammelte Schriften über Musik und Musiker*, 5th ed. Martin Kreisig, 2 vols., Leipzig 1914, Vol. 1, 26.

4 Quoted from Theodor W. Adorno: *Philosophie der Neuen Musik*, Frankfurt am Main 1958, 45. English translation: *Philosophy of Modern Music*, New York 1974.

5 Arnold Schönberg: *Harmonielehre*, Leipzig/Vienna 1911, 15. English translation: *Theory of Harmony*, ed. Roy E. Carter, Berkeley and Los Angeles 1978.

6 Wassily Kandinsky: *Das Geistige in der Kunst*, 1st ed.. 1912, 4th ed. 1952, 6th ed. (Introduction Max Bill) Berlin Bümpliz 1959, 54.

7 Ibid., 49.

8 Schönberg: *Harmonielehre*, 447.

9 Walter H. Sokel: *Der literarische Expressionismus. Der Expressionismus in der deutschen Literatur des zwanzigsten Jahrhunderts*, Munich n. d.)., 73-107.

10 Helene Berg in a letter to Hans Redlich. See Erich Alban Berg: *Bergiana*, in: Schweizerische Musikzeitung 120 (1980), 147-155, p. 152.

11 Adorno: *Philosophy of Modern Music*, 28ff.

12 Hans Werner Henze: *Musik und Politik. Schriften und Gespräche 1955-1975*, ed. Jens Brockmeier, Munich 1976, 195.

[13] Dieter Möller: *Jean Cocteau und Igor Strawinsky. Untersuchungen zur Ästhetik und zu »Oedipus Rex«* (Hamburger Beiträge zur Musikwissenschaft 24), 2 vols., Hamburg 1981, Part 1/2, 186-191.

[14] Ferruccio Busoni: *Von der Einheit der Musik. Verstreute Aufzeichnungen*, Berlin 1922, 275-279.

[15] Busoni: *Entwurf einer neuen Ästhetik der Tonkunst*. With Annotations of Arnold Schoenberg and a Afterword of H. H. Stuckenschmidt, Frankfurt am Main 1974.

[16] Wolfgang Rathert: *Das ist ja alles schon tot! Ein Kommentar zum Verhältnis Busoni-Hindemith*, in: Hindemith-Jahrbuch. Annales Hindemith 2004/ XXXIII, 214-233, especially p. 228.

[17] Schönberg's marginalia in: Busoni: *Entwurf einer neuen Ästhetik der Tonkunst* (n. 15), 63.

[18] Hans Heinz Stuckenschmidt: *Neue Musik (Zwischen den beiden Kriegen*, Vol. 2), Berlin 1951, 300f.

[19] Igor Strawinsky: *Poétique musicale*, Cambridge, Mass.1942. English translation 1947.

[20] Möller: *Jean Cocteau und Igor Strawinsky*, Part 1/2, 235-242.

[21] Strawinsky: *Poétique musicale* (The poetics of Music), 46. Cf. Ernst-Albrecht Stiebler: *Torniamo all'antico*: in: Musik-Konzepte 100. *Was heißt Fortschritt?* April 1998, 83-87.

[22] Strawinsky: *Musikalische Poetik*, 47.

[23] Stuckenschmidt: *Schönberg. Leben. Umwelt. Werk*, Munich-Mainz 1989, 462. On Adorno's criticism see his *Philosophie der Neuen Musik*, 148f., 160f.

[24] György Ligeti: *Die Zukunft der Neuen Musik*, in: Hanns-Werner Heister and Wolfgang Hochstein (Eds.): Kultur, Bildung, Politik. Festschrift für Hermann Rauhe zum 70. Geburtstag, Hamburg 2000, 60f.

[25] Adorno: *Philosophie der Neuen Musik*, 163f.

[26] On the following see Fred K. Prieberg: *Lexikon der Neuen Musik*, Munich 1958, 151-156.

[27] Ibid., 307-313.

[28] Busoni: *Entwurf einer neuen Ästhetik der Tonkunst*, 54.

[29] Hans Rudolf Zeller: *Ferruccio Busoni und die musikalische Avantgarde um 1920*, in: Musik-Konzepte Sonderband. Musik der anderen Tradition. Mikrotonale Tonwelten, Februar 2003, 9-18; Zeller: Veranstaltungen 1981, ibid., 220-223.

[30] About Iwan Wyschnegradsky see Hans Rudolf Zeller, ibid., 224-227.

[31] Manfred Stahnke: *Mein Weg zu Mikrotönen*, ibid., 125-140.

[32] Busoni: *Entwurf einer neuen Ästhetik der Tonkunst*, 11.

[33] Edgar Varèse: *Die Befreiung des Klangs*, in: Musik-Konzepte 6. Edgar Varèse. *Rückblick auf die Zukunft*, November 1978, 11-24; english: *The Liberation of Sound*, in: Perspectives of New Music, Vol. 5, no. 1, Princeton 1966, 11-19.

[34] Stuckenschmidt: *Neue Musik*, Vol. 2, 304.

[35] *Die Einheit der Stockhausen-Zeit...*, in: Musik-Konzepte 19. *Karlheinz Stockhausen ... wie die Zeit verging ...*, May 1981, 48.

[36] Ernst Krenek: *Vom Verfall des Einfalls* (1959), in: Krenek: *Im Zweifelsfalle. Aufsätze zur Musik*, Vienna/Munich/Zurich 1984, 190-197.

[37] Ligeti: *Pierre Boulez. Entscheidung und Automatik in der »Structure Ia«*, in: Die Reihe 4, Vienna/Zurich/London 1958, 38-63.

[38] Adorno: *Philosophy of Modern Music*, 23-26.

[39] Pierre Boulez: *An der Grenze des Fruchtlandes*, in: Die Reihe 1, Vienna 1955, 47-56; english translation: *At the Ends of Fruitful Land*, 1958.

[40] Jean-Noel von der Weid: *Die Musik des 20. Jahrhunderts. Von Claude Debussy bis Wolfgang Rihm*, Frankfurt am Main/Leipzig 2001, 281-296.

[41] Hans-Jürgen von Bose: *Suche nach einem neuen Schönheitsideal*, in: Darmstädter Beiträge zur Neuen Musik, Vol. 17, Mainz 1978, 35. Others who thought similarly at that time are Wolfgang von Schweinitz, Detlef Müller-Siemens und Wolfgang-Andreas Schultz, Ligetis postgraduate students at the Hamburger Musikhochschule.

[42] Almut Rößler: *Beiträge zur geistigen Welt Olivier Messians. Mit Original- Texten des Komponisten*, Duisburg 1984, 154.

[43] Musik-Konzepte 61/62. *Helmut Lachenmann*, Munich, October 1988, 63.

[44] Ibid., 129.

[45] Ligeti: *Die Zukunft der Neuen Musik* (see Note. 24), 60f.

**Arnold Schoenberg - Revolutionary, Humanist and Visionary**

[1] Arnold Schönberg: *Prager Rede auf Gustav Mahler* (1912), in: Schönberg: *Stil und Gedanke. Aufsätze zur Musik*, ed. Ivan Vojtech (Gesammelte Schriften, Vol. 1). Frankfurt am Main 1976, 17; S & I, 462.

[2] Willi Reich (Ed.): *Arnold Schönberg. Schöpferische Konfessionen*, Zurich 1964, 121f.

[3] Schönberg: *Aphorismen*, in: Die Musik, 9. (Vol. XXXVI), 1909/ 1910, 159-163, especially p. 162.

[4] Schönberg: *Texte*, Vienna/New York 1926, S. 39.

[5] Hans Ferdinand Redlich: *Alban Berg. Versuch einer Würdigung*, Vienna/Zurich/London 1957, 328f.

[6] See Constantin Floros: *Alban Berg. Musik als Autobiographie*, Wiesbaden/Leipzig/Paris 1992, 32-34.

[7] Quoted from Christopher Hailey, in: Nuria Schoenberg Nono (Ed.): *Arnold Schoenberg 1874-1951. Eine interaktive multimediale Ausstellung*, Venice 1996, 28.

[8] Thomas Zaunschirm (Ed.): *Arnold Schönberg. Das bildnerische Werk*, Klagenfurt 1991, 275 and 277.

[9] Arnold Schoenberg: *Moderne Psalmen*, ed. Rudolf Kolisch, Mainz 1956.

[10] Alois Melichar: *Musik in der Zwangsjacke. Die deutsche Musik zwischen Orff und Schönberg*, Vienna/Stuttgart 1958. Cf. Martin Vogel: *Schönberg und die Folgen. Die Irrwege der Neuen Musik*, Bonn 1984.

[11] Pierre Boulez: *Schönberg ist tot*, in: Boulez: *Anhaltspunkte. Essays*, Stuttgart/ Zurich 1975, 288-296.

[12] Schönberg: *Prager Rede auf Gustav Mahler*. Gesammelte Schriften, Vol. 1, 11; S & I, 454.

[13] Ibid., 165-168; S & I, 365-369.

[14] *The Berg-Schoenberg correspondence*, ed. Brand, Hailey & Harris, London 1987, 407.

[15] Schönberg: Gesammelte Schriften, Vol. 1, 237.

[16] Wassily Kandinsky: Die Bilder, in: Arnold Schönberg in höchster Verehrung, Munich 1912, 59-64.

[17] Karl Linke: Zur Einführung. Ibid., 16.

[18] Zaunschirm: Arnold Schönberg, 280 and 281.

[19] Par example Boris Blacher, Luigi Dallapiccola, Wolfgang Fortner, Roberto Gerhard, Hans Werner Henze, Richard Hoffmann, Hanns Jelinek, Ernst Krenek, Rolf Liebermann, Humphrey Searle, Matyas Seiber, Rudolf Wagner-Regeny, Winfried Zillig. See their statements in: Josef Rufer: Die Komposition mit zwölf Tönen, Berlin/Wunsiedel 1952, 161-180.

[20] Alban Berg: Warum ist Schönbergs Musik so schwer verständlich?, in: Arnold Schönberg zum fünfzigsten Geburtstage, 13. September 1924, Sonderheft der Musikblätter des Anbruch, 6, August-September 1924, 329-341. Quoted from Willi Reich: The Life and Work of Alban Berg, New York 1982, 189-204.

[21] Wolfgang Rihm: ausgesprochen. Schriften und Gespräche, ed. Ulrich Mosch, 2 vols., Winterthur/Schweiz 1997, Vol. 2, 353.

[22] Schönberg: Ausgewählte Briefe, 178f.

[23] For basics see Floros: Alban Berg, 93-97.

[24] Schönberg: Gesammelte Schriften, Vol. 1, 24; S & I, 471.

[25] Ibid., 132; S & I, 136.

[26] On this see Christian Meyer (Ed.): Arnold Schönberg und sein Gott. Bericht zum Symposium 26.-29. Juni 2002, Vienna 2003; Marc M. Kerling: » O Wort, du Wort, das mir fehlt«. Die Gottesfrage in Arnold Schön-bergs Oper »Moses und Aron«, Mainz 2004.


**"Music is not to be Decorative; it is to be True".**
**Towards an Aesthetic of the Second Viennese School**

[1] Aesthetics of the philosopher A. G. Baumgarten, whose two-volume Aesthetica appeared 1750 and 1785 in Frankfurt an der Oder.

[2] Immanuel Kant: Kritik der Urteilskraft (suhrkamp taschenbuch wissenschaft 57), Frankfurt am Main 1974, 269.

[3] Arthur Schopenhauer: Die Welt als Wille und Vorstellung, Zweiter Band, Drittes Buch, Kap. 39: "Zur Metaphysik der Musik".

[4] Natalie Bauer-Lechner: *Recollections of Gustav Mahler*, trans. Dika Newlin, Cambridge 1980, 233.

[5] Ibid., 52.

[6] Ibid., 30.

[7] *Gustav Mahler Briefe*. New edition, ed. Herta Blaukopf, Wien/Hamburg 1982, 122.

[8] Theodor W. Adorno: *Philosophie der Neuen Musik*, Frankfurt am Main 1958, 45.

[9] Arnold Schönberg: Probleme des Kunstunterrichts (1910), in: *Stil und Gedanke* (1976), 165-168, p. 165; S & I, 365.

[10] Eduard Hanslick: *Vom Musikakalisch-Schönen. Ein Beitrag zur Revision der Ästhetik der Tonkunst*, 1. ed. 1854, 12. ed. Leipzig 1918, 76.

[11] Arnold Schönberg: *Mahler*, in: Stil und Gedanke (1976), 7-14, p.11; S & I, 454.

[12] Anton von Webern: *Schönbergs Musik*, in: *Arnold Schönberg*, R. Piper, München 1912, 22-48, p. 2.

[13] Schönberg: *Probleme des Kunstunterrichts* (1976), 167; S & I, 368.

[14] Dazu Constantin Floros: *Alban Berg* (1992), 87-89.

[15] Schönberg: *Franz Liszts Werk und Wesen*, in: Stil und Gedanke, 169-173, p.170; S & I, 442-447.

[16] Schönberg: *Menschenrechte*, in: *Stil und Gedanke*, 140-145, p.144; Style and Idea, 511.

[17] See Floros: *Alban Berg* (1992), 93-97; Hartmut Krones: *„Alpine" Programme bei Werner Pirchner und Anton Webern*, in: 22. Slovenian Music Days 2007, 196-214.

[18] Unpublished letter. Quoted from my book about Berg, 88 f.

[19] Unpublished letter. Quoted from my book about Berg, 89.

[20] Krones: *„Alpine" Programme*, 199.

[21] Floros: *Alban Berg* (1992), 99.

[22] Adorno: *Philosophie der Neuen Musik* , 11.

[23] Theodor W. Adorno: *Ästhetische Theorie* (Gesammelte Schriften, Band 7), ed. Gretel Adorno and Rolf Tiedemann, Frankfurt am Main 1970, 182; *Aesthetic Theory*, transl. Robert Hullot-Kentor, Continuum 2004, pag. 160.

[24] Ibid., 184; english edition, 161.

[25] Ibid., 185; english edition, 161

[26] *Gustav Mahler Briefe* (1982), 254.

[27] Adorno: *Ästhetische Theorie*, 189; engl. edition, 165.

[28] Ibid., 192; engl. ed. 168.

[29] Ibid., 193; engl. ed., 169.

[30] Ibid., 197; engl. ed. 172.

[31] See p. 42

**The Problem of "German Music"**

[1] Friedrich Nietzsche: *Jenseits von Gut und Böse*, § 255, in: *Werke*, ed. Karl Schlechta, Vol. 3, Munich 1979, 723.

[2] Illustration in: Süddeutsche Zeitung from 1./2. Oct. 1988, Nr. 227, Feuilleton-Beilage, 147.

[3] Cf. Constantin Floros: *Musik als Botschaft*, Wiesbaden 1989, 19-25.

[4] Nietzsche: *Jenseits von Gut und Böse*, 724.

[5] Hubert Kolland: *"Undeutsche Musik"*. *Gesellschaftliche Aspekte im Musikgeschichtsbild konservativer Musikpublizistik in der Weimarer Republik dargestellt am Beispiel der »Zeitschrift für Musik«*, in: *Angewandte Musik. Zwanziger Jahre*, ed. Dietrich Stern, Berlin 1977 (= Argument-Sonderbände; AS 24), 147-167.

[6] Richard Wagner: *Deutsche Kunst und deutsche Politik*, in: ders.: Sämtliche Schriften und Dichtungen, Volksausgabe, 16 vols., 6th ed., Leipzig n. d. Vol. 8, 30-124, especially p. 46.

[7] Wagner: *Was ist deutsch?*, in: Sämtliche Schriften, Vol. 10, 36-53, especially p. 45.

[8] Anton Webern: *Der Weg zur neuen Musik*, ed. Willi Reich, Vienna 1960, 39 (Lecture 10. April 1933).

[9] David Josef Bach: *Arnold Schönberg und Wien*, in: Musikblätter des Anbruch, 3. (1921), 216-218.

[10] Bruno Schräder: *Musikbriefe aus Berlin*, in: Neue Zeitschrift für Musik, 85. (1918), 312.

[11] --: in: Neue Zeitschrift für Musik, 86. (1919), 43.

[12] Friedrich Haufe an Alfred Heuß, in: Zeitschrift für Musik, 90. Jg. (1923); Issue 17, 4.

[13] Alfred Heuß: *Auseinandersetzungen über das Wesen der neuen Musik*, in: Zeitschrift für Musik, 91. (1924), 7.

[14] Adolf Diesterweg: *Berliner Musik*, in: Zeitschrift für Musik, 91. Jg. (1924), 316.

[15] Cf. Martin Vogel: *Schönberg und die Folgen. Die Irrwege der Neuen Musik*, Bonn 1984 (ORPHEUS-Schriftenreihe zu Grundfragen der Musik; Vol. 35), 510ff.

[16] Volker Scherliess: *Alban Berg in Selbstzeugnissen und Bilddokumenten*, Hamburg 1975 (rowohlts monographien, 225), 75.

[17] Konrad Vogelsang: *Dokumentation zur Oper »Wozzeck« von Alban Berg. Die Jahre des Durchbruchs 1925-1932*, Laaber 1977, 30.

[18] I am very grateful to Dr Ernst Hilmar, former head of the music collection in the Wiener Stadt- und Landesbibliothek, who was kind enough to let me consult the typescript of the correspondence.

[19] Josef Rufer: *Schönberg - gestern, heute und morgen*, in: Schweizerische Musikzeitung, 105. Jg. (1965), 190-200, especially p. 199; *Schoenberg-Berg correspondence*, 217 f.

[20] Rufer: *Das Werk Arnold Schönbergs*, Kassel/Basel 1959, 26.

[21] Alban Berg: *Warum ist Schönbergs Musik so schwer verständlich?*, in: Arnold Schönberg zum 50. Geburtstage, 329-341, p. 341.

[22] Ibid.

[23] Schoenberg: Nationale Musik, in: Gesammelte Schriften (1976), Vol. 1, 250-254; Style and Idea, 172.

[24] Ibid., 173.

[25] Willi Reich: *Arnold Schönberg oder der konservative Revolutionär*, Wien/ Frankfurt am Main 1968; Taschenbuchausgabe (dtv 1041), Munich 1974.

[26] Unpublished letter.

**The Fate of Arnold Schoenberg and Alban Bergs after 1933**

[1] The full text of this letter, not previously published in its entirety, ist given above, p. 37ff

[2] Berg to Webern on 26 August 1933. Copy of the letter above, p. 39f

[3] Alban Berg: *Briefe an seine Frau*, Munich/Wien 1965, 628.

[4] Alban Berg 1885-1935. Ausstellung der Österreichischen Nationalbibliothek, Prunksaal, 23. Mai-20. October 1985, ed. Rosemary Hilmar, Vienna 1985, 184.

[5] Ibid., 188.

[6] Ibid.

[7] Berg to his wife Helene on 15. May 1933. See Berg: Briefe an seine Frau, 626f.

[8] Berg to Helene on 16. Mai 1933, ibid., 627.

[9] Katalog der Schriftstücke von der Hand Alban Bergs, der fremdschriftlichen und gedruckten Dokumente zur Lebensgeschichte und zu seinem Werk, ed. Rosemary Hilmar, Vienna 1985 (Alban Berg Studien; Vol. 1/2), 129.

[10] Ernst Hilmar: »Wozzeck« von Alban Berg. Entstehung - erste Erfolge - Repressionen (1914-1935), Vienna 1975,. 66.

[11] Ibid., 68.

[12] Volker Scherliess: Briefe Alban Bergs aus der Entstehungszeit der »Lulu«, in: Melos/Neue Zeitschrift für Musik, 2 (1976), 108-114.

[13] Quoted from Ernst Hilmar: Alban Bergs Selbstzeugnisse zu Entstehung und Aufführbarkeit der Oper »Lulu«, in: Alban Berg. Lied der Lulu. Faksimile- Ausgabe der Anton von Webern gewidmeten autographen Partitur, ed. Franz Patzer, Vienna 1985, 12-23, especially p. 23.

[14] Ibid., 17.

[15] Quotation from Erich Alban Berg: Der unverbesserliche Romantiker. Alban Berg 1885-1935, Vienna 1985, 139f. Willi Reich published Berg's provocative statement on Bach and Handel in the Viennese music journal 23, p. 4, in March 1935, and also applied it to Berg himself.

[16] Berg to Webern on 6. July 1933.

[17] Quotation from Willi Reich's open letter to Ernest Newman, in: 23, Nr. 28/30 (10. Nov. 1936), 27.

[18] Arnold Schönberg: Gesammelte Schriften, Vol. 1, 26; Style and Idea, 114.

[19] Schönberg: Ausgewählte Briefe, 234f.

[20] Ibid., 230.

[21] On this see Michael Mäckelmann: Arnold Schönberg und das Judentum. Der Komponist und sein religiöses, nationales und politisches Selbstverständnis nach 1921, Hamburg 1984 (Hamburger Beiträge zur Musikwissenschaft, Vol. 28), 468-476.

[22] Leonard Stein: A Note of the Genesis of the »Ode to Napoleon«, in: Journal of the Arnold Schoenberg Institute, Vol. II/1, 52-54.

[23] Josef Rufer: Das Werk Arnold Schönbergs, Kassel/Basel/London/New York 1959, 50-52.

[24] Willi Reich: *Arnold Schönberg oder Der konservative Revolutionär*, Munich 1974 (Deutscher Taschenbuch Verlag, Vol. 1041), 219.

[25] Schönberg: *Ausgewählte Briefe, 259f.*

[26] Rufer: *Das Werk Arnold Schönbergs*, Illustrations 6 and 7.

[27] Rufer: *Die Komposition mit zwölf Tönen*, Berlin/Wunsiedel 1952 (Stimmen des 20. Jahrhunderts, Vol. 2), 121 and 140-143.

[28] Rufer: *Das Werk Arnold Schönbergs*, 51.

[29] Constantin Floros: *Beethoven's Eroica.Thematic Studies*. Peter Lang: Frankfurt am Main/New York 2013

**Two Unknown Letters of Schoenberg and Berg**

[1] Extracts from this letter were published by Willi Reich (*Arnold Schönberg oder Der konservative Revolutionär*, Munich 1974, pp. 196/197) (Engl. trans. 1971 as *Schoenberg: a critical Biography*) after a transcript by Hans Heinz Stuckenschmidt (*Schönberg. Leben, Umwelt, Werk*, Zürich 1974, p. 334f.) .

[2] The three-act play *Der biblische Weg* dates from 1926/1927. See above, p. 65

[3] The reference is to the Concerto for String Quartet and orchestra after Handel's op. 6 no. 7. Schoenberg's transcrption was completed in Arcachon on 16. August 1933, and later published by G. Schirmer in New York.

[4] Görgi: Schoenberg's son Georg, born in 1906, struggled with professional and financial difficulties, and continued to be a concern to his father in later life.

[5] Mali: Weberns daughter Amalie.

[6] The famous architect and architectural theorist Adolf Loos died on 23 August 1933. A Schoenberg and his pupils felt a deep bond with him, and for the Festschrift marking his 60th birthday on 10 December 1930 Berg created a double acrostic distich where the beginning and end of each line spells out the names Adolf Loos and Alban Berg.

[7] The reference is to Webern's songs *Herr Jesus mein* op. 23 no. 3 and *Es stürzt aus Höhe Frische* op. 23 no. 2 from *Viae inviae* by Hildegard Jone.

**Beethoven and the Schoenberg School**

[1] Arnold Schönberg: *Komposition mit zwölf Tönen*, in: Stil und Gedanke, 72-96, p. 76; Style and Idea, 220.

[2] Schönberg: *Ausgewählte Briefe*, 214f.

[3] Schönberg: *Aphorismen*, in: Die Musik, 9 (1909/10), Issue 21, 159-163.

[4] Adolf Loos gave his famous lecture *Ornament and Crime* fist in 1908 and than repeated it on 21 January 1910 at the "Academic Union for Literature and Music" in Vienna. The lecture can be found in: Adolf Loos: *Trotzdem. 1900-1930*, Innsbruck 1931, reprinted unaltered, Vienna 1982, p. 78-88.

[5] Schönberg: *Gesammelte Schriften*, Vol. 1, 165-168; Style and Idea. 365.

[6] Frederick Deutsch Dorian: *Webern als Lehrer*, in: Melos, 27 (1960), 101-106, p. 102.

[7] Anton Webern: *Der Weg zur neuen Musik*, ed. Willi Reich, Vienna 1960, 14.

[8] Hans und Rosaleen Moldenhauer: *Anton von Webern. Chronik seines Lebens und Werkes*, Zurich 1980, 28f. and 43.

[9] Deutsch Dorian, *Webern als Lehrer, 102.*

[10] Alban Berg: *Verbindliche Antwort auf eine unverbindliche Rundfrage*, in: *Alban Berg, Glaube, Hoffnung und Liebe. Schriften zur Musik*, ed. Frank Schneider, Leipzig 1981, 221-226, p. 225f.

[11] Berg to Hermann Watznauer 16. July 1903 (Pierpont Morgan Library, New York). Quoted from Rosemary Hilmar: *Alban Berg. Leben und Wirken in Wien bis zu seinen ersten Erfolgen als Komponist*, Vienna/Cologne/Graz 1978, 27.

[12] Soma Morgenstern: *Im Trauerhaus*, in: 23. Eine Wiener Musikzeitschrift, Nr. 24/25 (Alban Berg zum Gedenken), 1. February 1936, 16.

[13] Schönberg: *Ausgewählte Briefe*, 158.

[14] Schönberg: *Nationale Musik*, in: Gesammelte Schriften, Vol. 1, 250-254; Style and Idea, 171.

[15] Webern, *Der Weg zur neuen Musik*, 34f.

[16] Ibid., 56.

[17] Hanns Eisler: *Materialien zu einer Didaktik der Musik*, Leipzig 1973, 30.

[18] Schönberg: *Bemerkungen zu den vier Streichquartetten* (December 1949), in: Gesammelte Schriften, Vol. 1, 409-436.

[19] Ibid., 411.

[20] On this, see Constantin Floros: *Das verschwiegene Programm des Kammerkonzerts von Alban Berg. Eine semantische Analyse,* in: Neue Zeitschrift für Musik, 148 (November 1987). 11-22.

[21] A facsimile of the sheet is held in the Austrian National Library in Vienna, Music Collection 21 Berg 74/XV fol. 3 verso.

[22] Schönberg, *Gesammelte Schriften*, Vol. 1, 254; Style and Idea, 174.

**Principles of Vocal Composition**

[1] Conversation with the singer Georg Henschel. Siehe Max Kalbeck: *Johannes Brahms*, Vol. 3, Berlin 1910, 87.

[2] Mahler's statement was recorded by Ida Dehmel, wife of the poet Richard Dehmel. See Alma Mahler: *Gustav Mahler. Erinnerungen und Briefe*, Amsterdam, 2nd ed. 1949, 120.

[3] Albert Wellek: *Musikpsychologie und Musikästhetik. Grundriß der systematischen Musikwissenschaft,* Frankfurt am Main 1963, 229.

[4] Gottfried Benn: *Probleme der Lyrik* (Vortrag an der Universität Mainz am 21. 8.1951), Wiesbaden 1951, 44f.

[5] Cf. Emil Staiger: *Der musikalische Sinn der Dichtung. Zum Kunstverständnis unserer Zeit,* in: *Musik und Dichtung*, Zurich 5th ed.. 1986, 315- 341, especially p. 333ff.

[6] Hugo Friedrich: *Die Struktur der modernen Lyrik. Von Baudelaire bis zur Gegenwart,* Hamburg 1956 (rowohlts deutsche enzyklopädie, Vol. 25), 139-143; Gustav René Hocke: *Manierismus in der Literatur. Sprach-Alchimie und esoterische Kombinationskunst,* Hamburg 1959 (rowohlts deutsche enzyklopädie, Vols. 82/83), 68ff.

[7] Cf. Elmar Budde: *Zitat, Collage, Montage,* in: Die Musik der sechziger Jahre, ed. Rudolf Stephan, Mainz 1972 (Veröffentlichungen des Instituts für Neue Musik und Musikerziehung Darmstadt, Vol. 12), 26-38, especially p. 38.

[8] On this see Wilfried Gruhn: *Musiksprache - Sprachmusik - Textvertonung,* Frankfurt am Main 1978 (Schriftenreihe zur Musikpädagogik).

[9] Albert Camus: *Der Mythos von Sisyphos. Ein Versuch über das Absurde,* Hamburg 1959 (rowohlts deutsche enzyklopädie, Vol. 90); 275-284.

[10] Harald Kaufmann: *Ein Fall absurder Musik. Ligetis »Aventures« und »Nouvelles Aventures«* in: ders.: *Spurlinien. Analytische Aufsätze über Sprache und Musik*, Vienna 1969, 130-158, especially p. 138.

[11] On this see Dieter Schnebel: *Sprache als Musik in der Musik,* in: *Literatur und Musik. Ein Handbuch zur Theorie und Praxis eines komparatistischen Grenzgebietes,* ed. Steven Paul

Scher, Berlin 1984, 209-220; Wolfgang Hufschmidt: *Sprachkomposition als musikalischer Prozeß*, in: *Reflexionen über Musik heute. Texte und Analysen*, ed. Wilfried Gruhn, Mainz 1981, 204-232; Claus Raab: *Sprachkomposition in Dieter Schnebels »Madrasha II«*, ibid., 233-245.

[12] Werner Klüppelholz: *Sprache als Musik. Studien zur Vokalkomposition seit 1956*, Herrenberg 1976, 198.

[13] Luigi Nono: *Text - Musik - Gesang*, in: *Texte. Studien zu seiner Musik*, ed. Jürg Stenzl, Zurich/Freiburg i. Br. 1975, 41-60, especially p. 60.

[14] See Christoph von Blumröder's commentary in the booklet accompanying cassette 10 of the recording documentation of the Deutscher Musikrat *Zeitgenössische Musik in der Bundesrepublik Deutschland*, Bonn 1983, 14f.

### Schoenberg's *Gurrelieder*

[1] For the history of the composition, premiere and reception of *Gurrelieder*, see Ernst Hilmar (Ed.): Arnold Schönberg. *Gedenkausstellung 1974*, Vienna 1974, 228-244; Rosemary Hilmar; *Alban Berg. Leben und Wirken in Wien bis zu seinen ersten Erfolgen als Komponist*, Vienna/Cologne/Graz 1978, 70-76. For a chronological account of the work's composition dates see Josef Rufer: *Das Werk Arnold Schönbergs*, 61 f., and Jan Maegaard: *Studien zur Entwicklung des dodekaphonen Satzes bei Arnold Schönberg*, Vol. I, Copenhagen 1972, 31f.

[2] For an accoount how Berg's guide came to be written, see Rosemary Hilmar: *Alban Berg* (1978), 65-68, und Rudolf Stephan und Regina Busch: *Alban Berg, Musikalische Schriften und Dichtungen*, Vol. 1 (Sämtliche Werke, III. Abteilung), Vienna 1994, p. XI-XXV.

[3] The term „floating" (in German „schwebend") tonality, meaning wavering between two keys, was coined by Schoenberg in his *Harmonielehre* (1911, 430f.).

### The Melodramas of *Pierrot lunaire*

[1] Arnold Schönberg: *Berliner Tagebuch* p. 33f. – Quoted from Reinhold Brinkmann (Ed.): *Arnold Schönberg. Melodramen und Lieder mit Instrumenten*, Part 1: Pierrot lunaire op. 21: Kritischer Bericht, Studien zur Genesis. Skizzen. Dokumente (Sämtliche Werke, Reihe B, Vol. 24, 1), Mainz/Vienna 1995, 228.

[2] Austrian National Library, Fonds Alban Berg. U.E. 5336 Copyright 1914 by Universal Edition.

[3] Alexander Zemlinsky: *Briefwechsel mit Arnold Schönberg, Anton Webern, Alban Berg und Franz Schreker*, ed. Horst Weber, Darmstadt 1995, 161.

4   For various aspects of Schoenberg's *Sprechgesang* see the articles in: Musik-Konzepte 112/113. *Schönberg und der Sprechgesang*, Munich July 2001.

5   This essay first appeared in the 1929 Yearbook of Universal Edition AG, Wien. Copy by Willi Reich: *Alban Berg*, Vienna/Leipzig/Zurich 1937, 164f.

6   Pierre Boulez: *Sprechen, Singen, Spielen, in: Werkstatt-Texte*, aus dem Französischen übersetzt von Josef Häusler, Frankfurt am Main/Berlin 1972, 124-141.

7   Schönberg: *Gesammelte Schriften*, 3-6; Style and Idea, 4. The essay first appeared in 1912 in the volume of *Der blaue Reiter* edited by Wassily Kandinsky and Franz Marc.

8   Following performances of *Pierrot* in Geneva, Amsterdam and Paris, three of the poems (»Madonna«, »Rote Messe« und »Kreuze«) were deemed blasphemous. Schoenberg protested against this claim in a letter of 30 December 1922 to Marya Freund, and asserted her that „I have never at any time in my life been anti-religious, indeed have never really been unreligious either. I seem to have had an altogether much naiver view if these poems than most people have." See *Arnold Schoenberg Letters* (ed. Erwin Stein), University of California Press, 1987, 82.

## "God's Eternity Opposes the Transience of Idols"
## On Schoenberg's *Moses und Aron*

1   Charlotte M. Cross and Russell A. Berman: *Political and Religious Ideas in the Works of Arnold Schoenberg*, New York & London 2000.

2   *Berg-Schoenberg correspondence*, 446.

3   On this see Karl H. Wörner: *Gotteswort und Magie. Die Oper »Moses und Aron« von Arnold Schönberg*, Heidelberg 1959; Michael Mäckelmann: *Arnold Schönberg und das Judentum* (Hamburger Beiträge zur Musikwissenschaft, Vol. 28), Hamburg 1984; Pamela White: *Schoenberg and the God-Idea. The Opera Moses und Aron*, Ann Arbor, Michigan 1983.

4   Theodor W. Adorno: *Sakrales Fragment. Über Schönbergs Moses und Aron*, in: Quasi una fantasia. Musikalische Schriften II, Frankfurt am Main 1963, 306-338.

5   Christian Martin Schmidt: *Schönbergs Oper »Moses und Aron«. Analyse der diastematischen, formalen und musikdramatischen Komposition*, Mainz 1988.

6   Schönberg: *Ausgewählte Briefe*, 163.

7   Schoenberg: *Letters*, ed. Erwin Stein, 172.

8   Faksimile of the draft in: *Arnold Schönberg, Moses und Aron* (Sämtliche Werke, Abteilung III: Bühnenwerke, Reihe B, Band 8, Teil 2), Mainz/Vienna 1998, 164.

[9] Schönberg: *Ausgewählte Briefe*, 188.

**Nationalism and Folklorism**

[1] *Ein Glück ohne Ruh'. Die Briefe Gustav Mahlers an Alma. Erste Gesamtausgabe.* Edited Henry-Louis de La Grange and Günther Weiß, Berlin 1995, 344 f.

[2] Zoltán Kodály: *Bartók als Folklorist* (1950), in: *Béla Bartók. Weg und Werk. Schriften und Briefe* (ed. Bence Szabolcsi), Kassel/Munich 1972, 83-92, p. 89. Quotation credit to Boosey and Hawkes in: *Zoltán Kodály: Bartók Remembered.* ed. Malcolm Gillies. Faber & Faber, 219.

[3] Béla Bartók: *Autobiography* (1921), in: Suchoff, Benjamin, ed. *Béla Bartók's Essays*, New York 1976, p. 409.

[4] Ibid., 410.

[5] Bartók: *The Influence of Peasant Music on Modern Music*, in: *Essays* (Note 3), 344.

[6] Ibid., 344.

[7] Bartók: *Ungarische Volksmusik und neue ungarische Musik* (1928), ibid., 158-163, p. 163. English: *The Folk Songs of Hungary*, idem, 331-339. Speech given in Portland, Oregon, 17 January 1928.

[8] On this see Constantin Floros: *Alban Berg. Musik als Autobiographie*, 81 f.

[9] Arnold Schönberg: *Ausgewählte Briefe*, 285 (Original in English).

[10] I am grateful to the Arnold Schoenberg Center in Vienna, who very kindly forwarded to me photocopies of several hitherto unpublished texts by Schoenberg.

[11] *Arnold-Schönberg-Gesamtausgabe. Abteilung V: Chorwerke, Reihe B, Vol. 18, 2. Kritischer Bericht zu Band 18A, Teil 2, Skizzen* (ed. Tadeusz Okuljar and Dorothee Schübel, Mainz/Vienna 1996, Documents, p. XXXVf.

[12] Richard Wagner: *Über das Dichten und Komponieren* (1879), in: *Sämtliche Schriften und Dichtungen*, Vol. X, 148. On this see Constantin Floros: *Brahms und Bruckner. Studien zur musikalischen Exegetik*, Wiesbaden 1980, 32.

[13] Schönberg: Zum Vorwort der Drei Satiren, in: *Dokumente* (see note 11), p. XXXVII.

[14] Ibid.

[15] Schönberg: *Why not Great American Music?* (Enddatum: 28. VI. 34), in: Gesammelte Schriften, Vol. 1, 304-308, especially p. 304 f.; S & I, 176f.

[16] Schönberg: *Volksmusik und Kunstmusik*. Unpublished manuscript, p. 2.

[17] *Documents* (see note 11), p. XXXVI.

[18] Suchoff, 345.

[19] Ibid., 347.

[20] Schönberg: *Symphonien aus Volksliedern*, in: Gesammelte Schriften, Vol. 1, 134-139, p. 137; S & I,165.

[21] Schönberg: *Neue Musik, veraltete Musik, Stil und Gedanke*, in: Gesammelte Schriften, Vol. 1, 24-34, p. 34: Style and Idea, 124.

[22] Rufer: *Das Werk Arnold Schönbergs*, 78.

[23] See the review by Lukas Haselböck, in: *Arnold Schönberg. Interpretationen seiner Werke* (ed. Gerold W. Gruber), 2 vols., Laaber 2002, Vol. II, 172-180.

[24] Matthias Henke: *Arnold Schönberg*, Munich 2001, 55.

[25] Dika Newlin: *Bruckner. Mahler. Schönberg*, Vienna 1954, 240f.

[26] Hartmut Krones, in: *Arnold Schönberg - Interpretationen*, Vol. I, 429- 446, especially p. 445.

**Nikos Skalkottas – A Schoenberg Pupil in Berlin**

[1] The quotation from Hans Keller at the opening of the chapter comes from *»Was immer aus seiner Feder kam, ist gold«. Ein Schönberg-Schüler in Berlin*, in: Neue Zeitschrift für Musik 162, May/Juni 2001, 58-61. Judit Alsmeier (Essen), Kostis Demertzis (Athen), Nina-Maria Jacklitsch (Vienna), Evangelia Mantzourani (London) und John Thornley (London) have all written disssertations on Skalkottas. An international convention on Skalkottas attended by researrches from various European countries was held in the Berlin Konzerthaus on 2./3. December 2000.

[2] List of Works by John Thornley: *Nikos Skalkottas*, in: The New Grove Dictionary of Music and Musicians, 2$^{nd}$ ed. London 2001, Vol. 23, 464-469.

[3] Johann G. Papaioannou: *Nikos Skalkottas*, in: MGG 1$^{st}$ ed., Vol. 12 (1965), Col. 744-747, especially Col. 745.

[4] Quoted from Charis Brontos: *For Nikos Skalkottas* (greek), Athens 1999, 100.

[5] Nikos Christodoulou recorded a number of works by Skalkottas with both the Malmö Symphony Orchestra and Iceland Symphony Orchestra for the Label BIS betwen 1997 and 1999: the Violin Conzerto (1938), Largo sinfonico and Seven Greek Dances for

strings (BIS-CD- 904), the fairy drama *May Spell* (1944/49), Double bass Concerto (1942) and Three Greeek Dances (1936) (BIS-CD-954) and the ballet suite *The Maiden and Death* (1938), the First Piano Concerto (1931) und the *Ouvertüre Concertante* (1944/45) (BIS-CD-1014). A discography is given in Hartmut Lück: *Einsamer Grieche. Immer noch ein Geheimtip: Nikos Skalkottas*, in: Neue Zürcher Zeitung of 7. July 1999, 35.

[6] Arnold Schönberg: *Symphonien aus Volksliedern*, in: Gesammelte Schriften, Vol. 1, 134-139; S & I, 161-166.

[7] David Drew: *Kurt Weill. A Handbook*, London/Boston 1987, 56.

[8] Kostis Demertzis in the booklet accompanying the disc of works by Skalkottas for violine and piano performed by Georgios Demertzis and Maria Asteriadou (BIS- CD-1024), 1999, 18.

[9] Ibid.

[10] Ferruccio Busoni: *Von der Einheit der Musik. Verstreute Aufzeichnungen*, Berlin 1922, 275-279.

[11] Philipp Jarnach: *Das Stilproblem der neuen Klassizität im Werke Busonis*, in: Musikblätter des Anbruch 3, January 1921, 6-19.

[12] Skalkottas shared with Busoni a passion for sonatine form. He composed no fewer than four sonatinas for violin and piano.

[13] Ten of these 32 Piano Pieces were published by Universal Edition in 1965 (U.E. 12958 LW).

[14] Weill's 1925 Concerto for Violin and Wind Orchestra, op. 12, rapidly became well known, and Skalkottas' Wind Concerto, composed in 1929 and first performed in Berlin in 1930 (but now sadly lost) was conceivably inspired by Weill's work.

[15] Peter Gradenwitz: *Arnold Schönberg und seine Meisterschüler. Berlin 1925- 1933*, Vienna 1998, 169-183.

[16] Schönberg: *Nationale Musik* (1931), in: Gesammelte Schriften, Vol. 1, 250-255, p. 253; Style & Idea, 169-174, p. 174.

[17] Cf. the excellent recordings of works for brass and piano with Heinz Holliger (Oboe), Hakan Hardenberger (Trompete), Klaus Thunemann (Fagott) and Bruno Canino (Piano). Philips 442 795-2 (1 CD).

[18] Schönberg: *Prager Rede auf Gustav Mahler* (1912), in: Gesammelte Schriften, Vol. 1, 11; S & I, 454.

**Beyond Schoenberg and Debussy – Nikos Skalkottas's 32 Piano Pieces**

[1] The Passacaglia from the 32 Piano Pieces was published by Universal Edition (London) in 1955 (U.E. 12370 L. W.) It was followed in 1965 by the 10 Piano Pieces, also published by Universal Edition U. E. 12958 L. W. Günther Schüller was responsible for the publication of the remaining pieces in three volumes under the title *Nikos Skalkottas.Piano Pieces*, Margun Music, Inc. in 1992.- Nikolaos Samaltanos has made an excellent recording of the 32 Piano Pieces (BIS CD- 1133/1134).

[2] Kostis Demertzis: *Nikolaos Skalkottas as composer of solo piano music* (greek), Chalkis 1991.

[3] Faksimile in the Universal Edition publication of the 10 Piano pieces.

[4] Theodor W. Adorno: *Alban Berg*, in: Klangfiguren. Musikalische Schriften I, Frankfurt am Main 1959, 125.

[5] Constantin Floros: *György Ligeti. Jenseits von Avantgarde und Postmoderne*, Vienna 1996, 172-196.

**A Conversation with Luigi Nono**

[1] Nono expressly added the words *per orchestra a microintervalli* to the title of the piece. See Rainer Zillhardt: *Überlegungen zu den äußeren und inneren Bedingungen mikrotonaler Strukturen anhand von Luigi Nonos Orchesterstück* A Carlo Scarpa ... („Reflexions on the external and internal requirements of microtonal structures based on Luigi Nono's orchestral piece *A Carlo Scarpa*...), in: Musik-Konzepte Sonderband. Musik der anderen Tradition. Mikrotonale Tonwelten, Munich February 2003, 141-166.

[2] Constantin Floros: *Das esoterische Programm der Lyrischen Suite von Alban Berg. Eine semantische Analyse*, in: Alban Berg. Kammermusik I (Musik-Konzepte 4), Munich 1978, 5-48.

[3] Christian Martin Schmidt: *Schönbergs »very definite - but private« Programm zum Streichquartett Opus 7*, in: Rudolf Stephan and Sigrid Wiesmann (Eds.): Bericht über den 2. Kongreß der Internationalen Schönberg-Gesellschaft »Die Wiener Schule in der Musikgeschichte des 20. Jahrhunderts«, Vienna 1986, 230-234.

[4] Floros: *Gustav Mahler*, 3 vols., 1. ed. Wiesbaden 1977; 2. ed. 1987

[5] Heinz-Klaus Metzger: *Wendepunkt Quartett?*, in: Musik-Konzepte 20. Luigi Nono, July 1981, 93-112. Außerdem: Hermann Spree: *»Fragmente-Stille, An Diotima«. Ein analytischer Versuch zu Nonos Streichquartett*, Saarbrücken 1992.

[6] Quoted from Ellen Kohlhaas: *»Römerbad - Musiktage Badenweiler: Schumann oder der Stachel in der Versöhnlichkeit*, in: Frankfurter Allgemeine Zeitung, 3. December 1980, 27.

[7] The allusion is to the sixth movement of *Il canto sospeso* (1955/56), which includes the words, *»Com'è duro dire addio per sempre alla vita cosi bella!«* („How hard it is to say farewell for ever to so beautiful a life!").

## Olivier Messiaen's "Theological Music"

[1] Leonardo Pinzauti: *Gespräch mit Olivier Messiaen*, in: Melos 5 (1972), 270ff.

[2] Claude Rostand: *Olivier Messiaen*, Paris 1956.

[3] The most comprehensive groundwork on Messiaen's »theological music« has been done by Aloyse Michaely: *Die Musik Olivier Messiaens. Untersuchungen zum Gesamtschaffen* (Hamburger Beiträge zur Musikwissenschaft. Sonderband), Hamburg 1987. Cf. Aloyse Michaely: *L'Abime. Das Bild des Abgrunds bei Olivier Messiaen*, in: Musik-Konzepte Issue 28. *Olivier Messiaen*, November 1982, 7-55. See also Siglind Bruhn (Ed.): *Messiaen's Language of Mystical Love*, New York/London 1998.

[4] Ingrid Hohlfeld-Ufer: *Die musikalische Sprache Olivier Messiaens*, Duisburg 1978, 84.

[5] Mention should be made in this context of his 1949 piano piece *Mode de valeurs et d'intensités*.

[6] Aloyse Michaely: *Verbum Caro. Die Darstellung des Mysteriums der Inkarnation in Olivier Messiaens Vingt Regards sur l'Enfant-Jesus*, in : Hamburger Jahrbuch für Musikwissenschaft, Vol. 6, Laaber 1983, 225-345.

[7] Almut Rößler: *Beiträge zur geistigen Welt Olivier Messiaens Mit Original-Texten des Komponisten*, Duisburg 1984, 10. Translation Almut Rößler. A facsimile of the composer's original text can ber found ibid. pp. 8/9.

## Pierre Boulez's Masterpiece *Le marteau sans maitre*

[1] Pierre Boulez: *Musikdenken heute 1*, in: Darmstädter Beiträge zur Neuen Musik, Vol. V, Mainz 1963.

[2] Boulez: *Werkstatt-Texte*, 139. See also p. 111ff

[3] *Orientations*, 341.

[4] Ibid., 339.

[5] Boulez: *Dichtung - Mittelpunkt und Ferne - Musik*, in: Werkstatt-Texte, 145-163.

[6] Ibid., 139.

[7] *Orientations*, 342.

[8] André Breton: *Les vases communicants*, Paris 1932, 129. For more on René Char's surrealist association technique see the extensive discussion of the poetry in Theo Hirsbrunner: *Pierre Boulez und sein Werk*, Laaber 1985, 86-98.

[9] Cf. Manfred Stahnke: *Struktur und Ästhetik bei Boulez*, Hamburg 1979 (Hamburger Beiträge zur Musikwissenschaft; Vol. 21), 128.

**Fascinated by the Music of Ligeti**

[1] On this, see *„Träumen Sie in Farbe?" György Ligeti im Gespräch mit Eckhard Roelcke*, Vienna 2003, 19.

[2] Constantin Floros: *György Ligeti* (1996), 70, 165.

**Ligeti's *Hölderlin-Phantasien*. A Letter from the Composer**

[1] Constantin Floros: *György Ligeti. Prinzipielles über sein Schaffen*, in: Musik und Bildung 10 (1978), 484-488.

[2] Nutida Musik 24 (1980/81), Issue 3, 3-7.

[3] Ligeti's *Atmosphères* was performed by the Philharmonisches Staatsorchester Hamburg under Aldo Ceccato in the Hamburg Musikhalle on 29/30 and 31 may 1983. Ligeti is here referring to the letter I wrote to mark the composer's 60th birthday, which appeared in the concert programme.auf.

[4] Prof. Rauhe: Professor Hermann Rauhe, President emeritus of the High School for Music in Hamburg, where Ligeti was Professor of Composition from 1973 to 1989.

[5] From the time of Pierre Bertaux' book *Hölderlin und die Französische Revolution* (2nd edition, Frankfurt am Main 1970) at least, Friedrich Hölderlin has seen something of a revival in Germany.

[6] The reference is to the *Magyar Etüdök* (Hungarian Studies) after poems by Sándor Weöres for 16-part a cappella choir.

[7] My Commentary about the *Hölderlin-Phantasien* was published in Nutida Musik 1983/84 No. 1, 14-16 in Schwedish and p. 18-20 in English. The german version is published for the first time in Neue Zeitschrift für Musik 146 (1985), Issue 2, 18-20.

**Iridescent Sound**

[1] Heinrich Husmann: *Einführung in die Musikwissenschaft*, Heidelberg 1958, 149f.

[2] For basis, see my book *György Ligeti. Jenseits von Avantgarde und Postmoderne*.

[3] Manfred Stahnke: *Über den Begriff »Mikrotonalität«, abgeleitet aus dem Werk György Ligetis*, in: Gütersloh '90. Hommage a György Ligeti, 29-33, p. 30.

[4] György Ligeti about the concert for violin. Conversation with Louise Duchesneau (Hamburg, October 1992), published in: *Gütersloh 94: Musikfest für György Ligeti*, 23-25.

[5] Gottfried Michael Koenig: *Ligeti und die elektronische Musik*, in: *György Ligeti. Personalstil - Avantgardismus - Popularität*, ed. Otto Kolleritsch (Studien zur Wertungsforschung; Vol. 19), Vienna-Graz 1988, 11-26.

[6] Some extracts were published in Erkki Salmenhaara: *Das musikalische Material und seine Behandlung in den Werken »Apparitions«, »Atmospheres«, »Aventures« und »Requiem« von György Ligeti* (Forschungsbeiträge zur Musikwissenschaft, Vol. 19), Regensburg 1969, 67f.

[7] Ove Nordwall: *György Ligeti. Eine Monographie*, Mainz 1971, 140.

[8] The marking *Dans la sonorité du debut* appears at the end of the piece.

[9] Mauricio Kagel: *Ton-Cluster, Anschläge, Übergänge*, in: Die Reihe 5 (1959), 23-37, p. 28.

[10] Nordwall: *György Ligeti*, 117.

[11] Ligeti himself differentiates between these three types in his notation in *Atmosphères*, in highly illuminating notes in Hungarian that Salmenhaara (see note 6), 177-179, published in German.

[12] Ligeti: *Musik und Technik. Einige Erfahrungen und subjektive Betrachtungen*, in: Günther Batel, Günter Kleinen und Dieter Salbert (Eds.); Computermusik. Theoretische Grundlagen. Kompositionsgeschichtliche Zusammenhänge. Musiklernprogramme, Laaber 1987, 9-35, p. 24.

[13] Jan Kasem-Bek: *Informationstheorie und Analyse musikalischer Werke*, in: Archiv für Musikwissenschaft, 35 (1978), 62-75, p. 72.

[14] Andreas E. Beurmann, Albrecht Schneider: *Struktur, Klang, Dynamik. Akustische Untersuchungen an Ligetis »Atmosphères«*, in: Hamburger Jahrbuch für Musikwissenschaft, Vol. 11 (1991), 311-334, p. 317, Diagram p. 318.

[15] Circled letters = Ligeti's markings; arabic numerals = sound fields according to Ligeti and Salmenhaara; roman numerals = structural markings from Sigrid Schneider: *Zwischen Statik und Dynamik. Zur formalen Analyse von Ligeti's »Atmosphères« (betweem Statics*

and Dynamism. Towards a formal analysis of Ligeti's *Atmosphères*), in: Musik und Bildung, 7 (1975), 506-510. The diagram is a depiction of *Atmosphères* by the Sinfonie-Orchester des Südwestfunks under Ernest Bour made in May 1966

16 Ernst Thomas: *Klang gegen Struktur? Problematische Aspekte auf den Musiktagen 1961*, in: Neue Zeitschrift für Musik, 122 (1961), 524f.

17 Walter Benjamin: *Das Kunstwerk im Zeitalter seiner technischen Reproduzierbarkeit*. Drei Studien zur Kunstsoziologie (edition suhrkamp 28), Frankfurt am Main 1966, 7-44, p. 13 and 15.

18 Theodor W. Adorno: *Ästhetische Theorie* (Gesammelte Schriften; Band 7), Frankfurt am Main 1970, 57 and 72-74.

19 Werner Klüppelholz in Conservation with György Ligeti, in: *Was ist musikalische Bildung?* (Musikalische Zeitfragen 14), Kassel/Basel/London 1984, 66-75, p. 70.

**"Folklore in Serious Music is a Lie" – Ligeti's Relationship with Béla Bartók**

1 György Ligeti: *Streichquartette und -duette*, in: György-Ligeti-Edition 1, 14.

2 Ove Nordwall: *György Ligeti. Eine Monographie*, Mainz 1971, 188-200.

3 *»Träumen Sie in Farbe?« György Ligeti im Gespräch mit Eckhard Roelcke*, Vienna 2003, 197.

4 See Constantin Floros: *György Ligeti* (1996), 82f.

5 Ibid., S. 83-85.

6 Cf.. Colin Mason: *Bartóks Streichquartette. Gestalt und Wandel*, in: Musik der Zeit. Eine Schriftenreihe zur zeitgenössischen Musik, Issue 3: Béla Bartók, Bonn 1953, 39-44.

7 See Floros: *György Ligeti*, 86-88.

8 Nordwall: *György Ligeti*, 141.

9 Commentary from the booklet accompanying the Ligeti cassette WER 60 095, p. 15f. The following quotes also come from this booklet.

10 For basics, see Floros: *György Ligeti*, 156-160.

11 Ibid., 179f. (with Facsimile).

12 Ibid., 165.

13 *"Träumen Sie in Farbe?"*, 170f.

[14] Denys Bouliane: *Stilisierte Emotion. György Ligeti im Gespräch*, in: Musik- Texte 28/29 (März 1989), 52-62, p. 55.

[15] *"Träumen Sie in Farbe?"*, 201.

## Multicultural Phenomena in the New Music

[1] Wolfgang Welsch: *Transkulturalität. Lebensformen nach der Auflösung der Kulturen*, in: Information Philosophie (May 1992), 5-20, p. 20.

[2] Charles Taylor: *Multiculturalism and »The Politics of Recognition«*, Princeton 1992, 63

[3] Naixiong Liao: *Im Prozeß des Ineinanderfließens. Nationale Musiktradition und Weltmusik*, in: Detlof Gojowy: *Quo vadis musica?* Proceedings of the Symposium of the Alexander von Humboldt-Foundation Bonn-Bad Godesberg 1988, Kassel 1990, 18-24.

[4] Harry Halbreich: *Olivier Messiaen*, Paris 1980, 60-66.

[5] Quoted from Klaus Schweizer: *Olivier Messiaen, Turangalila-Symphonie* (Meisterwerke der Musik, no. 32), Munich 1982, 61.

## "A Music of the Whole Earth, All Countries and Races": Karlheinz Stockhausen's Utopia of World Music

[1] Karlheinz Stockhausen: *Interview über Telemusik*, in: Texte zur Musik, 1963- 1970, Vol. 3, Cologne 1971, 79-84, p. 81.

[2] Georg Capellen: *Ein neuer exotischer Musikstil*, Stuttgart n. d. [1906], 46. For basics, see Peter Revers: *Das Fremde und das Vertraute. Studien zur musiktheoretischen und musikdramatischen Ostasienrezeption* (Beihefte zum Archiv für Musikwissenschaft, vol. XLI). Stuttgart 1997, 32-35.

[3] Stockhausen: *Telemusik* (see note 6), 75-77, p. 75.

[4] Ibid., 80.

[5] Stockhausen: *Hymnen mit Orchester* (1969), in: Texte zur Musik 1970- 1977, Vol. 4, Cologne 1978, 78f.

[6] Stockhausen: *Interview with Peter Bockelmann in Deutschlandfunk*, 2. July 1968, In: Texte III, 305-319, p. 308.

[7] Stockhausen: *Texte* IV, 468-476. On Stockhausen's Conception of Weltmusik see Michael Kurtz: *Stockhausen. Eine Biographie*, Kassel/Basel 1988, 189-212; Christoph von Blumröder: *Die Grundlegung der Musik Karlheinz Stockhausens* (Beihefte zum Archiv für Musikwissenschaft, vol. XXXII), Stuttgart 1993, 158 / n. 10.

[8] Luise Rinser/Isang Yun: *Der verwundete Drache. Dialog über Leben und Werk des Komponisten*, Frankfurt am Main 1977, 35.

[9] Ibid., 75.

[10] Ibid., 93f.

[11] Ibid., 111.

[12] Josef Häusler: *Musik im 20. Jahrhundert. Von Schönberg zu Penderecki*, Bremen 1969, 433.

[13] Rinser/Yun: *Der verwundete Drache*, 101.

[14] Ibid., 94.

[15] Hartmut Lück: *Rituelle Musik als Wendepunkt. Versuch über »Réak«* (1966), in: Hanns-Werner Heister/Walter-Wolfgang Sparrer (Eds): Der Komponist Isang Yun (edition text + kritik), Munich 1987, 152-157.

[16] Rinser/Yun: *Der verwundete Drache* (see n. 13), 100.

[17] Ibid., 74.

[18] Constantin Floros: *György Ligeti* (1996), 64-66.

[19] On this, see István Balázs: *Fragmente über die Kunst György Kurtágs*, in: Friedrich Spangemacher (Ed.): György Kurtág (Musik der Zeit. Dokumentationen und Studien 5), Bonn 1986, 65-87, p. 74.

[20] See Hartmut Lück: *»Dezembers Gluten, Sommers Hagelschläge ...«. Zur künstlerischen Physiognomie von Kurtág*, in: Spangemacher: György Kurtag (see note 24), 28-52, pp. 35, 37.

[21] Claudia Stahl: *Botschaften in Fragmenten. Die großen Vokalzyklen von György Kurtág*, Saarbrücken 1998, 74-96.

[22] Béla Bartók: *Harvard Lectures* IV, in: Benjamin Suchoff (Ed.): Béla Bartók Essays, London 1976, 383ff.

**The Philosophy of Time and Pluralistic Thought of Bernd Alois Zimmermann**

[1] Bernd Alois Zimmermann: *Musiker von heute* (1961), in: Intervall und Zeit. Aufsätze und Schriften zum Werk, ed. Christof Bitter, Mainz 1974, 24.

[2] Cf. Wulf Konold: *Bernd Alois Zimmermann. Der Komponist und sein Werk*, Cologne 1986, 28-35.

[3] *Intervall und Zeit*, 11-14.

[4] Ibid., 12.

[5] Zimmermann: *Vom Handwerk des Komponisten* (1968), in: Intervall und Zeit, 31-37.

[6] Zimmermann: *Zukunft der Oper* (1965), in: Intervall und Zeit, 38-46, p. 41.

[7] Konold: *Bernd Alois Zimmermann*, 198.

[8] See Aloyse Michaely: *Toccata - Ciacona - Nocturno. Zu Bernd Alois Zimmermanns Oper Die Soldaten*, in: Hamburger Jahrbuch für Musikwissenschaft, vol. 10 (Musiktheater im 20. Jahrhundert), Laaber 1988, 127-204, pp. 146ff.

[9] *Intervall und Zeit*, 106f.

[10] Quoted from Konold: *Bernd Alois Zimmermann*, 95.

[11] Ibid., 99.

[12] Jörn Peter Hiekel: *Bernd Alois Zimmermanns Requiem für einen jungen Dichter* (Beihefte zum Archiv für Musikwissenschaft, vol. XXXVI), Stuttgart 1995.

[13] *Intervall und Zeit*, 116.

[14] Ibid.

**Alfred Schnittke and Polystylism**

[1] List of Works and Discography in: Alfred Schnittke: *Über das Leben und die Musik. Gespräche mit Alexander Iwaschkin*, Munich/Düsseldorf 1998, 345-379.

[2] Alfred Schnittke: *Foreward to A Paganini*, 1983.

[3] Alfred Schnittke: *Polystilistische Tendenzen in der modernen Musik*, in: Musik-Texte 30, July/August 1989, 29f. – See Lutz Lesle: *Komponieren in Schichten. Begegnung mit Alfred Schnittke*, in: Zeitschrift für Musik 148, July/August 1987, 29-32.

[4] Bernd Alois Zimmermann: *Intervall und Zeit*, Mainz 1974, 34.

[5] Quoted from Tamara Burde: *Zum Leben und Schaffen des Komponisten Alfred Schnittke* (Musikgeschichtliche Studien, Vol. 1), Gehann-Musik-Verlag, Kludenbach 1993, 66.

[6] Ibid.

[7] Quoted from Tamara Burde: *Zum Leben und Schaffen*, 63.

**And Always for a Better World – Approaches to Hans Werner Henze**

[1] Ingeborg Bachmann: *Musik und Dichtung,* in: Musica viva, ed. K. H. Ruppel, Munich 1959, 163-166, p. 165.

[2] Hans Werner Henze: *Reiselieder mit böhmischen Quinten. Autobiographische Mitteilungen 1926-1995,* Frankfurt am Main 1996, 167.

[3] Ibid., 182f.

[4] Ibid., 201.

[5] Hans Werner Henze: *Musik und Politik. Schriften und Gespräche 1955-1984.* Foreword Jens Brockmeier, Munich 1984, 30.

[6] Ibid., 33.

[7] Ibid.

[8] Theodor W. Adorno: *Philosophie der Neuen Musik,* Frankfurt am Main 1958, 112ff.

[9] Henze: *Musik und Politik* (1984), 284f.

[10] For basics, see Peter Petersen: *Tanz-, Jazz- und Marschidiome im Musiktheater Hans Werner Henzes. Zur Konkretisierung des Stilbegriffs »musica impura«,* in: Musiktheorie 10, 1995, 73-86.

[11] See Peter Petersen, Hanns-Werner Heister und Hartmut Lück (Eds.): *»Stimmen« für Hans Werner Henze. Die 22 Lieder aus »Voices«,* Mainz 1966.

[12] Cf. Peter Petersen: *Hans Werner Henze. Ein politischer Musiker. Zwölf Vorlesungen,* Hamburg 1988.

[13] Jean-Paul Sartre: *Qu'est-ce que la litterature?,* Paris 1948; german edition: *Was ist Literatur?,* ed. Traugott König, Reinbek bei Hamburg 1981, 33 and 53.

[14] Ibid., 52.

[15] Henze: *Musik und Politik,* 314.

[16] Andrew McCredie: *Karl Amadeus Hartmann. Sein Leben und Werk,* Wilhelmshaven 1980, Illustrations p. XI, Illustration 11.

[17] For Hartmann's political engagement and his conception of art, see Constantin Floros: *Humanism, Love and Music,* Peter Lang, Frankfurt am Main/New York 2012, 65-72.

[18] Henze: *Musik und Politik,* 332-343.

[19] Ibid., S 336.

[20] Ibid., 30-32.

[21] »Eine Existenz wie die meine«. Speech given by Hans Werner Henze in Gütersloh on 16 September 1986 in, in: Journal. Theater in Ostwestfalen, Gütersloh, December 1986, 19-21.

[22] Henze: *Musik und Politik*, 247.

[23] Ibid., 254.

[24] Ibid., 267.

[25] Henze: *Reiselieder mit böhmischen Quinten*, 47.

[26] Ibid., 51.

[27] Henze: *Musik und Politik*, 40f.

[28] Henze: *Reiselieder mit böhmischen Quinten*, 20.

[29] *All Knowing Music. A Dialogue on Opera. Hans Werner Henze and Ian Strasfogel*, in: Dieter Rexroth (Ed.): Der Komponist Hans Werner Henze, Mainz 1986, 137-142, p. 140.

[30] For the speech-like character of Henze's music, see Constantin Floros: *Musik als Botschaft*, Wiesbaden 1989, 165-170.

[31] Henze: *Musik und Politik*, 246.

[32] Ibid., 245.

[33] Ibid., 368f. – Cf. p. 316.

[34] Thomas Mann: *Richard Wagner und der 'Ring des Nibelungen'* (1937), in: Ausgewählte Essays in drei Bänden, vol. 3 (Fischer Taschenbuch Verlag no. 1908), Frankfurt am Main 1978, 129.

[35] Hans Werner Henze: *Über die Entstehung der Musik zu Edward Bonds Orpheus. Aus einem Brief an Josef Rufer*, in: Generalintendanz der Württembergischen Staatstheater Stuttgart (Ed.): Orpheus, Materialien, Stuttgart 1979, 32-42, pp. 37ff.

[36] *All Knowing Music* (see note 29), 139.

[37] Cf. Caroline Mattenklott: *Figuren des Imaginären. Zu Hans Werner Henzes »Le miracle de la rose«*, Hamburg 1996.

[38] Henze: *Musik und Politik*, 246.

[39] Richard Wagner: *Oper und Drama*, in: Sämtliche Schriften und Dichtungen, Vol. III, 316.

[40] *All Knowing Music*, 140f.

[41] Ibid., 139.

[42] For basics, see my book *Musik als Botschaft* (note 30), 114-133.

[43] E. T. A Hoffmann: *Schriften zur Musik. Nachlese*, Winkler-Verlag Munich 1963, 36.

[44] Henze: *Musik und Politik*, 142.

[45] Ibid., 135.

[46] Peter Petersen: *Hans Werner Henze. Werke der Jahre 1984*-1993, Mainz 1995, 138.

**So-called Postmodernism**

[1] Hermann Danuser: *Die Postmodernität des John Cage. Der experimentelle Künstler in der Sicht Jean-Francois Lyotards*, in: Wiederaneignung und Neubestimmung. Der Fall »Postmoderne« in der Musik (Studien zur Wertungsforschung, Vol. 26), Vienna/Graz 1993, 142-159.

[2] Quoted from Ulli Götte: *Minimal Music. Geschichte - Ästhetik - Umfeld* (Taschenbücher zur Musikwissenschaft 138), Wilhelmshaven 2000, 223f.

[3] Wolfgang Gratzer: *Komponistenkommentare. Beiträge zu einer Geschichte der Eigeninterpretation,* Vienna/Cologne/Weimar 2003, 282.

[4] Peter Michael Hamel: *Durch Musik zum Selbst. Wie man Musik neu erleben und erfahren kann*, Munich 1980, 158.

[5] Götte: *Minimal Music*, 19.

[6] From the concert program for the Meta-Musik-Festival, Berlin 1974. Quoted from Hamel: *Durch Musik zum Selbst*, 160.

[7] Götte: *Minimal Music*, 16.

[8] Peter Oswald: Review in Neue Zeitschrift für Musik 2/1986, 57. Quoted from Götte: *Minimal Music*, 230/n. 24.

[9] Constantin Floros: *György Ligeti* (1996), 130f.

[10] Wolfram Schwinger: *Krzysztof Penderecki. Begegnungen, Lebensdaten, Werkkommentare*, Mainz 1994, 230-236.

[11] Quoted from Wolfgang Sandner, booklet accompagnying the EMC CD New Series 1275 (1984).

[12] Michael Kurtz: *Sofia Gubaidulina. Eine Biographie*, Stuttgart 2001.

[13] Floros: *György Ligeti*, 230.

[14] Peter Petersen: Article *Hans Werner Henze*, in: Die Musik in Geschichte und Gegenwart, 2nd ed., Personenteil, Vol. 8, Col. 1345-1349.

[15] Hans Werner Henze: *Übers Opernschreiben, ein Interview mit Barbara Zuberg*, in: Die Deutsche Bühne, October 1993, 21.

[16] Hans Zender in his commentary on the 25-year-old interview with Boulez in *Der Spiegel*, in: Neue Zeitschrift für Musik, July 1993, 28.

[17] For basics, see Floros: *Gustav Mahler. Visionary and Despot*, Frankfurt am Main/New York 2012, 189 f.

[18] Peter Ruzicka: *Die eigene Art ist des Menschen Dämon. Gedanken zur heutigen Mahler-Rezeption*, in: Das Orchester, December 2004, 30-35.

[19] Axel Fuhrmann: *Geschichte, Geschichten. Luciano Berio über das Verhältnis von Musik und Text*, in: Neue Zeitschrift für Musik, 152. Jg. May 1991, 31.

[20] Theodor W. Adorno: *Philosophie der Neuen Musik* (1958), S. 36-41.

[21] Cf. Reinhard Schulz: *Der Überdruß am Fortschritt. Die Materialdiskussion und die Postmoderne*, in: *Wiederaneignung und Neubestimmung. Der Fall »Postmoderne« in der Musik* (see note. 1), 160-175.

[22] Roland Barthes: *The death of the author*, in: Image, Music, Text, Essays, ed. Stephen Heath, New York 1977, 148.

[23] Wolfgang Gratzer: *Komponistenkommentare* (2003), 276-308.

[24] Claus-Steffen Mahnkopf describes Postmodernism as the „false compromise" of the ‚new' music". See his *Kritik der neuen Musik. Entwurf einer Musik des 21. Jahrhunderts* (Critique of the new music. Outline of a 21th-century music), Kassel 1998, 57-80.

"No Artist Works at a Distance from Humanity" – In Praise of Wolfgang Rihm

Eulogy given at the award ceremony of the Bach Prize of the Free and Hanseatic City of Hamburg on 21 September 2000

[1] Stefan Zweig: *Das Geheimnis des künstlerischen Schaffens*, Fischer Taschenbuch Verlag, Frankfurt am Main 1981, 244.

[2] Wolfgang Rihm: *ausgesprochen. Schriften und Gespräche*, ed. Ulrich Mosch (Veröffentlichungen der Paul Sacher Stiftung Vol. 6, 1 und 6, 2), 2 vols., Amadeus Verlag, Winterthur/Schweiz 1997, Vol. I, 48.

[3] Ibid., Vol. I, 120.

[4] Ibid., Vol. II, 79.

[5] Ibid., Vol. I, 143.

[6] Ibid., Vol. II, 287.

[7] Ivanka Stoianova: *Rihm und Artaud: das Musiktheater der Grausamkeit*, in: Musik-Konzepte. Neue Folge. Sonderband. Wolfgang Rihm, XII/2004, 135-151.

[8] Rihm: *ausgesprochen,* Vol. I, 390-396.

[9] Booklet accompagnying the Kairos CD 001207 (1999/2000)

[10] Rihm: *ausgesprochen,* Vol. I, 292.

## Afterword

[1] Luigi Nono: *Über Anton Webern* (1953), in: Heinz-Klaus Metzger and Rainer Riehn (Eds..): Darmstadt-Dokumente I. Musik-Konzepte. Sonderband, Munich January 1999, 69.

[2] Hans Mayer: *Kulturkrise und neue Musik*, ibid., 17-25.

[3] Ibid., 23.

[4] Ibid., 24.

[5] See Claudia Bullerjahn and Hans-Joachim Erwe (Ed.): *Das Populäre in der Musik des 20. Jahrhunderts. Wesenszüge und Erscheinungsformen,* Hildesheim/Zurich/New York 2001.

[6] Theodor W. Adorno: *Über den Fetischcharakter in der Musik und die Regression des Hörens,* in: Adorno: Dissonanzen. Musik in der verwalteten Welt, 2nd ed. Göttingen 1958, 9-45.

[7] György Ligeti: *Die Zukunft der Neuen Musik*, in: Hanns-Werner Heister and Wolfgang Hochstein (Ed.): Kultur, Bildung, Politik. Festschrift für Hermann Rauhe zum 70. Geburtstag, Hamburg 2000, 60f.

[8] Busoni: *Entwurf einer neuen Ästhetik der Tonkunst*. With Annotations of Arnold Schoenberg, 51.

[9] Friedrich Nietzsche: *Werke*, 5 vols., ed. Karl Schlechta, Frankfurt am Main/Berlin/Vienna 1979, Vol. III, 609.

[10] See Constantin Floros: *Humanism, Love and Music*, Frankfurt am Main/New York 2012, 199-204.

# Selective Bibliography

## Overviews

Adorno, Theodor W.: *Philosophie der Neuen Musik*, Frankfurt am Main 1958; engl translation: *Philosophy of Modern Music*, New York 1974
--: Dissonanzen. *Musik in der verwalteten Welt*, 2nd ed., Göttingen 1956
--: *Einleitung in die Musiksoziologie. Zwölf theoretische Vorlesungen*, Frankfurt am Main 1962 and 1968
--: *Ästhetische Theorie* (Gesammelte Schriften, Vol. 7), ed. Gretel Adorno and Rolf Tiedemann; englisch edition: *Aesthetic Theory*. transl. Robert Hullot-Kentor, Continuum 2004
Austin, William M.: *Music in the Twentieth Century*, New York 1966
Borio, Gianmario/Danuser, Hermann (Eds.): *Im Zenit der Moderne. Die Internationalen Ferienkurse für Neue Musik Darmstadt 1946-1966*, 4 vols., Freiburg im Breisgau 1997
Brindle, Reginald Smith: *The New Music*, Oxford 1974
Danuser, Hermann: *Die Musik des 20. Jahrhunderts* (Neues Handbuch der Musikwissenschaft, Vol. 7), Laaber 1984
--: Article »*Neue Musik*«, in Die Musik in Geschichte und Gegenwart, 2nd ed., Sachteil, Vol. 7, Kassel 1997, Col. 75-122
Danuser, Hermann (Ed.): *Die klassizistische Moderne in der Musik des 20. Jahrhunderts. Internationales Symposion der Paul Sacher Stiftung Basel 1996*, Winterthur (Schweiz) 1997
Danuser, Hermann/Gerlach, Hannelore/Köchel, Jürgen (Eds.): *Sowjetische Musik im Lichte der Perestroika*, Laaber 1990
Dibelius, Ulrich: *Moderne Musik nach 1945*, Munich 1998
Eggebrecht, Hans Heinrich (Ed.): *Zur Terminologie der Musik des 20. Jahrhunderts*, Stuttgart 1974
Götte, Ulli: *Minimal Music. Geschichte - Ästhetik - Umfeld* (Taschenbücher zur Musikwissenschaft 138). Wilhelmshaven 2000
Golea, Antoine: *Musik unserer Zeit. Eine kritische Darstellung ihrer Hauptströmungen*, Munich 1955
Gratzer, Wolfgang: *Komponistenkommentare. Beiträge zu einer Geschichte der Eigeninterpretation*, Vienna/Cologne/Weimar 2003
Griffiths, Paul: *Modern Music and after*, Oxford University Press 1995
Hamel, Peter Michael: *Durch Musik zum Selbst. Wie man Musik neu erleben und erfahren kann*, Bern/Munich/Vienna 1976, New Edition: Deutscher Taschenbuch Verlag Munich, Bärenreiter Verlag Kassel n.d.
Gojowy, Detlef: *Studien zur Musik des XX. Jahrhunderts in Ost- und Ostmitteleuropa*, Berlin 1990
Häusler, Josef: *Musik im 20. Jahrhundert. Von Schönberg zu Penderecki*, Bremen 1969
--: *Spiegel der Neuen Musik. Donaueschingen. Chronik - Tendenzen - Werkbesprechungen*, Kassel/Stuttgart 1996
Heister, Hanns-Werner (Ed.): *Geschichte der Musik im 20. Jahrhundert: 1945-1975* (Handbuch der Musik im 20. Jahrhundert, Vol. 3), Laaber 2005
Hill, Peter (Ed.): *The Messiaen Companion*, London: Faber & Faber 1995
Kämper, Dietrich (Ed.): *Der musikalische Futurismus*, Laaber 1999
Ivashkin, Alexander: *Alfred Schnittke*, London: Phaidon 1996

Krones, Hartmut (Ed.): *Stimme und Wort in der Musik des 20. Jahrhunderts* (Vol. 1 der Sonderreihe »Symposien zu WIEN MODERN«), Vienna/Cologne/ Weimar 2001
--: *Struktur und Freiheit in der Musik des 20. Jahrhunderts. Zum Weiterwirken der Wiener Schule* (Vol. 2 der Sonderreihe »Symposien zu WIEN MODERN«), Vienna/Cologne/Weimar 2002
Leeuw, Ton de: *Die Sprache der Musik im 20. Jahrhundert. Entwicklung, Strukturen, Tendenzen,* Stuttgart 1995
Lesle, Lutz: *Neue Hörwelten in Skandinavien, Polen und den baltischen Ländern,* Munich 2010
Loos, Helmut/Keym, Stefan (Ed.): *Nationale Musik im 20. Jahrhundert. Kompositorische und soziokulturelle Aspekte der Musikgeschichte zwischen Ost- und Westeuropa.* Konferenzbericht Leipzig 2002, Leipzig 2004
Mahnkopf, Claus-Steffen: *Kritik der neuen Musik. Entwurf einer Musik des 21. Jahrhunderts. Eine Streitschrift,* Kassel 1998
Metzger, Heinz-Klaus: *Musik wozu,* ed. Rainer Riehn, Frankfurt am Main 1980
Mießgang, Thomas: *Semantics - Neue Musik im Gespräch,* Hofheim 1991
Motte-Haber, Helga de la (Ed..): *Klangkunst. Tönende Objekte und klingende Räume* (Handbuch der Musik im 20. Jahrhundert, Vol. 12), Laaber 1999
Potter, Keith: *Four Musical Minimalists,* Cambridge 2000
Prieberg, Fred K.: *Lexikon der Neuen Musik,* Munich 1958
--: *Musica ex machina. Über das Verhältnis von Musik und Technik,* Berlin/ Frankfurt/Vienna 1960
Ross, Alex: *The Rest is Noise. Listening to the Twentieth Century,* New York 2007
Rufer, Josef: *Die Komposition mit zwölf Tönen,* Berlin/Wunsiedel 1952
Salmen, Walter und Schubert, Giselher: *Verflechtungen im 20. Jahrhundert. Komponisten im Spannungsfeld elitär- populär,* Mainz 2005
Stahnke, Manfred (Ed.): *Mikrotöne und mehr. Auf György Ligetis Hamburger Pfaden,* Hamburg 2005
Stuckenschmidt, Hans Heinz: *Neue Musik (Zwischen den beiden Kriegen,* Vol. II), Berlin 1951
Stürzbecher, Ursula: *Werkstattgespräche mit Komponisten,* Munich 1973
Taruskin, Richard: *Oxford History of Western Music,* 6 vols., Oxford University Press 2005 Vol.: *The Early Twentieth Century*: Vol. 5: *The Late Twentieth Century Toop, Richard: György Ligeti, Phaidon: London 1999*
Von der Weid, Jean-Noel: *Die Musik des 20. Jahrhunderts. Von Claude Debussy bis Wolfgang Rihm,* Frankfurt an Main and Leipzig 2001
Whitall, Arnold: *Exploring Twentieth-Centuty Music. Tradition and Innovation, Cambridge 2003*

**Letters and Writings by Composers**

Bartók, Béla: *Weg und Werk: Schriften und Briefe,* ed. Bence Szabolcsi, Kassel/Munich 1972
*Béla Bartóks Essays.* Selected and Edited by B. Suchoff, London 1976
Berg, Alban: *Briefe an seine Frau,* Munich/Vienna 1965
-- : *Glaube, Hoffnung und Liebe. Schriften zur Musik,* ed. Frank Schneider (Reclams Universal-Bibliothek), Leipzig 1981
Boulez, Pierre: *Penser la musique aujourd'hui,* Editions Gonthier 1963.
-- : *Werkstatt-Texte,* aus dem Französischen übersetzt von Josef Häusler, Frankfurt am Main/Berlin 1972

--: *Anhaltspunkte. Essays*, Stuttgart/Zurich 1975
--: *Wille und Zufall. Gespräche mit Célestin Deliège und Hans Mayer*, Stuttgart/Zurich 1977
--: *Orientations. Collected Writings*, ed. Jean Jacques Nattiez, Cambridge 1986
--: *Leitlinien.Gedanken eines Komponisten*, Kassel 2000
Busoni, Ferruccio: *Von der Einheit der Musik. Verstreute Aufzeichnungen*, Berlin 1922
--: *Entwurf einer neuen Ästhetik der Tonkunst. Mit Anmerkungen von Arnold Schönberg und einem Nachwort von H. H. Stuckenschmidt*, Frankfurt am Main 1974
-- : *Maximen und Aphorismen*, ed. Martina Weindel, Wilhelmshaven 2004
Cage, John: Silence, London 1968
-- : *An Anthology*, ed. Richard Kostelanetz, New York 1970
*Conversing with Cage* ed. Richard Kostelanetz, New York 1988
Feldman, Morton: *Essays*, ed. Walter Zimmermann, Cologne 1985
Hartmann, Karl Amadeus: *Kleine Schriften*, ed. Ernst Thomas, Mainz 1965
Henze, Hans Werner: *Musik und Politik. Schriften und Gespräche 1955-1975*, ed. Jens Brockmeier, Munich 1976; *Music and Politics. Collected Writings 1953-81*, trans. P. Labanyi, London 1982
-- : *Reiselieder mit böhmischen Quinten. Autobiographische Mitteilungen 1926-1995*, Frankfurt am Main 1996; *Bohemian Fifths: An Autobiography*, trans. Stewart Spencer, London 1998
Hindemith, Paul: *Unterweisung im Tonsatz*, 2nd ed.. Mainz 1940
-- : *Komponist in seiner Welt*, Zurich 1959
-- : *Aufsätze - Vorträge - Reden*, ed. Giselher Schubert, Zurich und Mainz 1994
Krenek, Ernst: *Im Zweifelsfalle. Aufsätze zur Musik*, Vienna/Munich/Zurich 1984
--: *Im Atem der Zeit. Erinnerungen an die Moderne*, Hamburg 1998
Lachenmann, Helmut: *Musik als existentielle Erfahrung. Schriften 1966-1995*, ed. Josef Häusler, Wiesbaden 1996
Ligeti, György: *Gesammelte Schriften*, ed. Monika Lichtenfeld, 2 vols., Basel/Mainz 2007
--: *»Träumen Sie in Farbe?« György Ligeti im Gespräch mit Eckhard Roelcke*, Vienna 2003
--: György Ligeti/Neuweiler, Gerhard: *Motorische Intelligenz. Musik und Naturwissenschaft*, ed. Reinhart Meyer-Kalkus, Berlin 2007
Messiaen, Olivier: *Technique de mon langage musical*, 2 vols., Paris 1944
--: *Traité de rythme, de couleur et d'ornithologie* (1949-1992), 7 vols., Paris 1994-2002
Nono, Luigi: *Texte. Studien zu seiner Musik*, ed. Jürg Stenzl, Zurich 1975
--: *Dokumente - Materialien*, ed. Andreas Wagner, Saarbrücken 2003
Rihm, Wolfgang: *ausgesprochen. Schriften und Gespräche*, ed. Ulrich Mosch, 2 vols., Winterthur/Schweiz 1997
Russolo, Luigi: *The Art of Noises*. trans. Barclay Brown, New York 1986
Schnittke, Alfred: *Über das Leben und die Musik. Gespräche mit Alexander Iwaschkin*, Munich/Düsseldorf 1998
Schönberg, Arnold: *Harmonielehre*, Leipzig/Vienna 1911; english translation Roy E. Carter, Berkeley and Los Angeles 1978
--: *Texte*, Vienna/New York 1926
--: *Ausgewählte Briefe*, ed. Erwin Stein, Mainz 1958; english translation Eithne Wilkins and Ernst Kaiser, London 1964
--: *Stil und Gedanke. Aufsätze zur Musik*, ed. Ivan Vojtech (Gesammelte Schriften, Vol. 1), Frankfurt am Main 1976; engl. edition: *Style and Idea. Collected Writings*, ed. Leonard Stein, trans. Leo Black, Faber & Faber: London 1975, Abbreviation: S & I
--: *Schöpferische Konfessionen*, ed. Willi Reich, Zürich 1964

--: *Briefwechsel Arnold Schönberg – Alban Berg*. ed. Juliane Brand, Christopher Hailey and Andreas Meyer, 2 vols., Mainz 2007
Strawinsky, Igor: *Musikalische Poetik*, Mainz 1949
Stravinsky, Igor, and Craft, Robert: *Dialogues and a Diary*, New York: Double day 1963
--: *Expositions and Developments*, New York: Double day 1962
--: *Memories and Commentaries*, New York: Double day 1960
--: *Retrospectivs and Conclusions*, New York: Knopf 1969
Webern, Anton von: *Der Weg zur Neuen Musik*, ed. Willi Reich, Wien 1960
Zimmermann, Bernd Alois: *Intervall und Zeit. Aufsätze und Schriften zum Werk*, ed. Christof Bitter, Mainz 1974
--: *Dokumente und Interpretationen*, ed. Wulf Konoid, Köln n. d. (1986)
--: *»Du und Ich und Ich und die Welt«. Dokumente aus den Jahren 1940 bis 1950*, ed. Heribert Henrich, Hofheim 1998

**Monographs**

Adorno, Theodor W.: *Berg. Der Meister des kleinsten Übergangs* (Österreichische Komponisten des XX. Jahrhunderts, Vol. 15), Vienna 1968; english translation Juliane Brand and Christopher Hailey, Cambridge 1991
Bruhn, Siglind (Ed..): *Messiaen's Language of Mystical Love*, New York and London 1998
Burde, Wolfgang: *Strawinsky. Monographie* 1982
--: *György Ligeti: Eine Monographie*, Zurich 1993
Chalmers, Kenneth: *Béla Bartók*, Press Phaidon London 1995
Cholopowa, Valentina/Cholopow, Juri: *Anton Webern. Leben und Werk*, Berlin 1989
Dibelius, Ulrich: *György Ligeti. Eine Monographie in Essays*, Mainz 1994
--: (Ed.): *Karl Amadeus Hartmann. Komponist im Widerstreit*, Kassel 2004
Frisch, Walter: *Schoenberg and His World*, Princeton University Press Princetzon 1999
Frisius, Rudolf: *Karlheinz Stockhausen I. Einführung in das Gesamtwerk. Gespräche mit Karlheinz Stockhausen*, Mainz 1996
Gradenwitz, Peter: *Arnold Schönberg und seine Meisterschüler. Berlin 1925-1933*, Vienna 1998
Griffiths, Paul: *Olivier Messiaen and the Music of Time*, Ithaka . New York 1985
Halbreich, Harry: *Olivier Messiaen*, Paris 1980
Hiekel, Jörn Peter/Mauser, Siegfried (Ed.): *Nachgedachte Musik. Studien zum Werk Helmut Lachenmanns*, Saarbrücken 2005
Hindemith-Institut, Frankfurt/Main (Ed.): *Hindemith-Jahrbuch. Annales Hindemith*, Mainz since 1971, 41 vols.
Hofer, Wolfgang (Ed.): *ausdruck zugriff differenzen. Der Komponist Wolfgang Rihm*, Mainz 2003
Konold, Wulf: *Bernd Alois Zimmermann. Der Komponist und sein Werk*, Cologne 1986
Kostakeva, Maria: *Im Strom der Zeiten und der Welten. Das Spätwerk von Alfred Schnittke*, Saarbrücken 2005
Kroö, György. *Bartók-Handbuch*, Vienna/Budapest 1974
Kurtz, Michael: *Sofia Gubaidulina. Eine Biographie*, Stuttgart 2001
Mahnkopf, Claus-Steffen (Ed.): *Mythos Cage*, Hofheim 1999
Maurer Zenck, Claudia: *Ernst Krenek - ein Komponist im Exil*, Vienna 1980
Metzger, Heinz-Klaus und Riehn, Rainer (Eds.): *Musik-Konzepte Issue 6. Edgar Varèse. Rückblick auf die Zukunft*, Munich November 1978
--: *Musik-Konzepte Issue 22. Béla Bartók*, Munich November 1981

--: Musik-Konzepte Issue 54/55. *Iannis Xenakis*, Munich May1987
--: Musik-Konzepte Issue 109/110. *Isang Yun. Die fünf Symphonien*, Munich July 2000
Meyer, Krzysztof: *Dmitri Schostakowitsch. Sein Leben, sein Werk, seine Zeit*, Bergisch Gladbach 1995
Michaely, Aloyse: *Die Musik Olivier Messiaens. Untersuchungen zum Gesamtschaffen* (Hamburger Beiträge zur Musikwissenschaft. Sonderband), Hamburg 1987
Moldenhauer, Hans und Rosaleen: *Anton von Webern. Chronik seines Lebens und Werkes*, Zurich/Freiburg i. B. 1980
Nauk, Gisela: *Dieter Schnebel. Lehrgänge durch Leben und Werk*, Mainz 2001
Nicholls, David (Ed.): *The Cambridge Companion to John Cage*, Cambridge 2002
Petersen, Peter: *Hans Werner Henze. Ein politischer Musiker. Zwölf Vorlesungen*, Argument-Verlag Hamburg 1988
--: *Hans Werner Henze. Werke der Jahre 1984-1993* (Kölner Schriften zur Neuen Musik, Vol. 4), Mainz 1993
Peyser, Juan: *Boulez. Composer, Conductor, Enigma*, London 1977
Rathert, Wolfgang, Rickenbacher, Karl Anton and Schneider, Herbert (Ed.): *Olivier Messiaen. Texte, Analysen, Zeugnisse*, Vol. 2: *Das Werk im historischen und analytischen Kontext*, Hildesheim 2013
Redlich, Hans Ferdinand: *Alban Berg. Versuch einer Würdigung*, Vienna/Zurich/ London 1957
Reich, Willi: *Alban Berg. Leben und Werk*, Zürich 1963
--: *Arnold Schönberg oder Der konservative Revolutionär*, Munich 1974
Revill, David: *Tosende Stille. Eine John-Cage-Biographie*, Munich/Leipzig 1995
Rufer, Josef: *Das Werk Arnold Schönbergs*, Kassel 1959
Schwinger, Wolfram: *Krzysztof Penderecki. Begegnungen, Lebensdaten, Werkkommentare*, Mainz 1994
Stenzl, Jürg: *Luigi Nono* (rowohlts monographien 50582), Reinbek bei Hamburg 1998
Stuckenschmidt, Hans Heinz: *Schönberg. Leben. Umwelt. Werk*, Munich/ Mainz 1989; english tranlation New York: Schirmer Books 1977
Taruskin, Richard: *Stravinsky. The composer and the Russian Traditions*, 2 vols., Oxford 1996
Tomaszewski, Mieczyslaw: *Krzysztof Penderecki and his Music. Four Essays*, Cracow 2003
White, Eric Walter: *Strawinsky. The Composer and his Works*, 2$^{nd}$ ed. London 1979

**Series of papers**

*Darmstädter Beiträge zur Neuen Musik*, ed. Wolfgang Steinecke, Ernst Thomas uad Friedrich Hommel, Mainz since 1958, until now 20 vols.
*Die Reihe. Informationen über serielle Musik*, ed. Herbert Eimert, 8 Issues, Vienna 1955-1962
*Komponisten der Gegenwart*, ed. Hanns-Werner Heister and Walter-Wolfgang Sparrer. Loseblatt-Lexikon, Munich since 1992
*Musik-Konzepte*, ed. Heinz-Klaus Metzger and Rainer Riehn, Munich since 1977, 122 Issues und mehrere Sonderbände; Neue Folge, ed. Ulrich Tadday, Munich since 2004
*MusikTexte. Zeitschrift für Neue Musik*, eds. Ulrich Dibelius, Gisela Gronemeyer and Reinhard Oehlschlägel, Cologne since 1983, until now more than 100 Issues
*Neue Zeitschrift für Musik*
*Nutida Musik*, Stockholm

*Perspectives of New Music*, eds. Benjamin Boretz, Robert Morris and John Rahn, Princeton/Seattle since 1963, until now more than 40 vols.
*Positionen. Beiträge zur Neuen Musik*, ed. Gisela Nauck, Leipzig/Berlin since 1988, until now more than 60 Issues
*Studien zur Wertungsforschung*, ed. Otto Kolleritsch, Vienna/Graz since 1968, until now more than 45 vols., since 2002 edited by Andreas Dorschel

**Works of the Author**

*Kompositionstechnische Probleme der atonalen Musik*, in: Kongreßbericht Kassel 1962, Kassel 1963, 257-260
*Probleme der Amalgamierung von Dichtung und Musik in der Kunst des 20. Jahrhunderts*, in: Zum Verhältnis von zeitgenössischer Musik und zeitgenössischer Dichtung (Studien zur Wertungsforschung vol. 20), ed. Otto Kolleritsch, Vienna/Graz 1988, 35-50
*Musik als Botschaft*, Wiesbaden 1989 (Chapters about Hans Werner Henze and Bernd Alois Zimmermann)
*Die Wiener Schule und das Problem der »deutschen Musik«*, in; Die Wiener Schule und das Hakenkreuz (Studien zur Wertungsforschung Vol. 22), ed. Otto Kolleritsch, Vienna/Graz 1990, 35-50
*Zum Beethoven-Bild Schönbergs, Berg und Weberns*, in: Beethoven und die Zweite Wiener Schule (Studien zur Wertungsforschung Vol. 25), ed. Otto Kolleritsch, Vienna/Graz 1992, 8-24
*Alban Berg. Musik als Autobiographie*, Wiesbaden/Leipzig/Paris 1992 (with full bibliography)
*Gustav Mahler, Alban Berg und das Österreichische in der Musik*, in: Bruckner- Symposion »Entwicklungen - Parallelen - Kontraste. Zur Frage einer österreichischen Symphonik« Linz 1993, Bericht Linz 1996, 165-173
*Alban Berg und Gustav Mahler*, in: Gustav *Mahler - »Meine Zeit wird kommen«. Aspekte* der *Gustav Mahler-Rezeption* (Schriftenreihe der Gustav Mahler Vereinigung Hamburg vol. 1), Hamburg 1996, 75-85
*György Ligeti. Jenseits von Avantgarde und Postmoderne*, Vienna 1996 (with extensice Bibliography)
*Musik als Bekenntnis. Karl Amadeus Hartmann und seine Sechste Symphonie*, in: Das Orchester 44, July/August 1996, 2-8
*Eine Weltsprache der Musik? Multikulturelle Phänomene der Neuen Musik nach 1945*, in: Das Orchester 44, December 1996, 2-9
*Schönbergs Gurrelieder*, in: *Festskript Jan Maegaard*, ed. Niels Bo Foltmann and Claus R0llum-Larsen, Copenhagen 1996, 33-42
*Der irisierende Klang. Anmerkungen zu Ligetis »Atmosphères«*, in: »Laß Singen, Gesell, laß rauschen«. Zur Ästhetik und Anästhetik in der Musik (Studien zur Wertungsforschung Vol. 32), ed. Otto Kolleritsch, Vienna/Graz 1997, 182-193
*Humanism, Love and Music*, Peter Lang, Frankfurt am Main/New York 2012 (with extensive Bibliography)
*Das Ende der Avantgarde?*, in: Musik und ... Vol. 3: *Kultur Bildung Politik. Festschrift für Hermann Rauhe zum 70. Geburtstag* (Schriftenreihe der Hochschule für Musik und Theater Hamburg), eds. Hanns-Werner Heister and Wolfgang Hochstein, Hamburg 2000, 729-733
*Arnold Schönberg - fünfzig Jahre nach seinem Tod*, in: Das Orchester 49, July/ August 2001, 21-25

»*Was immer aus seiner Feder kam, ist gold*«. *Ein Schönberg-Schüler in Berlin*, in: Neue Zeitschrift für Musik 162, May/Juni 2001, 58-61

*Alban Berg and Hanna Fuchs. The Story of a Love in Letters*, Indiana University Press 2008

*Und immer wieder für eine bessere Welt - Annäherungen an den Komponisten Hans Werner Henze*, in: *Hans Werner Henze. Die Vorträge des internationalen Symposions am Musikwissenschaftlichen Institut der Universität Hamburg 28. bis 30. Juni 2001*, ed. Peter Petersen (Hamburger Jahrbuch für Musikwissenschaft Band 20). Frankfurt am Main 2003, 195-204.

*György Ligeti. Klassiker der Moderne*, in: MUSIKforum 6, October-December 2008, 34-37

*Die Zweite Wiener Schule in den zwanziger Jahren*, in: Hamburger Jahrbuch für Musikwissenschaftt Vol. 26, Frankfurt am Main 2009, 143-148

*Alban Berg, Anton Webern und die Neue Musik*, in: J. Bungardt, M. Helfgott, E. Rathgeber, N. Urbanek (Eds.): *Wiener Musikgeschichte. Festschrift für Hartmut Krones*, Vienna/Cologne/Wiemar 2009. 487-501

*Zum Mozart-Bild von Alban Berg*, in: Hartmut Krones and Christian Meyer (Eds.): *Mozart und Schönberg. Wiener Klassik und Wiener Schule*, Vienna/Cologne/Weimar 2012, 301-307

## List of Music Examples and Illustrations

| | |
|---|---|
| ME 1, p. 34: | Used by permission of Belmont Music Publishers |
| ME 2, p. 34: | The author's own schematic illustration |
| ME 3, p. 64: | Universal Edition (UE 5334) |
| ME 4, p. 76: | The author's schematic illustration |
| ME 5, p. 82: | Private print |
| ME 6, p. 89: | Universal Edition (UE 7627) |
| ME 7, p. 90: | Universal Edition (UE 12958 LW) |
| ME 8, p. 91: | Universal Edition (UE 7627) |
| ME 9, p. 92: | The author's schematic illustration |
| ME 10, p. 93: | Margun Music, Inc. (USA), 1992 |
| ME 11a & b, p. 94: | Margun Music, Inc. (USA), 1992 |
| ME 12, p. 121: | Quoted from Andreas E. Beurmann / Albrecht Schneider: Struktur, Klang, Dynamik. Akustische Untersuchungen an Ligetis »Atmosphères«, in: Hamburger Jahrbuch für Musikwissenschaft, Vol. 11 (1991), p. 318 |
| ME 13, p. 123: | Universal Edition (UE 11 418) |

**Plates**

Arnold Schoenberg
Published with kind permission oft he Arnold Schoenberg Center Vienna

Alban Berg

Béla Bartók

Olivier Messiaen

Pierre Boulez

Luigi Nono
with kind permission of Graziano Arici

György Ligeti
with permission of Music Schott Mainz

Bernd Alois Zimmermann
with permission of Music Schott

with kind permission of Jürgen Köchel

Wolfgang Rihm
with kind permission of Eric Marinitsch (Universal Edition)

Hans Werner Henze with Constantin Floros and Jens Brockmeier

# Index

Adorno, Theodor W. 4, 6, 9, 18, 20, 21, 88, 122, 154, 164, 172, 205, 208, 173
Andre, Carl ........................................... 161
Apollinaire, Guillaume ....................... 4, 5
Arnold, Robert Franz ............................ 52
Artaud, Antonin ................................... 168
Askitopoulos, Nelly ............................... 81
Auber, Daniel-François-Esprit ............... 26
Bach, Johann Sebastian .... 1, 16, 23, 27, 31, 43, 44, 45, 73, 81, 82, 113, 117, 141, 147, 149, 158
Banfield, Volker .................................. 109
Barlow, Clarence ................................. 110
Barraqué, Jean ......................................... 7
Barthes, Roland ................................... 164
Bartók, Béla ...... VI, 19, 71, 72, 74, 77, 80, 125, 126, 127, 128, 129, 130, 131, 140, 141, 172, 206, 208, 219
Bayer, Konrad ..................................... 145
Beckett, Samuel .................................... 49
Beethoven, Ludwig van .. V, 11, 16, 20, 21, 23, 25, 27, 33, 35, 41, 42, 43, 44, 45, 73, 85, 98, 125, 156, 158, 159, 169, 210
Bekker, Paul ................................... 3, 5, 173
Bellini, Vincenzo .................................. 26
Benn, Gottfried ..................................... 48
Berger, Roman ................................ 2, 165
Bergson, Henri ................................... 144
Berio, Luciano ............................... 149, 164
Berlioz, Hector ............................... 26, 159
Beurmann, Andreas E. ......................... 121
Bizet, Georges ................................. 26, 134
Blacher, Boris ...................................... 138
Bose, Hans-Jürgen von .......................... 10
Boulez, Pierre ...... V, 7, 8, 9, 13, 15, 59, 60, 101, 105, 106, 107, 109, 122, 128, 139, 140, 153, 158, 167, 206, 209, 221
Brahms, Johannes 4, 27, 29, 31, 43, 44, 45, 47, 73, 97, 158
Brand, Max ............................................ 7
Breton, André ..................................... 106
Bruckner, Anton ................... 3, 97, 122, 210
Büchner, Georg ...................................... 4
Busoni, Ferruccio ...... 5, 7, 81, 82, 172, 207
Byron, George Gordon, 6. Baron (Lord Byron) ........................................ 33, 35

Cacciari, Massimo ................................ 98
Cage, John. 9, 139, 161, 164, 207, 208, 209
Cahill, Thaddeus ..................................... 7
Camus, Albert ...................................... 49
Capellen, Georg .................................. 137
Ceccato, Aldo ..................................... 113
Char, René ................................... 105, 106
Chopin, Frédéric .................... 61, 158, 162
Cocteau, Jean .................................. 4, 5, 8
David, Félicien .............................. 134, 209
Debussy, Claude V, 23, 25, 54, 85, 95, 101, 111, 118, 125, 131, 134, 206
Dehmel, Ida .......................................... 47
Delacroix, Eugène ............................... 134
Delannoy, Marcel ................................... 7
Delius, Frederick .................................. 25
Demertzis, Kostis ............................ 81, 85
Dessau, Paul ....................... 148, 154, 158
Deutsch Dorian, Frederick .................... 42
Dieterle, Charlotte ................................ 41
Döhl, Friedhelm ............................... 2, 164
Dounias, Minos ..................................... 79
Duchesneau, Louise ............................ 118
Dutilleux, Henri ...................................... 7
Dvořák, Antonín .............................. 45, 73
Eidlitz, Walter ....................................... 68
Eimert, Herbert ....................... 8, 127, 209
Einstein, Albert ..................................... 30
Eisler, Hanns ........................... 44, 59, 148
Enkel, Fritz ............................................ 8
Ericson, Eric ....................................... 113
Falla, Manuel de ................................... 71
Farkas, Ferenc .................................... 140
Ferneyhough, Brian ............................... 10
Filippi, Amadeo de ............................... 72
Frescobaldi, Girolamo ........................ 126
Furtwängler, Wilhelm ..................... 29, 31
Genet, Jean ......................................... 158
George, Stefan ..................................... 75
Gershwin, George ................................. 75
Gerstl, Richard ..................................... 76
Giraud, Albert ......................... 59, 61, 62
Glass, Philip ................................ 161, 162
Goehr, Walter ....................................... 79
Goethe, Johann Wolfgang von ... 23, 33, 47
Goeyvaerts, Karel ................................... 8

229

Goldmark, Karl ........................................73
Goncourt, Edmond Huot de .................134
Goncourt, Jules Huot de.......................134
Górecki, Henryk Mikołaj ......................163
Göring, Hermann ..................................31
Götte, Ulli .....................................161, 205
Gradenwitz, Peter...........................83, 208
Grieg, Edvard........................................71
Grillparzer, Franz..................................11
Gubaidulina, Sofia ................163, 165, 208
Haas, Joseph.........................................30
Hába, Alois ............................................7
Hadjinikos, George ...............................79
Hamel, Peter Michael........................2, 205
Handel, Georg Friedrich .................31, 147
Hannenheim, Norbert von.......................83
Hartleben, Otto Erich ............................59
Hartmann, Karl Amadeus ....103, 145, 154, 155, 158, 169, 207, 208, 210
Haßler, Hans Leo ................................158
Häusler, Josef119, 128, 139, 205, 206, 207
Haydn, Joseph .......................................73
Hefferman, Helen..................................32
Heidegger, Martin ...............................144
Helmholtz, Hermann von..........................8
Henze, Hans Werner ..... VI, 2, 4, 103, 140, 148, 153, 154, 155, 156, 157, 158, 159, 163, 164, 169, 172, 207, 209, 210, 211, 227, 173
Hertzka, Emil ..................................51, 53
Hertzka, Hella ................................31, 53
Herzl, Theodor ......................................65
Hess, Willy ...........................................80
Heym, Georg.........................................50
Hindemith, Paul .....5, 29, 30, 95, 101, 143, 172, 207, 208
Hoffmann, Ernst Theodor Amadeus .....159
Höller, York .........................................50
Honegger, Arthur ...................................7
Husserl, Edmund ................................144
Indy, Vincent d´ .....................................7
Ionesco, Eugène ....................................49
Ives, Charles.......................................149
Jacobsen, Jens Peter...............51, 52, 53, 56
Jarnach, Philipp..............................81, 82
Jone, Hildegard ....................................39
Joyce, James..................................105, 144
Juon, Paul........................................80, 81

Kadosa, Pál ........................................140
Kagel, Mauricio ..............................49, 118
Kahn, Robert...................................80, 81
Kalomiris, Manolis ...............................71
Kandinsky, Wassily ...................4, 13, 173
Kant, Immanuel ..............................17, 25
Kasem-Bek, Jan ..................................120
Kaufmann, Harald................................49
Klebe, Giselher......................................8
Kleiber, Erich.................................30, 91
Klemperer, Otto ....................................41
Klüppelholz, Werner.............................50
Kodály, Zoltán ...............................71, 125
Koenig, Gottfried Michael.......................8
Kolisch, Gertrud ...................................76
Kolisch, Rudolf...............................15, 38
Kolland, Hubert ..............................23, 24
Křenek, Ernst ........................................8
Kreutziger-Herr, Annette ......................97
Krones, Hartmut ....................76, 206, 211
Kurtág, György ................2, 131, 140, 141
Lachenmann, Helmut.....10, 103, 164, 167, 207
Leibowitz, René ...................................33
Lenz, Jakob Michael Reinhold .............145
Leonardo da Vinci ..........................12, 169
Liao, Naixiong ....................................134
Ligeti, GyörgyVI, 2, 6, 8, 9, 10, 49, 60, 95, 109, 110, 111, 112, 113, 115, 117, 118, 119, 120, 121, 122, 123, 125, 126, 127, 128, 129, 130, 131, 140, 162, 163, 164, 172, 206, 207, 208, 210, 211, 223, 173
Linke, Karl .......................................... 14
Liszt, Franz ........................... 3, 19, 24, 159
Loos, Adolf................... 19, 38, 39, 42, 206
Loriod, Yvonne ...................................102
Lutoslavski, Witold..............................140
Lyotard, Jean-François .......................164
Machaut, Guillaume de .......................149
Maderna, Bruno ..........8, 98, 139, 153, 154
Madge, Geoffrey...................................85
Mahler, Gustav ....3, 11, 15, 16, 17, 18, 19, 20, 21, 25, 27, 29, 42, 43, 47, 52, 71, 97, 98, 122, 143, 147, 149, 155, 158, 164, 210
Malipiero, Francesco ...........................98
Mallarmé, Stéphane .................49, 63, 105
Manet, Edouard...................................134

Mann, Thomas ..................68, 157, 171
Marinetti, Filippo Tommaso ....................6
Marmion, Columba ............................102
Martynow, Iwan ............................1, 173
Mayakovsky, Vladimir .......................145
Mayer, Hans ...............................171, 207
Mendelssohn Bartholdy, Felix ........83, 159
Merimée, Prosper ..............................134
Messiaen, Olivier ......V, 10, 101, 102, 103,
 105, 111, 131, 134, 135, 140, 141, 172,
 205, 207, 208, 209, 220
Meyer, Krzysztof .............................2, 209
Meyerbeer, Giacomo ............................26
Meyer-Eppler, Werner .............................8
Michaely, Aloyse .........................102, 209
Milhaud, Darius ...................43, 140, 172
Monteverdi, Claudio .............141, 155, 158
Morgenstern, Soma ...............................43
Mozart, Wolfgang Amadé ...11, 27, 33, 43,
 44, 45, 73, 148, 149, 155, 158, 211
Nancarrow, Conlon .............................130
Napoleon I. (Napoleone Buonaparte) ....16,
 33, 34, 35
Nedbal, Oskar ................................25, 26
Neruda, Pablo .....................................154
Newlin, Dika ........................................76
Niculescu, Stefan ....................................2
Nietzsche, Friedrich ..............................23
Nono, Luigi ...V, 2, 8, 50, 97, 98, 100, 103,
 139, 153, 154, 164, 167, 169, 171, 207,
 209, 222
Offenbach, Jacques ..............................75
Oswald, Peter .....................................162
Palestrina, Giovanni Pierluigi da ..........117
Papaioannou, Marika .......................85, 91
Papaioannou, Yiannis ...............79, 80, 85
Papandreou, Andreas ..........................144
Pärt, Arvo .....................................2, 163, 165
Partch, Harry .........................................7
Penderecki, Krzysztof..140, 149, 162, 163,
 165, 172, 205, 209
Pergolesi, Giovanni Battista ....................5
Petersen, Peter ..............159, 163, 209, 211
Petschnig, Emil ....................................12
Pfitzner, Hans ................................29, 39
Picasso, Pablo .......................................5
Pound, Ezra .......................................144
Pousseur, Henri ....................................8

Pratella, Francesco Balilla .....................6
Prokofiev, Sergej .........................5, 147, 172
Rauhe, Hermann ...................113, 114, 210
Ravel, Maurice..10, 63, 101, 111, 125, 134
Reger, Max ..........................................27
Reich, Steve ................................161, 162
Reich, Willi ........................33, 207, 208
Respighi, Ottorino ................................71
Riadis, Emilios .....................................71
Rihm, Wolfgang ..VI, 2, 14, 167, 168, 169,
 172, 206, 207, 208, 226
Riley, Terry ................................161, 162
Rimbaud, Arthur ..................................49
Rosbaud, Hans ...................................121
Rossini, Gioachino .........................26, 42
Roussel, Albert .....................................7
Rufer, Josef ...............26, 37, 138, 206, 209
Russolo, Luigi ................................7, 207
Ruzicka, Peter ................................2, 164
Sartre, Jean-Paul ................................154
Satie, Erik ......................................4, 161
Schaeffer, Pierre ....................................7
Schiller, Friedrich ...........................23, 33
Schillings, Max von .............................29
Schnebel, Dieter ....................49, 164, 209
Schneider, Albrecht .....................121, 209
Schnittke, Alfred VI, 2, 147, 148, 149, 150,
 164, 165, 205, 207, 208
Schoenberg, Arnold ....V, 2, 3, 4, 5, 6, 8, 9,
 11, 12, 13, 14, 15, 16, 18, 19, 21, 24, 25,
 26, 27, 29, 31, 32, 33, 35, 37, 38, 39, 41,
 42, 43, 44, 45, 46, 50, 51, 52, 53, 54, 55,
 56, 57, 59, 60, 61, 62, 63, 64, 65, 66, 67,
 68, 69, 72, 73, 74, 75, 76, 77, 79, 80, 81,
 83, 84, 85, 87, 88, 89, 90, 91, 93, 95, 96,
 97, 101, 105, 106, 109, 125, 127, 131,
 143, 148, 169, 171, 208, 217
Schoenberg, Gertrud (geb. Kolisch).37, 76
Schoenberg, Mathilde (born von
 Zemlinsky) ............................75, 76, 97
Schoenberg, Nuria .....................2, 37, 38
Schönberg, Arnold .......133, 205, 207, 208,
 209, 210, 211, 173
Schreker, Franz ...............................51, 81
Schubert, Franz ...11, 27, 45, 149, 206, 207
Schuller, Gunther ............................79, 92
Schultz, Wolfgang Andreas ....................2
Schütz, Heinrich ................................141

231

Schwarz-Schilling, Reinhard ................ 138
Schweinitz, Wolfgang von ........................ 2
Scriabin, Alexander ...................... 111, 147
Sessions, Roger ......................................... 32
Shostakovich, Dmitri ... 147, 149, 172, 209, 173
Sibelius, Jean ............................................ 71
Skalkottas, Nikos V, 77, 79, 80, 81, 82, 83, 84, 85, 86, 87, 88, 89, 90, 91, 92, 93, 95
Sokel, Walter H ................................. 4, 173
St Augustine ........................................... 144
Stahmer, Klaus .......................................... 2
Stahnke, Manfred ................. 2, 7, 118, 206
Stockhausen, Karlheinz... VI, 8, 15, 49, 50, 101, 105, 128, 131, 134, 137, 138, 139, 140, 148, 149, 153, 165, 167, 208
Stoianova, Ivanka .................................. 168
Strasfogel, Ian ........................................ 156
Strauss, Johann ........................................ 75
Strauss, Richard ........................... 19, 24, 27
Stravinsky, Igor 5, 6, 10, 14, 43, 63, 71, 72, 73, 74, 77, 80, 95, 101, 105, 143, 147, 149, 156, 172, 208, 209
Strobel, Heinrich ..................................... 30
Stuckenschmidt, Hans Heinz ..... 6, 35, 206, 207, 209, 173
Thibaut, Anton Friedrich Justus ............ 117
Tietjen, Heinz .......................................... 31
Varèse, Edgard .......................... 7, 81, 208
Verdi, Giuseppe ............... 5, 6, 73, 98, 156
Veress, Sándor ....................................... 140
Vieru, Anatol ............................................. 2
Vishnegradsky, Ivan .................................. 7
Vitry, Philippe de ...................................... 3
Wagner, Richard 3, 4, 5, 11, 12, 19, 23, 24, 25, 26, 27, 42, 44, 48, 51, 52, 54, 68, 73, 109, 122, 156, 157, 158, 207
Washington, George ................................ 34
Webern, Amalie von (Mali) ................... 38
Webern, Anton von .... 3, 14, 15, 18, 19, 20, 21, 25, 27, 29, 30, 31, 32, 37, 38, 39, 42, 43, 44, 51, 63, 79, 84, 87, 105, 125, 134, 140, 147, 148, 153, 171, 208, 209, 211
Weill, Kurt ...................... 81, 82, 83, 148
Weiner, Leó ........................................... 140
Wellek, Albert ......................................... 47
Weöres, Sándor ..................................... 114
Werckmeister, Andreas ......................... 117
Widor, Charles-Marie .............................. 7
Windisch, Fritz ......................................... 5
Wittgenstein, Ludwig ........................... 144
Wolf, Hugo .............................................. 73
Wronski, Hoëné ........................................ 8
Xenakis, Iannis ............... 85, 110, 140, 209
Yesenin, Sergei ..................................... 145
Young, La Monte ................................... 161
Yun, Isang ..... 131, 138, 139, 140, 141, 209
Zehme, Albertine .................................... 59
Zemlinsky, Alexander von ..................... 59
Zimmermann, Bernd Alois .... VI, 101, 115, 143, 144, 145, 146, 148, 149, 207, 208, 210, 224
Zola, Émilie ........................................... 155
Zschorlich, Paul ....................................... 25